T0174706

PHILOSOPHY AND THE ADVENTURE OF THE VIRTUAL

The concept of the virtual has recently assumed a remarkable level of importance, spanning a diverse range of different disciplines and approaches. Yet in spite of the attention it has received, its precise ontological status is mysterious for many and the extent of its application to time, perception, and memory is largely unexplored and unknown. *Philosophy and the Adventure of the Virtual: Bergson and the time of life* brings the virtual to centre stage and argues for its importance in thinking anew the central philosophical questions of being and time.

Keith Ansell Pearson examines the nature of continuity, probes relativity, pursues a notion of creative evolution, and outlines a novel approach to perception and memory. Staging a series of encounters between Bergson and philosophers as diverse as Kant, Nietzsche, Russell, Popper, Denett, Badiou, and Sartre, the book provides some genuinely insightful readings of Bergson and endeavours to revitalize Bergsonism for a contemporary audience.

Philosophy and the Adventure of the Virtual is a lucidly written and imaginatively argued volume of essays, and will be of interest to philosophers across the analytic and continental divide and to anyone open to the possibilities of thinking.

Keith Ansell Pearson is Professor of Philosophy at the University of Warwick. His previous books with Routledge include *Viroid Life* (1997) and *Germinal Life* (1999).

PHILOSOPHY AND THE ADVENTURE OF THE VIRTUAL

Bergson and the time of life

Keith Ansell Pearson

London and New York

First published 2002
by Routledge
11 New Fetter Lane, London EC4P 4EE

Simultaneously published in the USA and Canada
by Routledge
29 West 35th Street, New York, NY 10001

Routledge is an imprint of the Taylor & Francis Group

© 2002 Keith Ansell Pearson

Typeset in Times New Roman by Exe Valley Dataset Ltd, Exeter
Printed and bound in Great Britain by
TJ International Ltd, Padstow, Cornwall

All rights reserved. No part of this book may be reprinted or
reproduced or utilized in any form or by any electronic, mechanical,
or other means, now known or hereafter invented, including
photocopying and recording, or in any information storage or
retrieval system, without permission in writing from the publishers.

British Library Cataloguing in Publication Data
A catalogue record for this book is available from the British Library

Library of Congress Cataloging in Publication Data
Ansell-Pearson, Keith, 1960–
Philosophy and the adventure of the virtual: Bergson and the time
of life / Keith Ansell Pearson.
p. cm.
Includes bibliographical references and index.
1. Bergson, Henri, 1859–1941. 2. Time. I. Title.
B2430,B43 A57 2001
110–dc21 2001031994

ISBN 0–415–23727–0 (hbk)
ISBN 0–415–23728–9 (pbk)

The best images and parables should speak of time and becoming.

(F. Nietzsche, 'On the Blissful Islands',
Thus Spoke Zarathustra, 1883)

The only crime is time itself.

(G. Deleuze, *Cinema 2: The Time-Image*, 1985)

The One expresses in a single meaning (*sens*) all of the multiple. Being expresses in a single meaning all that differs.

(G. Deleuze and F. Guattari, *A Thousand Plateaus*, 1980)

CONTENTS

CONTENTS

ACKNOWLEDGEMENTS

A version of essay three first appeared in Robin Durie's edited volume *Time and the Instant* (Clinamen Press, 2000). A slightly different version of essay four first appeared in *Pli: The Warwick Journal of Philosophy*, volume 11, 2001. A much shorter and more primitive version of essay five appeared in issue 6 (2000) of *Tekhnema: A Journal of Philosophy of Technology*, devoted to the theme of 'Teleologies: scientific, technical, critical', guest edited by G. Banham and S. Malik. I am grateful to the editors of these publications for allowing me to draw on this material for the purposes of this volume.

INTRODUCTION

Problems or Ideas emanate from imperatives of adventure or
from events which appear in the form of questions.
(Deleuze, *Difference and Repetition*, 1968)

The appeal to the originating goes in several directions: the
originating breaks up, and philosophy must accompany this
break-up, this non-coincidence, this differentiation.
(Merleau-Ponty, *The Visible and the Invisible*, 1959–60)

To neglect differences of nature in favour of genres is thus to
belie philosophy. We have lost the differences of nature.
(Deleuze, 'Bergson's Conception of Difference', 1956)

In this volume of essays I approach the question of time and the question of
life through the elaboration of a philosophy of the virtual (the conjunction
of the two questions constitutes the enigma of the book). In recent years the
notion of the virtual has assumed a degree of extraordinary importance for
attempts to articulate new experiences of the real (see, for example, the
studies by Heim 1993, Levy 1998, Hayles 1999). As a conceptual innovation
within philosophic modernity the notion is associated with the work of
Bergson and assumes a role of vital importance in the texts of Deleuze.
Indeed, Alain Badiou has gone so far as to claim that it is the principal name
of Being in Deleuze's thinking. Within Bergson and Deleuze we have the
distinction between virtual (continuous) multiplicities and actual (or discrete) multiplicities, a conception of the evolution of life as involving an
actualization of the virtual in contrast to the less inventive or creative
realization of the possible; the attempt to show that both perception and
memory involve virtual images; and, in the case of Deleuze, a thinking of the
event as virtual (pure reserve). Deleuze's conceives the virtual as a productive
power of difference, a simplicity and potentiality, which denotes neither
a deficient nor an inadequate mode of being. Hence the key formula,
borrowed from Proust's *Time Regained*: *the virtual is real without being*

1

actual, ideal without being abstract. The virtual presents an ontological challenge to our ordinary conceptions of perception and memory, of time and subjectivity, and of life in its evolutionary aspects. As we shall see in this series of studies, the virtual has important ontological referents and is allied to problems that have been central to philosophy from the beginning. But the notion also works in the context of specific set of modern problems regarding the nature of time, memory, consciousness, and evolution.

This volume takes as its focus certain key texts of Bergson and the writings of Deleuze on Bergsonism (especially the 1956 and 1966 readings and the two volumes on cinema from the 1980s), and it offers a set of close readings of the movements of Bergsonian thought and of key texts such as *Matter and Memory* (henceforth abbreviated to *MM*) and *Creative Evolution* (henceforth abbreviated to *CE*). I write out of the conviction that these texts merit being placed at the centre of our appreciation of twentieth-century philosophy and that they continue to have an important contribution to make to the staging of philosophical problems today. Deleuze's *Bergsonism* of 1966 is significant since it was the first reading to see that what unites the whole of Bergson's thinking from the treatment of psychic states in *Time and Free Will* (henceforth abbreviated to *TFW*) to the presentation of a new conception of evolution in *Creative Evolution* is the idea of a virtual multiplicity. This volume has set itself a fairly specific task, however. It is not making any contribution to a contemporary thinking of the virtual inspired by the new sciences of chaos and complexity theory. I encourage readers interested in contemporary applications and utilizations of the virtual, in current architectural theory and practice, and in the domain of new theory in general, to look at the texts by Cache (1995) and Rajchman (1998 and 2000), and, in relation to chaos and complexity theory, the forthcoming text of Manuel de Landa. My specific, and limited, task in this volume is twofold: to contribute to the correction of Bergson's erasure from our image of post-Kantian philosophy, and to contribute to our comprehension of Deleuze's unique conception and vision of philosophy.

The virtual remains for many people, including readers of Bergson and Deleuze, something of a mysterious and tricky notion. In this volume I seek to clarify its status and demonstrate the kind of philosophical work it is doing and can contribute to. The first essay introduces the notion of a virtual multiplicity in relation to time and how we think continuity and I attempt to provide an introduction to its essential features. The second essay tries to make sense of Bergson's idea of 'single time' by examining the nature of his engagement with Relativity. The third essay takes the problematic of duration and evolution and explores how the difference between the virtual and the possible might be important for how we construe the creative or inventive character of evolution. The fourth essay looks at the notion of the simple virtual and from the point of view of a renewed ontology of the One. Here I take to task Badiou's reading of Deleuze's thinking as a Platonism of the virtual and seek to demonstrate that the renewed thinking of the One Deleuze undertakes constitutes an intrinsic part of his overriding commitment to pluralism. The fifth essay examines Bergson's response to Kant in an effort to clarify key aspects of his thinking and argues that, conceived as an image of thought, the *élan vital* does not simply remain within the problematic of finality as established by Kant's critique of teleological judgement (given that it is the notion of virtuality that Bergson replaces finality with this essay too is on the virtual). The sixth and seventh essays are devoted to Bergson's *Matter and Memory*, first in relation to the question of the image and the figuration of the real, which covers chapters 1 and 4 of the book, and secondly with respect to the presentation of the virtuality of memory in chapters 2 and 3 of the book.

It is inadequate to describe Deleuze as a Bergsonian, not simply because of the many and varied sources he draws upon, but rather because of the highly innovative character of his Bergsonism. Essay seven provides an insight into Deleuze's innovations with respect to the Bergsonian project and seeks to demonstrate the complex operations he performs on Bergson's thinking of time. As a thinker of time Deleuze is both profoundly Bergsonian and radically different from Bergson. In this essay I aim to provide insight into Deleuze's attempt to think time beyond any 'presentism', as he called it, and show how he is able to think a time of the pure past and a time of the open future irreducible to any present. This thinking of time takes us beyond the human condition – which is how Bergson defined the philosophical task – and it does so in a most dramatic manner and with extraordinary results.

In his 1966 text entitled *Bergsonism* Deleuze insisted that a 'philosophy such as this' requires that the notion of the virtual stop being 'vague and indeterminate'. This appears to overlook the fact that the virtual is by nature something intrinsically vague and indeterminate. The challenge Deleuze presents in *Bergsonism* and other writings, however, is to show that it can be credited with determinations and differentiations. We cannot simply say, however, that the virtual has its own specific mode of reality. Deleuze wants to make the strong claim, which he endeavours to substantiate through precise philosophical thinking, that it is the mode of *what is*. The virtual is not, therefore, almost real but wholly real and the real is, in fact, unencounterable and unthinkable without it. Admittedly, the sense of the notion is a shifting one and cannot be restricted to a single level. Moreover, its precise reality varies in accordance with these different levels: the virtual reality of the *élan vital* is quite different than the virtual reality that defines the existence of a pure memory. There are, however, common features: in these two cases an actualization of the virtual is involved. Bergson himself will often use the notion in a rather neutral manner, barely marking a difference between the possible and virtual; this is in contrast to Deleuze who will insist that any confusion between the two proves disastrous. Deleuze constructs an entire philosophy of life – conceived as a philosophy of difference (life as self-differentiation) – and of memory on its basis. Is the notion, then, an invention of Deleuze's Bergsonism? Jacques Maritain was one early commentator, and former disciple, who understood Bergson to be a thinker of pure actuality. In denying the virtual as some ideal pre-existent possibility Bergson shows, he argued, that things become what they are by passing from one state of actuality to another (Maritain 1943: 71) We begin to see the innovative character of Deleuze's Bergsonism: there is all the difference in a thinking of the *Being* of difference between the virtual and the possible. The virtual is not of the order of preformed possibility. An adequate reading of Bergson's texts demonstrates this.

As an innovation within philosophical thinking the notion of the virtual presents an ontological challenge to conceptions of the one and the many, substance and subject, time and space. It does this by providing a new way of thinking *multiplicity*. The matter is complicated, as we shall see as this study unfolds, because while a virtual multiplicity enables us to think beyond a certain opposition between the one and the many it is also the case that this multiplicity can be credited with a One that is peculiar to it. The notion of the virtual first appears in Bergson's first major publication, *Time and Free Will*. In this early text (1889) Bergson develops a typology of multiplicities as a way of thinking the distinction between the continuous and the discrete. The virtual is used to mark a distinction between the subjective and the objective. Bergson inverts the way we might normally think this distinction, with the 'subjective' denoting anything that is held to be completely and adequately known and the 'objective' being applied to what is known in a way that recognizes new impressions could be substituted and added to our idea of a thing. However, Bergson maintains that it is the objective – matter, for example – that is without virtuality. This is because although an object can be divided in a myriad of ways the divisions are grasped in thought before being made. The divisions do not, therefore, require changing anything in the total aspect of an object since even when not realized such changes are always 'possible' and then they are either actually perceived or are capable of being perceived in principle. The object and 'objective' give us only quantitative differentiation or differences of degree. They are without virtuality which belongs to duration or the 'subjective' as that which divides in terms of a differentiation and supposes changes in kind. The arithmetical unit provides the model of a division which involves no changing in kind. As Bergson notes, the units by which numbers are formed are 'provisional' units that can be subdivided without limit and the division of a unit into as many parts as we like shows that the potentially infinite division is merely of an extensive kind. Duration, by contrast, is not simply indivisible since it is a *multiplicity*, but it is one which has the potential to change in kind since whenever it is actualized the actualization requires and involves a qualitative differentiation. In Bergson's first book it is psychical life which provides us with a case of difference in nature or kind since in it there is always otherness but without there ever being number or the opposition of one and the many (the one can be a many and the many can be a collection of ones). At any moment in our lives we are neither simply one nor many but an unfolding and enfolding virtual multiplicity: the time of our lives is both continuous and heterogeneous. We should note, however, that in calling the virtual or duration 'subjective' the attempt is not being made to restrict its provenance to the purely or merely psychological. As will be argued in the first essay, and demonstrated in other essays in the volume, duration is ontological and psychological duration is one determined case which itself needs to open out onto an ontological duration. In addition, and as will be demonstrated in essay seven, even when we are thinking the time of subjectivity it is possible to open up an ontology of the virtual, in this case the virtual being of memory, which takes us from psychology and beyond it.

Deleuze will insist that duration or the virtual is what differs from itself (self-difference, internal difference, difference in itself) and it is thus 'the unity of substance and subject' (Deleuze 1999: 48). Now, although biology is able to show us processes of differentiation at work in embryology and the evolution of species, Deleuze insists that even though difference is 'vital' its concept is *not* biological. What does this mean and why insist upon this point? While we can develop the idea of 'Life' as the domain of difference (variation, diversity, divergence, etc.), it is philosophy's task to demonstrate the nature of difference and the complications of it (determining differences of nature, locating the differences of nature in nature, showing how the difference of nature becomes a nature, etc.). The biological science of life can only show us a mechanism of evolution in terms of an exogenous causality and an accidental determination and can only think in terms of differences of degree. For Deleuze by contrast, 'Duration by itself is consciousness, life by itself is consciousness, but it is so *by right*' (ibid.: 52). The virtual – and by implication, duration – must be developed as a *concept*.[1] Why this is necessary can be grasped by reflecting on the inadequacy of a thinking of difference exclusively in terms of differentiation (*différenciation*) taken as an action or an actualization. If differentiation was sufficient then there would be no need for a concept of difference. The reason why it is not sufficient is because what differentiates itself is first what differs with respect *to itself*, and this is the virtual (whether in terms of a virtual multiplicity, life as creative evolution, or memory). Deleuze argues: 'Differentiation is not the concept, but the production of objects which find their reason in the concept' (54). Now, if the virtual has this power to differ with itself, so providing us with the only truly adequate concept of difference, then it must mean that it enjoys an 'objective consistency which enables it to differentiate itself and to produce such objects' (ibid.).

To illustrate this, Deleuze gives a reading of Bergson on colours. Bergson invites us to pose the question: how do we determine what colours have in common? Two ways of philosophizing on the issue present themselves. In the first we extract the abstract and general idea of colour, so taking away from red what makes it red, from blue what makes it blue, from green what makes it green, and so on. The result of such extraction is that we end up with a concept of colour but one which is nothing more than a *genre*. Several objects all have the same concept and we end up with a unity that rests on a general and abstract idea. Arrived at and articulated in this way the concept of colour is a negative in the sense that it can be defined only by saying that it does not represent anything specific (this red, this blue, this green). Conceived as a general idea, says Bergson, the concept is 'an affirmation made up of negations, a form circumscribing vacuum' (Bergson 1965: 225). Moreover, we have now produced a duality of concept and object in which the relation of object to concept is strictly one of subsumption. But note how this operation has been performed and what it leads us to: the concept rests on *spatial* distinctions in which difference is *exterior* to the thing. Is there another way of proceeding? Bergson shows that there is. The example given is that of passing the colours of a rainbow, the shades of blue, violet, green, yellow, and red, through a convergent lens which brings them on to a single point and from which is obtained pure white light that brings out the difference between tints in terms of an indefinite variety of multi-coloured rays (see Bergson 1965: 225).

Why does this example serve to demonstrate the concept of the virtual? Because it gives us different colours no longer subsumed under a concept but rather as nuances or degrees of the concept itself conceived as an intensive, undivided unity: 'degrees of difference and not differences of degree' (Deleuze 1999: 54). We no longer have subsumption but participation in which white light serves as a concrete universal. Concept and thing are no longer opposed and the thing itself is no longer a kind or a generality. Bergson suggests that more 'concentrated truth' is to be attained from the contemplation of an antique marble than is to be found in a whole philosophical treatise. This gives us the object and task of metaphysics as one of recapturing 'in individual existences and to follow even to the source from which it emanates the particular ray which, while it confers on each one its own particular shade, attaches it by that means to the universal light' (Bergson 1965: 225–6).

The significance of this example of colour for Deleuze is that it gives us *internal* difference, that is 'the concept become concept of difference'. To pursue this 'superior philosophical aim' requires that we give up on thinking in space and let go of spatial distinctions. Difference and the concept must placed 'in time' (Deleuze 1999: 54). Differences between subject and object, body and spirit, matter and memory, are temporal differences and, as such, they are indeed matters of degree. But this does not mean that they are, therefore, also simple differences 'of' degree: the differences belong to internal difference and not to an exterior difference that would abstractly and generally measure their degree. As the adequate concept of difference the virtual is the 'possible coexistence of degrees or nuances' (55). The conclusion cannot be avoided: the virtual defines 'an absolutely positive mode of existence'. We can posit it realizing itself and becoming what it is – pure otherness and pure difference – without any need to appeal to either a logic of contradiction and negation or to an abstract universality or generality. Indeed, Deleuze argues that it is only by virtue of an *ignorance* of the virtual that we continue to adhere to a doctrine of contradiction and negation: 'The opposition of two terms is only the realisation of the virtuality which contained them both: which is to say that difference is more profound than negation, than contradiction' (53). The virtual is a simple power as we shall demonstrate in essay four. Conceived in itself it is the mode of the 'non-active' since it only acts and comes to be what it is (otherness) in differentiating itself, *both* ceasing to be itself and retaining something of itself, and it is in this very respect that it can be considered to be 'the mode of *what is*' (ibid.). Bergson's challenge to thinking consists in the claim that this is not to move thought in the direction of an abstract metaphysics. Indeed, he insists that the contrary is the case (Bergson 1965: 223–4). The virtual is not, then, a general idea, something abstract and empty, but the concept of difference (and of life since it is vital) rendered adequate. The concept of the virtual gives us the *time* of life.

Why, then, have we *lost* the differences of nature? Because we have lost time, we do not know how to think in terms of duration. For Deleuze Bergsonism involves a criticism of metaphysics and a criticism of science on this point: metaphysics constructs only differences in degree between a spatialized time and eternity, in which eternity is assumed to be primary and time becomes nothing more than a deterioriation and diminution of being, with all beings getting defined on a scale of intensity between the extremes of perfection and nothingness; in science mechanism relies completely on a spatialization of time in which beings present only differences of degree (of position, of dimension, and of proportion). For example, in Darwinian evolutionism we have a unilinear evolution which takes us from one living organization or system to another by simple intermediaries, transitions, and variations of degree. If 'vital differences' or variations are interpreted solely in terms of a purely external causality and mechanism then in their nature they are nothing more than 'passive effects' and elements to be abstractly combined or added together. Deleuze argues that the error of evolutionism is to conceive vital variations 'as so many actual determinations that should then combine on a single line' (1991: 99). He lays down three conditions for a *philosophy* of life: (a) that vital difference needs to be thought as internal difference in which the *tendency* to change would not be, and could not be, accidental (this gives us an adequate conception of *evolution*); (b) that the variations do not enter into relationships of association and addition but rather ones of *dissociation* and *division*; (c) that they involve a virtuality that can be actualized in divergent lines, with the result that evolution cannot be

7

conceived as moving 'from one actual term to another actual term in a homogeneous unilinear series, but rather from a virtual term to the heterogeneous terms that actualize it along a ramified series' (ibid.: 100). If the first condition provides us with an adequate conception of evolution then the latter two provide us with an interesting and remarkable conception of *creative* evolution.

Taken as a 'whole' this volume seeks to demonstrate how the virtual works both as an ontology (the Being of beings, the univocity of Being) and in terms of a reconfiguration of the notion of the transcendental, so providing us with the virtual conditions of actual beings (individuation) and of actual experience (perception, memory, etc.). In both cases we need to show that the virtual is not of the order of transcendence; with respect to ontology the power of the virtual has to be conceived as an immanent and not an eminent power, while with respect to the field of experience the virtual shows us how it is possible to develop a conception of experience enlarged and gone beyond. In the essays that follow these crucial insights into the virtual will be pursued and opened up by staging a series of specific encounters of thought. Taking this adventure into the virtual requires overcoming certain habits of representation, thinking across different planes of experience, and bringing into rapport diverse fields of knowledge. The route I have chosen to follow in this series of studies is not an obvious one. It does not adopt a chronological approach to Bergson's texts but instead begins by opening up a problematic and then stages a series of encounters between Bergsonism and other modes of thought and with the key matters of Bergson's thought. If I have an ambition for this volume it is that it will contribute to the task of overcoming lazy and self-satisfied appraisals of Bergson's philosophical standing which guarantee that only sad encounters are produced with his ideas and texts. Bergson is not a simple vitalist or a mystical intuitionist but *both* a radical empiricist and a truly great metaphysician: the true metaphysician must be a radical empiricist and the radical empiricist must be a metaphysician.

1

INTRODUCING TIME AS A VIRTUAL MULTIPLICITY

In reality there is no one rhythm of duration; it is possible to imagine many different rhythms which, slower or faster, measure the degree of tension or relaxation of different kinds of consciousness. ... To conceive of durations of different tensions is perhaps both difficult and strange to our mind, because we have acquired the useful habit of substituting for the true duration an homogeneous and independent Time.

(Bergson, *Matter and Memory*, 1896)

Difference is of two kinds ... The first is call'd a difference of *number*; the other of *kind.*

(Hume, *A Treatise of Human Nature*, 1739–40)

Introduction

In this essay I want to provide some insight into the distinctive features of a Bergsonian mode of thinking. I will begin by introducing some of the essential features of duration. These may initially strike the reader as abstruse and possibly mystifying. By the end of the volume I hope they will strike the reader less so. Our starting point and persistent source of inspiration is this comment from Deleuze:

In *Time and Free Will* the fundamental idea of *virtuality* appears, which will be taken up again and developed in *Matter and Memory:* duration, the indivisible, is not exactly what cannot be divided, but what changes in nature in dividing itself, and what changes in this way defines the virtual or the subjective. But it is above all in *Creative Evolution* that we will find the necessary information.

(Deleuze 1999: 50)

Duration is experience (it is something lived if not adequately intuited), but equally it is experience enlarged and gone beyond. To think this duration is to think 'beyond the human condition' (Bergson 1965: 50, 193), that is, beyond our dominant habits of representation in which time is conceived in terms of space. My duration is disclosed by other durations, both 'inferior' and 'superior', which it is implicated in and that unfold it (ibid.: 184; Deleuze 1991: 28).[1] Take the example Bergson gives of mixing a glass of water with sugar and waiting until the sugar dissolves, which he says is a 'little fact big with meaning' (Bergson 1983: 9; see also p. 339). The time I have to wait is not a mathematical time which we could apply to the entire history of the material world as if it was spread out instantaneously in space; rather, it coincides with an impatience that constitutes a portion of my duration and which I cannot protract or contract at will. This is an experience that is lived and denotes not a relative but an absolute. Moreover, the experience supposes that the glass of water, the sugar, and the dissolving of the sugar in the water, are all abstractions cut out by my senses and understanding from a whole that implicates them. Further, my duration has the power to disclose other durations and to encompass them and itself *ad infinitum* (Deleuze 1991: 80). Bergson gives the example of a simultaneity of fluxes in which while sitting on the bank of a river, the flowing of the water, the flight of a bird, and the uninterrupted murmur in the depths of our life, can be treated as either three things or a single one (Bergson 2000: 36). Here there is an apportioning without dividing, a being of the one and the many at the same time. My duration both encompasses and discloses other durations.

The significance of Bergson's attempt to think duration in a new way, an attempt that only marks a beginning for philosophy, but one it can freely take up again as a repetition of concealed potentialities, was recognized and perhaps best appreciated by Levinas who wished to underline the importance of Bergsonism 'for the entire problematic of contemporary philosophy'. This is because, he argued, it puts into question the ontological confines of *esprit* by not returning to the 'assimilating act of consciousness' the alterity of novelty. It is no longer a thought of the equal and of a 'rationality revealing a reality which keeps to the very measure of a thought'. In effecting a 'reversal' of traditional philosophy by contending the priority of duration over permanence Bergson has provided thought with 'access to novelty, an access independent of the ontology of the Same' (Levinas 1987: 132). With respect to time philosophy must endeavour to remain faithful to its absolute alterity. The attempt to bring our duration in relation to other durations, both 'inferior' and 'superior' to our own, constitutes for Deleuze the very meaning of philosophy since it is only through an adequate thinking of time *qua* duration that we can hope to attain a level of precision in our thinking. It is on account of our human condition that we are condemned to dwell among badly analysed composites and 'to be badly analyzed composites ourselves' (Deleuze 1991: 28). Why is this so?

The human condition refers not to an existential predicament but to accrued evolutionary habits of thought and patterns of action which prevent us from recognizing our own creative conditions of existence and which restrict the domain of praxis to that of social utility. Bergson insists upon the need to provide a genesis of the human intellect – as will be shown in essay five this takes the form of a *double* genesis of matter and intellect – and, in large measure, this constitutes the chief aspect of his response to Kant's Copernican Revolution. This is a revolution which, in spite of its innovations, binds us to an unacceptable and unnecessary relativity of knowledge. Bergson's thinking of the absolute, which is bound up with a thinking of the whole (and of wholes), provides the basis for a novel alliance between science and metaphysics insofar as both, working in concert, are able to discover the real or 'natural articulations' of the universe that have been carved artificially by the abstract intellect. As Deleuze notes of Bergson's project, 'scientific hypothesis' and 'metaphysical thesis' are constantly combined 'in the reconstitution of complete experience' (Deleuze, Afterword 1991: 118). Duration is presented by Bergson as a 'metaphysical correlate of modern science' and the new science of space-time requires a metaphysics of 'immanent and constantly varying duration' if it is to avoid remaining abstract and deprived of meaning (ibid.: 116).

Philosophy attempts to think in accordance with the 'real' or the 'whole'. The precise nature of this real and this whole – one that is neither given nor giveable (if it was it would be an issue of space and not time) – can only be unfolded by pursuing the move beyond habits of representation and expanding the horizons of perception. What cannot be dogmatically upheld is the natural priority of science over metaphysics, in which the task of critique is simply to establish the boundaries and limits of metaphysics by according an unwarranted privilege to mechanism. It is necessary to give an account of our categories of being and spatial habits of representation, to show how they are part of human evolution and adaptation, and show how it is possible to think in other ways. The categories of stable being are not simple illusions but have their anchorage in the conditions of our evolutionary existence; space, for example, is a schema of matter which represents the limit of a movement of expansion that would come to an end as an external envelope of all possible extensions. In this sense it is inadequate to say matter and extensity are 'in' space, it is rather the other way round.

Given the tags of mysticism and spiritualism that Bergsonism has acquired over the years, we perhaps need to be reminded of the fact that in his own day Bergson was read primarily as an empiricist whose thinking amounted to, in the words of his former pupil and later harsh critic, Jacques Maritain, a 'wild experimentalism' (Maritain 1955: 66). Indeed, Maritain accused Bergson of realizing in metaphysics 'the very soul of empiricism' and of producing an ontology of becoming not 'after the fashion of Hegel's panlogism' but rather 'after the fashion of an integral empiricism' (1943: 65). As a rationalist Julien Benda vigorously protested against Bergson's demand for new ways of thinking and new methods in philosophy and called for a return to Spinoza (see Benda 1954 and the study by Niess, 1956: 112–13; see also James on Bergson, 1909: 237ff. and, more recently, the remarks in Mullarkey 1999: 158–9).

Deleuze uses the phrase 'superior empiricism' on different occasions to define the philosophies of Spinoza, Nietzsche, and Bergson (on the latter see Deleuze 1999: 46; see also Deleuze 1994: 57 and 143–4), and as he continues to develop his project he never ceases to uphold the rights of a radical or superior empiricism centred on events, relations, and pre-individual singularities (Deleuze and Guattari, 1994: 47–8). There are affinities between this 'superior' empiricism and James's 'radical empiricism'. What makes empiricism radical according to James is that instead of chopping up experience into atomistic sensations, which can then only be brought into union with one another in terms of a purely abstract principle that 'swoops down upon them from high' and folds them 'in its own conjunctive categories', it recognizes a continuity and concatenation between things (a synechism). He thus defends a 'through-and-through union of adjacent minima of experience, of the confluence of every passing moment of concretely felt experience with its immediately next neighbors' (James 1909: 326–7). James repeatedly insists that this commitment to continuity entails a pluralistic empiricism and is to be sharply distinguished from Hegelian monism. The resemblances between the two doctrines, evident in their critiques of atomism, are merely apparent and what is crucial are the differences between them. Bergson himself make some prudent comments on radical empiricism in letters to James dated 15 February 1905 and 30 April 1909 (see Bergson 1972: 652 and 791). His cautious attitude towards the doctrine in relation to his own project stems from the fact that in granting such a crucial role to the non-conscious and the unconscious (a key dimension of the virtual in fact) it is unable to simply go along the path of seen and felt (visual and tactile) experience. Sight and touch are what make it difficult for us to acknowledge and conceive a change that does not involve *things* that change or a movement without a mobile. Sight is our sense *par excellence*, in which the eye has developed the habit of separating in the visual field relatively invariable figures which change place without changing form and in which 'movement is taken as super-added to the mobile as an accident' (Bergson 1965: 147). Sight contrives to relate to things in this way as an 'advance-guard' for our sense of touch and in this way it helps prepare our action upon the external world. We do better with our sense of hearing. For example, if we allow ourselves to be lulled by a melody we gain access to pure qualitative movement conceived as a virtual multiplicity.

Like phenomenology, Bergsonism has an obsession with the pure.[2] Deleuze argues that in Bergson this is part of the attempt to restore differences in kind. For example, we can divide a composite or mixture according to qualitative and qualified tendencies, such as the way in which it combines duration and extensity defined as directions of movements, giving us 'duration-contraction' and 'matter-expansion'. Such a method of division (intuition in effect) might be compared to a form of transcendental analysis in that it takes us beyond experience as inexplicably given toward the conditions of experience. We frequently locate only differences in degree (more or less of the same thing), when in actuality the most profound differences are the differences in kind. Or, we do not how to draw the line between differences in degree (matter and its perception) and differences in kind (perception and memory). Experience itself offers us nothing more than composites, such as time imbued with space and mixtures of extensity and duration. To go beyond our sedimented habits, which give us only badly analysed composites, we require a method of intuition. Only intuition can take us beyond the abstractions and reifications of the intellect and show us how it is possible to think *in terms of duration*. As Deleuze notes, without this method and cultivating praxis duration would remain a simple psychological experience. Intuition is not itself duration but rather 'the movement by which we emerge from our own duration' and 'make use of our own duration to affirm . . . and recognize the existence of other durations', passing beyond both idealism and realism in the process (Deleuze 1991: 33; see essay six for a demonstration of this passing beyond). In practising philosophy in this manner we go beyond experience towards its conditions (actual experience itself gives us only composites). However, unlike the transcendental procedure of Kant, with which it has certain affinities as we have noted, this does not refer to the conditions of all possible experience; rather, it is moving 'toward the articulations of the real' in which the conditions are neither general and abstract nor are they broader than the conditioned (Deleuze 1991: 26–7). The transcendental is no longer bound up simply with securing conditions of possible experience but with the more demanding task of showing the conditions of real experience in all its peculiarities and of experience enlarged and gone beyond. When we make the turnings in experience, and thus go beyond any naïve conception of lived experience and what we take this to be, there takes place 'an extraordinary broadening out that forces us to think a pure perception identical to the whole of matter' and 'a pure memory identical to the totality of the past' (Deleuze 1991: 27; for a demonstration of pure memory see essay seven). All of this supposes that it is possible to take the turn in experience beyond the bias that is always directed towards utility. It is beyond this specific turn that we reach the point 'at which we finally discover differences in kind' and no longer subsume the real within utilitarian groupings (ibid.).

The two multiplicities

It is the conception of duration as a virtual multiplicity that unites Bergson's thinking from *Time and Free Will*, where the distinction between discrete multiplicities and continuous multiplicities is first introduced (renamed 'actual' and 'virtual' multiplicities by Deleuze), to *Creative Evolution*, where the evolution of life itself is approached in terms of a virtual multiplicity.

Let us begin with the point we wish to get to and arrive at: duration cannot be made the subject of a logical or mathematical treatment. This is owing to its character as a virtual multiplicity. Towards the end of part three of *Creative Evolution* Bergson turns to address the status of his construal of life in terms of an 'impetus' (the notorious *élan vital*). He explicitly conceives it in terms of a 'virtual multiplicity' (*virtuellement multiple*). He acknowledges that describing life in terms of an impetus is to offer little more than an image (a non-dogmatic image of thought). The image, however, is intended to disclose something about the essential character of life, namely, that it is not of a mathematical or logical order but a psychological one. The term psychological might appear to be a troubling one to use in this context. But Bergson uses it for a specific reason, as the following reveals: 'In reality, life is of the psychological order, and it is of the essence of the psychical to enfold a confused plurality of interpenetrating terms' (Bergson 1983: 257). The contrast he is making is with space in which the multiplicity posited or found therein will be of a distinct kind, that is, one made up of discrete elements or components that are related to one another in specific terms, namely, relations of juxtaposition and exteriority. Bergson argues that 'abstract unity' and 'abstract multiplicity' are determinations of space *and* categories of the understanding (that is, they are schemas imposed upon the real in order to make it something uniform, regular, and calculable for us). In this respect it is legitimate for him to claim that 'spatiality and intellectuality' have been molded upon each other. He then goes on to argue that what is psychical in nature cannot entirely correspond with space or fit neatly into categories of the understanding. Take, for example, the question: is a person at any moment one or manifold? The opposition between unity and multiplicity is one posited by the understanding. There is a correspondence between my 'inner life' and 'life in general'. After having noted the correspondence, Bergson then writes in an important passage:

> While, in its contact with matter, life is comparable to an impulsion or an impetus, regarded in itself it is an immensity of virtuality, a mutual encroachment of thousands and thousands of tendencies which nevertheless are 'thousands and thousands' only when regarded as outside each other, that is, when spatialized. Contact with matter is what determines this dissociation. Matter divides actually what was but a virtual multiplicity; and, in this sense, individuation is in part the work of matter, in part the result of life's own inclination. Thus, a poetic sentiment, which bursts into distinct verses, lines and words, may be said to have already contained this multiplicity of individuated elements and yet, in fact, it is the materiality of language that creates it.
>
> (ibid.: 258)

There is a great deal in this passage that needs commenting on. What, precisely, is the relation between life and matter? What is the relation between an intensive virtual multiplicity of tendencies – the tendencies that characterize life in its impulsive form – and an actualization of materiality? How does matter come to divide and actualize what exists as a virtual multiplicity? These are crucially important questions and will be addressed in subsequent essays in the volume that focus specifically on Bergson's conception of creative evolution (see essays three and four).

I indicated above that the term 'psychological' is an awkward one for Bergson to use. Deleuze is one reader, for example, who insists on the primacy of ontology over psychology within Bergson, arguing that unless this point is appreciated then all the new insights contained in Bergson's thinking on time and memory will be lost (memory belongs to the Being of the virtual, not simply to the psychological subject). But at this point in *Creative Evolution* where he is speaking of life in terms of a plurality of interpenetrating tendencies Bergson is simply referring back to his treatment of psychic states in his first published work, *Time and Free Will*, in which he had sought to show that the actuality of our psychic states presupposes a virtual multiplicity of duration. The different degrees of a mental state correspond to qualitative changes, changes that do not admit of simple measure or number. When we ordinarily speak of time we think of a homogeneous medium in which our conscious states are placed alongside one another as in space, and so form a discrete multiplicity. The question is whether the multiplicity of our psychic states resembles the multiplicity of the units of a number and whether duration has anything to do with space. If time is simply a medium in which our conscious states are strung out as a discrete series that can be counted, then time would indeed be space. The question Bergsonism poses is whether time can legitimately be treated as such a medium.

It is in chapter 2 of *TFW* that Bergson will make central to his argument the distinction between two kinds of multiplicity. The distinction he draws between the discrete and the continuous represents a reworking of a distinction initially introduced by the mathematician G. B. Riemann who had utilized the distinction in his 1854 *Habilitationsschrift* entitled 'On the hypotheses which provide the grounds for geometry'. Geometry assumes and takes as given the notion of space and the first principles of construction in space. It gives merely nominal definitions of them with specific determinations assuming the forms of axioms. The task is to determine the extent to which the connections between our assumptions and principles are necessary ones and whether they are, in fact, possible *a priori*. Riemann held that the general notion of 'multiply extended magnitudes', which includes space-magnitudes, was in need of a greater elaboration than had hitherto been the case. A multi-dimensional (*Mannigfältigkeit*) magnitude, he argued, is capable of different measure-relations, in which space is only a particular

15

case of such a magnitude. This also means that the propositions of geometry cannot be derived from general notions of magnitude; rather, the properties which distinguish space from other extended magnitudes can only be deduced from experience. We must, therefore, discover the simplest matters of fact which will enable us to determine the measure-relations of space. We face the problem, however, that we have to admit that there may be several systems of fact which are sufficient to determine these relations (Euclid's system being one such system among many probable ones). Such 'matters of fact' can only be treated as hypotheses, and the critical task consists in deciding upon their extension beyond the limits of observation on the side of both the infinitely great and the infinitely small. Riemann's solution is to distinguish between a discrete multiplicity or manifoldness that contains the principle of its metrical division (the measure of one part is given by the number of elements in a multiplicity) and a continuous multiplicity in which the metrical principle is located in the binding forces which act upon it.[3] Definite or distinct portions of a multiplicity are distinguished by a mark or a boundary. In the case of both multiplicities, therefore, we are dealing with an issue of 'Quanta'. In the case of a discrete magnitude we make the comparison with quantity by counting, and in the case of a continuous one by measuring. The measure consists either in the superposition of the magnitudes to be compared (which requires a means of using one magnitude to act as the standard for another) or, where this is not possible, comparing two magnitudes when one is a part of the other (in this case it is possible only to determine the more or less and not the how much). This makes for an interesting case of magnitudes since it refers us to ones that cannot be treated independently of position or as ever expressible in terms of a unit, but rather as 'regions in a manifoldness'.

Deleuze argues that Bergson was well aware of the contribution of Riemann and that an indirect engagement with him informs the treatment of Relativity in *Duration and Simultaneity* (Relativity is said to be dependent on Riemannian ideas) (Deleuze 1991: 39). Bergson's contribution is to transform the nature of the distinction between the two multiplicities by linking the continuous with the realm of duration. Deleuze's claim is that:

> . . . for Bergson, duration was not simply the indivisible, nor was it the nonmeasurable. Rather, it was that which divided only by changing in kind, that which was susceptible to measurement only by varying its metrical principle at each stage of the division. Bergson did not confine himself to opposing a philosophical vision of duration to a scientific conception of space but took the problem into the sphere of two kinds of multiplicity. He thought that the multiplicity proper to duration had, for its part, a 'precision' as great as that of science; moreover, that it should react upon science and

open up a path for it that was not necessarily the same as that of
Riemann and Einstein.[4]

(ibid.: 40)

Deleuze maintains that Bergson's usage of multiplicity is not part of the
traditional vocabulary, especially when thought in relation to a continuum. I
myself would wish to contend that the thinking contained in the notion of
virtual multiplicity is not peculiar to Bergson but will be found in any
metaphysics that wishes to think beyond the limits of the understanding (one
will thus find it in substance if not in name in Hegel, for example).[5] As
Robin Durie astutely points out, Bergson 'does not begin with a pre-
determined concept of time', from which could then be derived the nature of
temporal relations. Instead, the procedure is to discover 'the formally
determinate relations which determine the "objects" comprising differing
provinces' and from this discovery the two concepts of time (duration and
spatial time) are articulated on the basis of the relations determining the
multiplicities.[6] Let us note some of the salient features of a virtual or
continuous multiplicity:

a   With a nonnumerical multiplicity we can speak of 'indivisibles' at each
     stage of the division: a multiplicity like a qualitative duration divides but
     each time it does so it changes in kind. In this way there 'is *other* without
     there being *several*; number exists only potentially' (Deleuze 1991: 42).
     Let us also note that duration contains both movement and alteration,
     thereby meeting the conditions laid down by Socrates for a coherent and
     sustainable conception of change or a 'flowing' time (Plato, *Theaetetus*
     182c; Plato 1987: 83).
b   This means that the 'other' within a multiplicity is *virtual* and a change
     will always be qualitative. Division is of the order of differentiation
     conceived as a change in kind and not merely degree. This is because a
     nonnumerical multiplicity is both continuous *and* heterogeneous and
     qualitative. We cannot simply say this is because there is more than is
     actually present at any single moment since the issue is not one of
     perspectivism. The virtual does not name or refer to the *whole* of a
     possible experience. Rather, the qualitative movement of a virtual
     multiplicity is bound up with the very nature of this kind of multiplicity
     (fusion, intensive change, etc.).
c   The most important insight for Deleuze about this virtual kind of
     multiplicity is that it is bound up with an actualization. There are two
     orders of the real and the virtual is real and wholly real. A multiplicity is
     virtual insofar as it is actualized and is inseparable from the movement
     of its actualization. Moreover, this actualization comes about through a
     differentiation which requires the creation of divergent lines and that
     produce differences in kind. This doubling of the virtual with actualiz-

ation and its strict separation from the 'possible' will come to play a crucial role in Deleuze's Bergsonism (both in the 1966 text and a text like *Difference and Repetition*) and, more recently, it has come to play a crucial role in the interpretation of Deleuze's work and its legacy (the reading of Deleuze by Alain Badiou, for example). Let us simply note for now that Deleuze is clearly trying to show that the virtual is not to be reified as some pre-existing universal or as some global power (which would Platonize or spatialize it).

d   In a nonnumerical multiplicity not everything is actual. In contrast, in a numerical multiplicity everything is actual although it may not be realized. Thus, when something does get realized it simply gets existence added to it, it does not change its nature (a demonstration of this in connection with a thinking of evolution will be attempted in essay three). In a virtual multiplicity, by contrast, there is a temporal movement from a condition of virtuality to an actualization in which lines of differentiation as lines of non-resemblance are created. In short, we must make a unilateral distinction between the virtual and the *possible* and posit an asymmetry between the virtual and the actual. For Deleuze it is disastrous to confuse the virtual with the possible since they are bound up with two completely different processes. 'Possibility' is the source of many false problems in our thinking and needs to be restricted to analyses of closed systems; 'virtuality', on the other hand, is the peculiar feature of open systems and is the notion upon which Bergson will go on to establish a philosophy of memory and life.

The time of number

In *TFW* Bergson sought to show that in thinking through the distinction between two kinds of multiplicity much rests on our conception of number since the unit of arithmetics is a model of what divides without changing in kind. In this respect it is an example of an actual or discrete multiplicity. Number generates the illusion of the 'object' and conceals its own operations. How does this happen? Chapter 2 of *TFW* opens with a discussion of number,[7] which comes immediately after the denouement to the book's opening chapter that has treated the relation between intensity and multiplicity, in which Bergson seeks to show that our idea of intensity is situated 'at the junction of two streams', one of which is the idea of extensive magnitude (something we can compare and measure precisely, such as the difference in size between two blocks of wood) and the image of an 'inner multiplicity'. His question is whether something like a psychic state can be treated as a magnitude: does it make sense, for example, to say that today I am twice as happy or joyous as I was yesterday? While we can distinguish between experiencing a twinge of jealousy and being obsessed by a jealous passion, would it make sense to say that the jealousy of Othello should be understood as being made up of innumerable twinges of jealousy? (Moore 1996: 45; see Bergson 1960: 73).[8] Bergson asks: 'why do we say of a higher intensity that it is greater? Why do we think of a greater quantity or a greater space?' (7). His contention is that states of consciousness cannot be isolated from one another but should be approached in terms of a 'concrete multiplicity', in which there is fusion and interpenetration, in short, a qualitative heterogeneity. The reason for this fusion and interpenetration is that the states of consciousness unfold themselves in duration and not, like the units of arithmetic, in space. An increasing intensity of a mental state is inseparable from a qualitative progression and from a becoming of time. As Deleuze points out, the notion of an intensive magnitude 'involves an impure mixture between determinations that differ in kind' with the result that our question 'by how much does a sensation grow or intensify?' takes us back to a badly stated problem (Deleuze 1991: 19).

Let us see how Bergson seeks to expose the illusion of number. This is the illusion that generates a confusion of quality with quantity, of intensity with extensity. Chapter 2 of *TFW* begins with the claim that number may be defined as a synthesis of the one and the many conceived as a collection of discrete units, in which every number is the 'one' of a simple intuition. The unity of a number is that of a sum in that it covers a multiplicity of parts each of which can be taken separately. However, this characterization is insufficient since it fails to recognize that the units of a collection of numbers are *identical*. In other words, the question has to be posed: just what is the *difference* between the units of a number if the units are identical? Bergson's answer is that numbering or counting relies upon the intuition of a multiplicity of identical parts or units, so that the only difference between them can reside in their position in space.[9] The components or elements of an actual or discrete multiplicity have to be differentiated, otherwise they would form a single unit.

Bergson gives the example of a flock of sheep and invites us to carry out the following operation: we can count them and say there are fifty and in counting them as a collection of units we neglect their individual differences (which are known to the farmer whose flock they are); then we can say that although we have a grouping of sheep they differ in that they occupy different positions in space. Now this requires an intuition of space. This is what Kant sought to demonstrate in his transcendental aesthetic by showing that space has an existence independent of its content and arguing that it cannot be treated as an abstraction like other abstractions of sensation. This is a demonstration that Bergson regards as correct as far as it goes (1960: 92–5). How do I form the image of a singular collection of things? Do I place the sheep side by side in an ideal space or do I repeat in succession the image of a single one? It is certain that I am building up a composite picture in which I retain the successive images and this retention is required if the number is to go on increasing in proportion to my building up of the collection of units. Bergson's contention is that this act, in which I am juxtaposing the images being built up, takes place not in duration but in space. It is not that we do not count in duration; rather, the point is that we count the moments of duration by means of points in space.[10]

Number is curious in that every number is both a collection of units (the number one being a sum of, or divisible into, fractional quantities) and is itself a unit. Taken as a unit in itself the whole of any number can be grasped by a simple and indivisible intuition. Such intuition leads us to the belief that all numbers are made up of indivisible components; all we are doing here, however, is building up levels of discreteness (adding, subtracting, multiplying, and dividing discreteness). Any unit of number is potentially implicated in an actual or discrete multiplicity, and within such a multiplicity when the elements change they do not change in kind (they might grow smaller or bigger, but this is pure quantity and not quality). When I equate the number three to the sum of $1+1+1$ there is nothing to stop me from regarding each of the units as indivisible, but the reason for this is simply that I choose not to make use of the multiplicity that is enclosed within each of the units (I could choose to compose the number from halves or quarters). If it is conceivable that a unit can be divided into as many parts as we want then it is shown to be extended as a magnitude. It is only when a number assumes a completed state that we come to think that the whole displays the features of continuity, and this then settles into a general illusion with respect to numbering (we overlook the discontinuity of number). This explains why Bergson is keen to draw our attention to the difference between number in the process of formation and a formed number: 'The unit is irreducible while we are thinking it and the number is discontinuous while we are building it up; but, as soon as we consider number in its finished state, we objectify it, and it then appears to be divisible to an unlimited extent' (1960: 83). Number applies to the sphere of 'objectivity' in the sense that new elements or components can be added or substituted at any time but without this addition or subtraction changing anything in kind vis-à-vis the object (of a multiplicity). This is why Bergson holds that such a multiplicity has no virtuality to it. It is from this consideration of the peculiar operations of number that Bergson is led to his distinction between 'two very different kinds of multiplicity'.

Bergson goes on to draw a distinction between the perception of extensity and the conception of homogeneous space. Only among beings of intellect do we find the independence of the latter. In many animals there is only a perception of extensity. Space does not assume a homogeneous form for them. The faculty of conceiving a space without quality is not so much a faculty of abstraction as more of a faculty which enables the human intellect to count, to abstract, and to posit clean-cut distinctions. Space is a principle of quantitative differentiation that enables us to distinguish a number of identical and simultaneous sensations from one another, and it covers up the 'heterogeneity that is the very ground of our experience' (ibid.: 97). There is a danger of reification in the way in which Bergson draws this distinction between a conception of homogeneous space and a perception of extensity and one that he does not expose, and overcome, until *MM*. Abstract space has to be seen as a limit-conception, that is, as a result of the needs of action and not reified as an indomitable feature of the human standpoint.[11] I will return to this point later in the essay.

We can now return to the central argument of *TFW*: we perfectly comprehend the sense of there being a number that is greater than another, but can the same be said of an intensive sensation? How can a more intense sensation contain one of less intensity? Unlike the law of number the relations among intensities cannot be adequately approached in terms of those of container and contained with different intensities being superposed upon one another. Adequately understood an intensity cannot be assimilated to magnitude.

Is time space?

The question to be posed now is the following: can duration be treated as a discrete multiplicity, that is, are states of consciousness external to one another and spread out in time as a spatial medium? Looked at from the perspective of pure duration our states can be seen to permeate and melt into one another without precise outlines and without any affiliation with number, in which past and present states form a whole, 'as happens when we recall the notes of a tune, melting, so to speak, into another' (1960: 100; see also Husserl's discussion of melody [1964: 30: 43–4, 58–60], which is strikingly close to Bergson on this issue). These are involved in qualitative changes that disclose a 'pure heterogeneity' (continuous variation). When we interrupt the rhythm of a tune by perhaps dwelling longer than is customary on one note, it is not the exaggerated length that signals the mistake to us but rather the qualitative change caused in the whole of the piece of music.

> We can thus conceive of succession without distinction, and think of it as a mutual penetration, an interconnexion and organization of elements, each one of which represents the whole, and cannot be distinguished or isolated from it except by abstract thought.
>
> (Bergson 1960: 101)

Duration is nonrepresentational and as soon as we think it we necessarily spatialize it (which clearly presents a major, if not insuperable, problem for any thinking of duration; see Weyl 1987: 87ff.). It could be called an intensive magnitude 'if intensities can be called magnitudes' (1960: 106). Bergson hesitates on this point because he does not wish to treat duration as a quantity. Because we have the idea of space we set our states side by side so

21

as to perceive them simultaneously: we project time into space, express duration in terms of extensity, and succession assumes the form of a continuous chain. A decisive movement or shift takes place in our thinking, albeit one we are ordinarily not aware of:

> Note that the mental image thus shaped implies the perception, no longer successive, but simultaneous, of a *before* and *after*, and that it would be a contradiction to suppose a succession which was only a succession, and which nevertheless was contained in one and the same instant.
>
> (ibid.)

The important point is this: we could not introduce order into terms without first distinguishing them and then comparing the places they occupy. As Bergson writes, 'if we introduce an order in what is successive, the reason is that succession is converted into simultaneity and is projected into space' (102). Moreover, since the idea of a reversible series in duration, even of a certain *order* of succession in time, itself implies the representation of space it cannot be used to define it.

Reducing time to simple movement of position is to confuse time with space. It is this confusion between motion and the space traversed which explains the paradoxes of Zeno.[12] The interval between two points is infinitely divisible, and if motion is said to consist of parts like those of the interval itself, then the interval can never be crossed. But the truth of the matter is different:

> . . . each of Achilles's steps is a simple indivisible act . . . after a given number of these acts, Achilles will have passed the tortoise. The mistake of the Eleatics arises from their identification of this series of acts, each of which is *of a definite kind and indivisible*, with the homogeneous space which underlies them.
>
> (113)

Because this space can be divided and put together again according to any kind of abstract law, the illusion arises that it is possible to reconstruct the movement of Achilles not with his step but with that of the tortoise.[13] In truth, we have only two tortoises that agree to make the same kind of steps or simultaneous acts so as to never catch one another. Let us now take the paradox of the flying arrow which at any point is not in flight. If the arrow is always at a point when is it ever in flight or mobile? Instead, we might ask, what is it in this example that leads us to saying that the arrow *is* at any point in its course? (Of course it might be but only in the sense of it passing and stopping at a particular point, at which point it would come to rest and its flight would cease.) Within any posited motionless trajectory it is possible to count as many immobilities as we like. What we fail to see is that 'the trajectory is created in one stroke, although a certain time is required for it; and that although we can divide at will the trajectory once created, we cannot divide its creation, which is an act in progress and not a thing' (Bergson 1983: 309).[14]

The key insight concerns the difference between extensity and intensity: the space traversed is a matter of extension and quantity (it is divisible), but the movement is an intensive act and a quality. Bergson is insistent that it is 'through the quality of quantity that we form the idea of quantity without quality', not the other way round. Qualitative operations are even at work in the formation of numbers (the addition of a third unit to two others alters the nature, the rhythm, of the whole, even though our spatial habits lead us to disregard the significance of these varying aspects) (1960: 123).

In Bergson's first published text duration, conceived as a pure heterogeneity, is presented as an aspect of a synthesizing consciousness, that is, its reality is something solely psychological. Bergson contrasts psychic time with clock time. It is the latter that treats time as a magnitude (1960: 107–8). Motion, however, in so far as it is a passage from one point to another, 'is a mental synthesis, a psychic and therefore unextended process ... If consciousness is aware of anything more than positions, the reason is that it keeps the successive positions in mind and synthesizes them' (111). The conclusion is reached in *TFW* that the 'interval of duration' exists only for us and on account of the interpenetration of our conscious states (116). Outside ourselves we find only space, and consequently nothing but simultaneities, 'of which we could not even say that they are objectively successive, since succession can only be thought through *comparing* the present with the past'. The qualitative impression of change cannot, therefore, be felt outside consciousness. Duration and motion are not objects but 'mental syntheses' (120). In our consciousness states permeate one another, imperceptibly organize themselves into a whole, and bind the past to the present. Conceived as a virtual, qualitative multiplicity this duration 'contains number only potentially, as Aristotle would have said' (121).

This restriction of duration to consciousness is one that Bergson will seek to overcome in subsequent texts. The importance of the move he makes will be treated later in the essay. For now, let us note that it requires breaking down the form/matter opposition that structures his account of mind and the world in *TFW*. Even in this work Bergson is already aware of the problems connected with any account which construes the relation between mind and world in terms of a form simply being imposed upon matter: 'assuming that the forms alluded to, into which we fit matter, come entirely from the mind, it seems difficult to apply them constantly to objects without the latter soon leaving their mark on them ... forms applicable to things cannot be entirely our own work ... if we give much to matter we probably receive something from it ...' (1960: 223). As we shall see in essay six, in

Matter and Memory Bergson will provide a very different account of matter and perception.

To draw this section to a close I wish to return to the conception of space we find in *TFW*. The danger in the account Bergson gives, one which he appears to implicitly acknowledge, is that it fails to appreciate the extent to which even a homogeneous space presupposes *dimensions* of space that have qualitative differences. As Lindsay points out, if we take away the possibility of determinations in space then space itself becomes nothing and cannot provide the basis of counting (Lindsay 1911: 133). Certainly space has to be regarded as that which has infinite divisibility, but such a characterization only serves to indicate that each division is made in definite ways and that a definite division of provisional units implies some kind of heterogeneity. If objects were, as a matter of fact, completely identical and devoid of qualitative differences then no discrimination would be possible at all: 'Without counting and discrimination we could not have the conception of that which is merely divisible' (ibid.: 134). So, while we can think of qualitative differences becoming more and more like mathematical points, if they disappeared completely so too would the ground upon which spatial relations are constructed. Lindsay then notes that if the same is true of time then, *mutatis mutandis*, 'time and space may be homogeneous media and yet sufficiently distinguished as the limits of duration and extensity; as the limits of two mathematical functions may be nothing and yet distinguishable in terms of the functions which they limit' (ibid.). Space and time cannot then be taken to be, in their homogeneous aspect, *a priori* realities (intuitions of sensibility) but have to be seen as emergent and exigent features of social action. As the mental diagram of infinite divisibility abstract space and abstract time are the result of the solidification and division we effect on a moving continuity in order to secure a fulcrum for our action and to introduce into it real changes. The necessity of making this move is clearly argued for, and contra Kant, by Bergson in *Matter and Memory* (1991: 211). The real is made up of *both* extensity and duration, but this 'extent' is not that of some infinite and infinitely divisible space, the space of a receptacle, that the intellect posits as the place in which and from which everything is built. It is necessary, then, to separate a concrete extension, diversified and organized at the same time, from 'the amorphous and inert space which subtends it' (ibid.: 187). This is the space that we divide indefinitely and within which we conceive movement as a multiplicity of instantaneous positions. Homogeneous space is not, then, logically anterior to material things but posterior to them.

Bergson and Russell on continuity

I now turn to examine the nature of Russell's critique of Bergsonism and his espousal of a purely mathematical treatment of continuity. This may help us to acquire a better grasp of the issues at stake in our thinking of time and comprehension of the virtual type of multiplicity.

In Lecture V of his *Our Knowledge of the External World* on 'The Theory of Continuity' Russell proclaims that continuity is a purely mathematical subject and not, strictly speaking, part of philosophy. A notion of change must fit into a logical framework, with the result that logical necessity compels us to a conception of 'instants without duration' (Russell 1914 [1922]: 158). In the section on time in the essay on 'Mysticism and Logic' from the same year Russell holds time to be 'an unimportant and superficial characteristic of reality' and in the process he sets himself in opposition to a variety of modern teachings on time, including Nietzsche, pragmatism, Bergson, and Darwin and evolutionism (Russell 1914 [1986]: 42, 43–5).[15] Also in evidence in this essay is the superficial nature of aspects of Russell's appreciation of Bergson, as when he declares his philosophy of intuition rests on a complete condemnation of the knowledge that is derived from science and common sense (38). Bergson defends a common-sense realism against the scepticism of philosophy in the Introduction to *Matter and Memory* and conceives science as providing knowledge of one half of the absolute. Neither are simply condemned. Russell has, in fact, a number of affinities with Bergson and to which his prejudices blinded him. Russell's negotiation with realism in 'On Matter' (1912) is, for example, quite close to aspects of Bergson's position in *MM*. Having noted this, however, in this essay Russell insists that our knowledge of matter is solely descriptive and reveals nothing about its intrinsic nature – it remains, in other words, purely on the level of exposing 'the logical character of its interrelations' (Russell 1914 [1992]: 95). Although Russell was not at all happy with subjectivism – which he equated with Kant's endeavour to restrict philosophy to our mental habits – he failed to see that his own logicism remains, ironically, caught up in subjectivism.

In addition to his critical, but often incisive and fair-minded, reception of Bergson published in *The Monist* in 1912, Russell also engages with Bergson throughout the lectures that make up *Our Knowledge of the External World*. It needs to be made clear: in privileging a mathematical treatment of continuity Russell is not contesting Bergson's stress on continuity and falling back on discontinuous states; rather, the difference is over how continuity is to be thought and mapped out. This explains why he is able to appreciate the force of Bergson's exposition of Zeno's paradoxes while at the same time insisting on the need to think the continuity of motion in a different way to the 'interpenetration' argument of Bergson. For Russell, however, the force of Bergson's exposition only holds if we accept the initial force of Zeno's paradoxes, and he doesn't: 'A cinematograph in which there are an infinite number of films, and in which there is never a *next* film because an infinite number come between any two, will perfectly represent a continuous motion. Wherein, then, lies the force of Zeno's argument?' (1912: 339).[16] Before we explore this further by looking at the lecture on the theory of continuity, let us just pause to note the paradoxical nature of Russell's own position (he has answered Zeno by substituting one paradox for another). In evincing the argument that motion can be shown to be continuous because there is never anything that comes next, Russell has deprived the movement of time itself, as a movement of virtual time (the coexistence or immanence of past and present), of any efficacy and replaced this movement with an infinite number of discrete motions. In short, he is seeking to construct continuity out of discreteness. As we shall now see, that Russell has replaced a philosophical treatment of time (a virtual multiplicity) with a mathematical one (a numerical multiplicity) accounts for the difficulties on change and time that he reaches in his 1914 lecture on continuity: are they something real or is their status solely a logical one?

In this lecture Russell is concerned to reconcile the philosophical and the logical: how can the mathematical treatment of time in terms of points and instants be squared with our feeling, intimated at by many philosophers, that time is a continuity? His response is to say that while it is wrong to divide time into a *finite* number of points and instants the correct way forward, one that will stop us from falling back into Bergson's confused response to Zeno, is to appeal to an *infinite* number of these points and instants. But surely won't infinitely numerous points and instants simply provide us with a jerky motion and a succession of different immobilities? Russell raises this question himself and answers it by saying that to assume this to be the case is to fail to realize, both imaginatively and abstractly, the nature of a continuous series as understood in mathematics. In short, we lack the *intuition* to conceive of such a continuity and we need to learn how, says Russell, to *feel* its complete adequacy and validity (1914 [1922]: 136).

Russell seeks to show that when mathematics thinks continuity it does so in terms of it being a property of a series of terms, which is to suppose an 'order' or arrangement of time, in which something comes before something else (though this is not required, he notes, in the case of the cardinal number). Thus, continuity does not belong to a set of terms themselves but to a set in a certain order (in this case we can say that in the example of continuity the relations established are always external to their terms).[17] Russell then introduces his idea of 'compactness' as a way of accounting for the lowest degree of continuity within the arrangement of any series: 'A series is called "compact" when no two terms are consecutive, but between any two there are others' (138), and he gives the simple example of a series of fractions in order of magnitude. Between any two fractions, however small the difference, there can be posited an infinite number of other fractions. Now while mathematical space and time have the property of compactness, it is not clear that we can extend this to actual space and time. It seems as if mathematics reaches an empirical limit at this point. But this is not enough to stop Russell from persisting with this logicizing of space and time and inviting us to feel and intuit the validity of this logic.

26

In short, Russell reaches the view that there are no discontinuous leaps in something changing from one state or position to another; rather, continuity is to be thought in terms of an infinite number of positions. This explains why it is illegitimate, he argues, to say what something will be at the next instant or where it will be in its next position – there are no such 'nexts'. The movement of time is to be conceived then not in terms of *consecutive* points and instants but rather in terms of a *continuous series* of infinite points and instants. It is important we get Russell right on this point and not commit a logical blunder. It would be mistaken to suppose that he is arguing with this model that between the positions and states of things there are infinitesimal distances in space or periods of time, and that it is this which allows us to multiply indefinitely the points and instants. This is clearly not the case. His argument is rather that in a continuous motion the interval between any two positions and instants is always finite; the continuity lies solely in the fact that, however near together the two positions or instants are taken to be, 'there are an infinite number of positions still nearer together, which are occupied at instants that are also still nearer together' (142). This means that a moving body 'never jumps from one position to another, but always passes by a gradual transition through an infinite number of intermediaries' (ibid.). No instant, therefore, can be said to last for a finite time and neither can it be said that an instant has a beginning and an end. The conclusion is reached that although the facts or logic itself do not necessitate this model of continuous motion in terms of a particular conception of points and instants, it is at least 'consistent' with the facts and with logic (whether this defence rests on a vicious circle I will not explore here). I contend that time has been thought away on this mathematical model, which, in spite of its criticism of the consecutive, is still a model of points and instants in accordance with a discrete or an actual multiplicity.

We might now ask, what is the relation between this mathematical treatment of continuity and actual space and time? Again, it is an issue that is raised by Russell himself. He adopts the position that while points and instants cannot be taken to be actual physically existing entities we can posit an analogy between the continuity of actual space and time and the continuity that mathematics works with. However, he also wishes to stress that the theory of mathematical continuity is an abstract logical theory, the validity of which is *not* dependent upon any properties of actual space and time (Russell 1914 [1922]: 135–58, 137). But this is not the whole of Russell's position, for he also argues that the logical theory has more empirical purchase than any other theory, including what he takes to be its major rival, that of Bergson's. He speaks of translating the propositions of physics into propositions about objects given to us in sensation 'by a sort of dictionary' (147). Although he has no such basis upon which to make the claim, he argues that within the sphere of immediate sense-data it is both necessary and more consonant with the facts than any other view to distinguish states of objects as instantaneous ones which form a compact series. What he will not allow for is that Bergson's conception of time as a virtual multiplicity has any empirical purchase whatsoever; it is rather to be understood solely in terms of an illusion of experience and a mistaken inference from available sense-data. Now, this is clear evidence of an outright dogmatism on the part of Russell's logicism. This is so because he has clearly stated that we know very little from the evidence of our sense-data about the empirical character of space and time, and yet he is insistent that the choice to be made is not between a philosophical thinking of time and a mathematical one, but rather choosing between various mathematical alternatives. Thus, instead of developing a genuine empiricism of thinking, Russell simply rests content with a restricted empiricism, one that is dogmatically stated in spite of Russell's appeal to the virtue of simplicity which results when one adopts Occam's razor. For Russell the empirical data can be read in all sorts of ways, and this means that we are simply dealing with overcoming certain *logical* difficulties, such as our failure of imagination and abstraction when it comes to appreciating how a continuous series can be thought in terms of infinite numbers within mathematics. This means, in effect, that while the mathematical account of continuity is not dependent for its validity upon any properties of actual space and time, it arrogates to itself the right to dictate what should be the proper *philosophical* account of space and time.

One time and one space

Kant's presentation of time in the *Critique of Pure Reason* is for Bergson a classic instance of the conversion of time into space. Kant seems to provide such an image of time when he says that because an inner intuition cannot yield a shape we have to represent a time-sequence by analogy with space, drawing it as a line in space that progresses to infinity: 'We represent the time-sequence by a line progressing to infinity, in which the manifold constitutes a series of one dimension only; and we reason from the properties of this line to all the properties of time' with the exception of substituting simultaneity with succession as the mode of relation between parts (A 33/B 50; see also B 155–6, B 292).[18] We shall complicate Kant's image of time in essay seven of the volume. For now, I shall examine Kant on time in the context of Bergson's critique of the habit of treating time as if it was space.

There is more than one presentation of time in the first Critique. First we have the treatment offered in the transcendental aesthetic, and second we have the treatment in the transcendental analytic. As one recent commentator has succinctly argued, there is no fundamental inconsistency in Kant's argument: in the first presentation Kant is offering an account of the forms of space and time on the level of immediate intuition, while in the second he is seeking to explain how it is possible for us to have cognition of specific and determinate regions of space and stretches of time (Gardner

1999: 84; see also the entry on 'time' in Caygill 1995: 398). The difference is, if one likes, between Space and spaces and Time and times, or between their unity and their multiplicity, the one and the many. Putting it like this, however, is misleading since in both presentations Kant is keen to uphold the thesis of there being only the *one* space and only the *one* time. Kant is not being inconsistent, then, when after having argued for the intuition of a one-whole of space and time he goes on to account for their divisions and parts. In the aesthetic his concern is with the indeterminate character of the pure intuitions of space and time; in the analytic his concern shifts to accounting for their determinate character 'through being subjected to conceptual synthesis, which necessarily begins with the spatial and temporal positions of appearances' (Gardner 1999: 85).

Kant begins the transcendental aesthetic by stating that intuition denotes the immediate relation between our mode of knowing and objects. For intuition (*Anschauung*) to take place an object has to be given to us and this means that the mind must be affected in some way. This capacity for receiving representations (*Vorstellungen*) in this affective mode is what we can call 'sensibility' (*Sinnlichkeit*). Although concepts are needed in order to think what is given to us there can be no knowledge without this primary basis in affective sensibility. Objects and things that appear to us and which we sense do so within an empirical intuition. Here Kant makes a distinction within such an appearance between its 'matter' and its 'form'. The former denotes the *a posteriori* material sensation, the latter the *a priori* ordering and organization of the same sensation in the mind. It is the *a priori* element of sensation that necessitates for Kant the introduction of a *pure* intuition. Every intuition has a manifold aspect to it, but the arrangement of it in terms of relations amounts to a pure form of sensibility, that is, it is 'of' sensation but independent of it. We can think, for example, of a body as being composed of an empirical intuition of its secondary qualities such as hardness and colour, but we can also think of it in terms of an extension and a figure (primary qualities) that remain over once the empirical element has been taken away. Thus, if we remove the actual sensations we are still left in the mind with a pure intuition as a *form* of sensibility. This pure element within sensation is what Kant names the 'transcendental aesthetic', and his claim is that there are two pure forms of sensible intuition, space and time conceived as forms of outer and inner sense. By means of the former we are able to represent to ourselves objects external to us and by means of the latter the mind can intuit its inner states.

Neither space nor time can be empirical concepts that could be derived from actual experiences, Kant argues; rather as the conditions of possible experience they provide the grounds for any actual experience. Actual experience would be impossible without there being first the conditions of a possible experience. Without such conditions it would be blind. Take space as an example: unless I am able to represent things outside of me in certain relations, such as juxtaposition and externality, I would not even be able to refer my sensations of objects to anything outside of myself. Thus, 'the representation of space must be presupposed' (*CPR*: A 23/B 38). Although we can think space as devoid of objects we can never represent to ourselves an absence of this homogeneous space within which we construct relations between objects. As a pure intuition space can only be represented as the *one* space (Kant will say the same of time). Of course we can and we do speak of a diversity of different spaces but these are all parts of one and the same space (space is nothing other than divisibility, partitioning, etc.). All the parts of space coexist into infinity which is why, Kant argues, we can treat it as an 'infinite *given* magnitude' (A 25/B 40). The reason why space and time can be said to be infinite magnitudes that are given is because both are unified wholes and provide the 'exclusive ground for possible limitations' (Heidegger 1997a: 83). In other words, and as Heidegger points out, such a whole cannot be generated out of the parts; the whole has, therefore, a 'being' that is independent from, and different, to its parts. Kant reaches the conclusion that space is the form of all the appearances of outer sense and as such it is a subjective condition of sensibility: 'It is, therefore, solely from the human standpoint that we can speak of space, of extended things, etc.' (B 43). Kant then makes a key point about the status of space which he will also attribute to that of time: the 'empirical reality' of space is possible owing to its 'transcendental ideality'. What he means by this is that space does have an objective validity with respect to the subjective conditions of sensible experience. It is not that we are dreaming or being held in illusion when we intuit the form of things in terms of space and time; space and time are indeed 'real' but only in the sense that they are the transcendental and 'ideal' conditions of any actual experience. Whether this is enough to save Kant's Critique from hopeless confusion and a mire of indecision about the 'true' reality of time and space was an issue at the forefront of the reception of Kant by his contemporaries.[19] What is clear is that for Kant both the empirically real and the transcendentally ideal are valid only for the human standpoint. This is why he insists that the ground of metaphysics lies in a negative science he calls 'general phenomenology'.[20]

Let me now turn to Kant's presentation of time in the aesthetic. This presentation strictly follows what has been said already of space. Like space, time cannot be an empirical concept derivable from experience; it is rather a condition of sensible experience by which we are able to represent to ourselves a manifold of things as existing at one and the same time (simultaneity) and at different times such as one after the other (succession). In this opening statement on time we can see the assumption at work which Bergson is so keen to draw our attention to, namely, that time is being conceived in terms of space: to conceive of things as taking place in terms of a succession of positionings ('before', 'after', etc.) is to presuppose a faculty of space. Time is being thought in terms of a discrete multiplicity governed by relations of juxtaposition (simultaneity) and externality (succession). Kant goes on to argue that although we can think time as void of appearances (as void of actual things being related either simultaneously or successively) we cannot remove time itself from our conditions of sensibility. Time is a 'universal condition of the possibility of things' in the mode of their appearance to us. The axioms or principles of time cannot be derived from experience simply because if they were they would not be able to give to experience either strict universality or apodeictic certainty (B 47). Again, like space, time is essentially one. The single dimension of time for Kant is that of different times all taking place in terms of succession: 'Different times are part of one and the same time' (ibid.). This proposition, says Kant, is a synthetic one contained in our intuition and representation of time. So when we speak of an infinitude of time – that time is without limit – this means nothing other than that every determinate magnitude of time 'is possible only through limitations of one single time that underlies it' (B 48). This representation must be *given* as unlimited: '. . . when an object is so given that its parts, and every quantity of it, can be determinately represented only through limitations, the whole representation cannot be given through concepts, since they contain only partial representations; on the contrary, such concepts must themselves rest on *immediate intuition*' (B 48, my emphasis). The infinity of time resides solely in our intuition and not anywhere else.

Kant goes on to place the concepts of alteration and motion within this intuition and representation of time: time is the *form* of change that does not itself change (alteration itself cannot, therefore, be counted among the data of transcendental experience). This point is demonstrated again later in the 'analytic' part of the Critique. Here Kant construes time as the permanent substratum of inner intuition (A 182/B 225), and he speaks of it as an 'underlying ground' that must exist *'at all times'* (A 182/B 226). As the ground of change time, *qua* substrate or permanent substance, *abides* (*Bleibendes*). The notion of duration – again, conceived in terms of laying out the transcendental conditions of the possibility of experience – gives us the permanent substratum by which we are able to represent changes in time. Consequently, Kant can say: 'change does not affect time itself, but only appearances in time' (A 183/B 226). And he points out that if the mode of time is succession then this rules out *coexistence* as a mode of time, 'for none of the parts of time coexist' (ibid.). It is only when we cognize the permanence of time that we can develop the correct understanding of alteration: 'Coming to be and ceasing to be are not alterations of that which comes to be or ceases to be' (A 187/B 230). If substances could come into being and go out of being the one condition that can guarantee the empirical unity of time would be removed, and this would mean that appearances would be able to relate to two different times with existence flowing in two parallel streams – 'which is absurd', Kant says. Thus, there can only be the one time in which all different times are locatable (a time of succession and not coexistence). It should be noted that when Kant talks of substances he is doing so on the level of the field of appearance. Substance, one might say, is the being of what appears and not the being of what is. This is not to attribute to Kant a straightforward opposition between the phenomenological and the ontological; rather, we might suggest that what the Critique has sought to demonstrate is the phenomenological conditions of ontology: '. . . the most the understanding can achieve *a priori* is to anticipate the form of a possible experience in general. . . . Its principles are merely rules for an the exposition of appearances, and the proud name of an Ontology . . . must, therefore, give place to the modest title of a mere Analytic of pure understanding' (A 247/ B 303).

Again, like space, time is to be credited with both empirical reality and transcendental ideality, for although time is also a subjective condition of experience its phenomenological being is objective for all appearances and for all the things that can enter into our experience. We should not say things are 'in' time but rather that things *appear* for us as implicated in certain temporal relations (past, present, future, etc.) and must appear so if sensible experience is to be an intelligible experience. Time cannot, then, be granted an absolute reality but only a relative one: its reality is relative to our intuition and cannot be said to subsist or inhere in things themselves. Kant insists that time is real not as an 'object' but as a 'mode of representation'. He insists upon this point in order to counter the inference that he is suggesting that time is a mere hallucination or that an appearance is the same as an illusion. It is the 'possibility of experience' which gives 'objective reality' to *a priori* modes of knowledge (A 156/B 195). Kant distinguishes his transcendental idealism from two other kinds of idealism: what he calls the 'problematic idealism' of Descartes (which contends that the 'cogito' contains the only indubitable empirical assertion available to us and holds back from ascribing any empirical reality to things outside the existence of the I) and the 'dogmatic idealism' of Berkeley (which does not equivocate but dogmatically holds that things in space are imaginary entities). Kant argues that the proof required to refute dogmatic idealism must show that we have real experience of outer things and not merely their imagination; in short, it needs to be shown that inner experience, in its indubitable aspect, 'is possible only on the assumption of outer experience' (B 275). Thus, 'the consciousness of my existence is at the same time an immediate consciousness of the existence of other things outside me' (B 276). It is important to appreciate the formal character of Kant's project: it does not aspire to determine in transcendental fashion the actual materiality of experience but provides us only with its form.

As we have seen, there is a notion of duration at work in Kant's presentation of time. However, this is in the context of a transcendental determination of the possibility of experience. In order to ascribe succession to time it is necessary to posit another time in which the sequence is possible:

Only through the permanent does existence in different parts of the time-series acquire a magnitude which can be called duration (*Dauer*). For in bare succession existence is always vanishing and recommencing, and never has the least magnitude. Without the permanent there is therefore no time-relation.

(*CPR*: A 183/B 226)

However, because we cannot perceive time in itself but only in terms of an intuitive representation, in which we remain solely on the level of appearances, this permanent conceived as the substratum of all determinations of time has to be viewed as a condition of the possibility of the synthetic unity of perceptions, in short, of experience. Duration, then, is not itself change; rather, change in time is 'a mode of the existence of that which remains and persists' (A 184/B 227). Moreover, the permanence that is this duration is 'simply the mode in which we represent to ourselves the existence of things in the [field of] appearance' (A 186/B 229). Duration, then, belongs to this field. It is important to note that there is in Kant's presentation of time a distinction between a temporal order of representations and a temporal order of objects. The account Kant gives of notions such as causality and substance in the analogies of experience is designed to show the need for a phenomenological positing of an 'objective time-order' (Gardner 1999: 172). If this was not the case then it would be impossible for a subject to locate and position *objects* in any determinate temporal manner, all it would have would be the experience of its own inner states and representations. However, this determination of the objective order of objects and events in time – such as a flash of lightning followed by the sound of thunder – is operating strictly on a phenomenological level in relation to the field of appearance and is objective only in relation to a universal subject.[21]

Let me now briefly examine what Kant has to say about time as a magnitude in the transcendental analytic. I have drawn on some of this material already *vis-à-vis* the matter of substance. In the 'axioms of intuition' Kant deals with appearances in their quantitative aspects (extensive magnitudes) and in the 'anticipations of perception' he deals with them in their qualitative aspects (intensive magnitudes). The relevant aspect for us of the 'anticipations' concerns Kant's conception of space and time as '*quanta continua*'. In the previous section on the 'axioms' he has argued that the formal aspects of appearance contain an intuition in space and time which conditions them *a priori*. This involves a synthesis of the manifold within which the representations of a determinate space and time are generated, in terms of a 'combination of the homogeneous manifold and consciousness of its synthetic unity' (B 203). In this respect all appearances without exception can be called extensive magnitudes. A magnitude can be called extensive when the representation of the parts makes possible and precedes that of the whole. Kant gives the example of representing a line: to do this requires first of all that we draw it in thought by generating from a point all of its parts one after the other: 'Only in this way can the intuition be obtained' (A 163). Similarly, I can only generate a time-magnitude by thinking a successive advance from one moment to another, however small the parts of time may be conceived. This means for Kant that all appearances are intuited as *aggregates*, that is, 'as complexes of previously given parts' (B 204). In order to appreciate Kant's point about space and time being continuous quanta we now have to think intensive magnitudes. An intensive magnitude is one that is apprehended as a unity and within which the multiplicity of degrees is represented in terms of an 'approximation to negation=0' (A 168). Kant argues that within the field of appearance every reality has such a magnitude (degrees of heat, colour, etc.). This is a magnitude of degree since any intensive magnitude can always be diminished: 'Between reality and negation there is a continuity of possible realities and of possible smaller perceptions' (B 211). Now the property of a magnitude in which no part of it can be the smallest possible is what we call continuity. We can conceive space and time in terms of continuous quantities because 'no part of them can be given save as enclosed between limits'. These are limits that Kant conceives in terms of points and instants in which each part is itself a space and a time, which leads Kant to say that 'Space consists only of spaces, time solely of times'. Points and instants act as limits in the sense that they provide positions with which to limit space and time. Now Kant goes on to say something further which initially make strike us as profoundly Bergsonian. This is the point he makes about it being impossible to construct space or time out of positions that are viewed as mere constituents capable of being given prior to space and time. This cannot be so, he maintains, because what comes first is the *a priori* intuition of Space and Time, and this is an intuition that admits of degrees or parts of space and time (a space of spaces and a time of times) but which cannot be derived from them. We might also call these magnitudes 'flowing' (*fliessende*) insofar as the act of mental synthesis at work in their production – what Kant calls the productive imagination – takes place in terms of a 'progression in time'. However, this conception of a continuity of time is not exactly equivalent to Bergson's duration simply because it seems to rest on a progressive continuity of instants only, albeit one that is not constructed out of these instants but within the intuition of the one Time.

Clearly there are some crucial differences between Kant and Bergson on the question of time. When Bergson argues that there is a 'single time' common to my inner experience and the life of things, this is not the same as Kant's stress on there being the 'one' single time. The single time of Bergson refers to a virtual multiplicity; the time of the one in Kant refers to the whole *of* discreteness which anticipates any and all actual experience (precisely what the 'single time' amounts to in Bergson will be brought out in the next essay). In Bergson my duration is disclosed by other tensions and rhythms of duration and this requires not simply the form of possible experience but the materiality of real experience. In Kant continuity is posited in terms of an order of magnitude; in Bergson, by contrast, intensity is never magnitude, or, rather, intensities only become such through a spatialized representation. The intensity of a state is not a quantity (more or less of something) but its 'qualitative sign'. His concern is twofold: with what happens to our notion of time when we think it exclusively in terms of space; and with the distorted image it produces of our psychical life, which can only be inadequately understood when it is conceived in terms of increasing or diminishing quantitative magnitudes.

Unlike Kant, Bergson argues that time involves a virtual coexistence of past and present and not simply a continuity of succession. Pure duration 'is the form which the succession of our conscious states assumes when our ego lets itself *live*, when it refrains from separating its present state from its former states' (Bergson 1960: 100). As an account of the time of the self in the dimensions of its becoming, however, Bergson's account proves inadequate. A novel synthesis of Bergson and Kant will be presented in essay seven as a way of providing a more adequate conception of this time. This involves showing that Kant's straight line of time can be folded in novel and surprising ways. It provides a way of thinking the 'empty form' of time. This peculiar 'form' can be located in Kant's image of time as the form of change that does not itself change: the straight line becomes a labyrinth and the time of the self can be shown to be a vertiginous one. We are no longer dealing with simple discreteness in any spatial sense but rather with a topology of time that allows for critical points (singularities), an enfolding time as well as an unfolding one; in short, this operation on time, utilizing the combined resources of Kant and Bergson, is able to provide us with becomings 'in' time which present a virtual self (a self that is never actual to itself 'in' time). This requires enlarging our conception of what it means to be a being in time – time as subject – and to endure time.

Although Bergson sharply distinguishes his conception of duration from Kant's treatment of time in *TFW*, he nevertheless considers it to be a feature of a synthesizing consciousness; outside of us there is only space and simultaneity. His thinking is now forced to find ways of overcoming the fundamental antinomy that has been set in place between mind and world. Duration cannot simply be a form that the mind imposes on the world.

Towards an ontology of duration

Bergson's thinking of time undergoes some major and quite dramatic shifts after *TFW*. In the first work he is clearly adhering to the view that the experience of duration requires an act of mental synthesis and thus time is a phenomenon of consciousness and something solely inner or psychological (external reality is simply space). The innovation of this work lies in its conception of time as a nonspatial and continuous multiplicity. In *MM* he speculates whether nonspatial time or duration can be extended to external things – do they endure in their own way? – and although he ends producing a vision of matter that he believes will fatigue our intellect, he remains undecided on the issue. By the time of *CE* he has reached the view that duration is 'immanent to the universe', and aims to show that duration is the key notion for thinking the idea of a creative (nonmechanical and non-finalist) evolution.[22] He seeks to show that physics deals with closed and artificial systems in which time has been left out of the picture. Once we apply ourselves to the movement of the 'whole' then duration has to be admitted into our account of the evolution of life.[23]

Deleuze argues that in Bergson duration comes to be seen as less and less reducible to a psychological experience and becomes instead the 'variable essence of things'; in short, it becomes an ontology of the complex (Deleuze 1991: 34). The question 'do external things endure?' can only remain indeterminate from the standpoint of psychological experience. If external things do not endure and duration is a phenomenon of consciousness only, then the danger arises of it being readily treated as a subjective determination (that of a mere appearance). Deleuze cites Bergson himself on the issue: 'Although things do not endure as we do, nevertheless there must be some incomprehensible reason why phenomena are seen to *succeed* one another instead of being set out all at once' (ibid.: 48; quoting from Bergson 1960: 227). For Deleuze the task is to demonstrate that movement belongs to things as much as to consciousness. In this way movement will not be confused with psychological duration; rather, 'Psychological duration should be only a clearly determined case, an opening onto *ontological* duration' (ibid.: 48–9).

Two key questions that need addressing for Deleuze are: what kind of multiplicity is this ontological duration? And, in what sense can it be said there are several durations and in what sense can it be shown that, over and above the plurality of different durations (rhythms, tempos, contractions, etc.), there is a single time? As Deleuze notes, *MM* goes furthest in affirming a radical plurality of durations, in the sense that the universe is said to be made up of modifications, perturbations, changes of tension and energy. These are different rhythms of duration. Psychological duration is seen to be only one case among others, as a certain well-defined tension. Deleuze, however, does not hesitate to affirm the monism of Time, and to do so in contrast to the hesitations of Bergson's own texts. Bergson wavers between at least three different positions: the first, that the multiplicity of our own durations is not to be extended to the rest of the material universe; the second, that material things outside us are to be distinguished not as absolutely different durations but by the relative way they participate in our duration and give it shape and pattern; third, there is only a single time or duration in which everything participates, including our consciousness, living beings, and the whole material world. This latter position is the one Deleuze wants to uphold and it can only be seen as Bergson's true position by working through the encounter with Relativity.

The articulation of duration as immanent to the whole of the universe informs Bergson's stress in *CE* on the study of life or living systems over the claims of physics and chemistry which, he contends, deal only with closed or isolated systems. Evolution has a history and an irreversibility to it. Whereas in the first book, *TFW*, he had seen only psychic states as nonmechanical and nondetermined, contesting in the process the application of the law of the conservation of energy to the domain of psychology, in *CE* he now wants to extend this to claims about the evolution of life. He thus engages once again with the first and second laws of thermodynamics but this time in terms of their implications for thinking a creative evolution.[24] Let me explore this a little further.

'The universe endures' is the key opening claim of the book. Bergson then writes: 'The more we study the nature of time, the more we shall comprehend that duration means invention, the creation of forms, the continual elaboration of the new' (that is, it is not a mere rearrangement of parts) (Bergson 1983: 11). Just as key is this claim: 'There is no reason why a duration, and so a form of existence like our own, should not be attributed to the systems that science isolates, provided such systems are reintegrated into the Whole' (ibid.). Consider the way in which our perception construes an object in terms of distinct outlines. This distinct individuality of an object is no more that the design of a certain kind of influence we exert on a certain point of space. The universal interaction between things is halted (this provides us with an insight into what Bergson means by the 'whole'). Science does the same in constituting isolable systems, that is, it extracts them from the movement of the whole that they are implicated in: 'let me say I am perfectly willing to admit that the future states of a closed system of material points are calculable and hence visible in its present state. But this system is extracted, or abstracted, from a whole, which, in addition to inert and unorganized matter, comprises organization' (Bergson 1965: 103). Now, Bergson does not deny that the material world is made up of individuated bodies (organisms) or that nature itself has carved out relatively closed systems, but this is not the whole of the picture and conforms in large part to our mental habits and evolutionary needs, in short, to our diagrammatic designs upon reality. The categories of the understanding – categories that also inform science to a large measure – provide us with access to one line of the real but it also blocks off access to other lines, which are treated as merely 'metaphysical' and in need of a critique.

What needs to be overcome, then, are certain ingrained habits of the mind, habits which also inform how science approaches the real, such as:

a   the view that change is reducible to an arrangement or rearrangement of parts or that change merely involves a change of position regarding unchangeable things.

b that the irreversibility of time is only an appearance relative to our ignorance and that the impossibility of turning back is only a human inability to put things in place again.

c that time has only as much reality for a living system as an hour-glass. We are fixated on reducing time to instants (mathematical points). This is to deny time any positive reality and to think it spatially. In the theory of Relativity, for example, what is measured is the abstract and quantitative simultaneity of two clock readings and according to a convention for determining under which circumstances they should be called simultaneous.

A prevailing conception of evolution is one where duration and invention are lacking; there are merely preformed possibilities which are then brought into being by being realized. Of course Bergson appreciates the important contribution Darwinism makes to a theory of evolution, but argues that every generation of form is bound up with a unique history that reflect specific durational conditions of existence (Bergson 1983: 28). In other words, the Darwinian conditions of life, such as adaptation, are built into the evolving life-form, 'they are peculiar to that phase of its history in which life finds itself at the moment of producing the form'. Let us suppose that life is indeed mechanism. This still leaves the question of what kind of mechanism it is: 'the mechanism of parts artificially isolated within the whole universe, or is it the mechanism of the real whole?' What does Bergson mean? If we posit the 'real whole' as an indivisible continuity then the systems we cut out within it would not, strictly speaking, be parts but rather *partial views* of the whole' (Bergson 1983: 31).

The whole of duration

We have invoked the notion of the whole without reflecting on its exact status. Can it not be taken as a clear sign that Bergsonism is indulging in abstract metaphysics? And, in the attempt to think it, are we not simply refusing to accept the limits of (finite) human thinking?

Bergsonism is first and foremost a pluralism and an empiricism. Its complicated character as a practice of philosophy stems from the fact that it also makes use of typically idealist categories like the 'whole', the 'One', and the 'image'. [25] As we shall see in the essays that follow, such notions are really part of an attempted 'superior' empiricism. The 'whole', for example, cannot be approached in terms of ready-made criteria of an organic totality.[26] The pluralist and the empiricist will thus invoke and appeal to a whole that is only ever the whole of an acentred mobile continuity, a continuity of moving parts and wholes in which the 'whole' that they are implicated in does not refer to any pre-given organic unity. Neither is such a whole of the real to be thought in dialectical terms of mediation, negation, and sublation. When we think the whole on the level of life and its evolution it is not necessary to posit it a logical or dialectical development.[27] As we shall see in essay four, Deleuze's ontology of the virtual operates completely outside these Hegelian terms.

'It is clear that there is a Whole of duration', Deleuze writes in the 1966 text on *Bergsonism* (1991: 105). In his return to Bergsonism in *Cinema 1* Deleuze clarifies the nature of this whole. Although the whole is neither given nor giveable this does mean that it is simply a meaningless or abstract notion. If the whole is not given to us in any sense then 'it is because it is the Open, and because its nature is to change constantly, or to give rise to something new, in short, to endure' (1986: 9). Every time that we disclose our duration, or one is disclosed to us, 'we may conclude that there exists somewhere a whole which is changing, and which is open somewhere' (Deleuze ibid.). Duration cannot simply be the property of a phenomenological consciousness since such a consciousness exists only insofar as it opens itself upon a whole which is, as Deleuze says, a whole of duration. Similarly if a living being considered as a whole in and for itself can be compared to the whole of the universe this is not because we are dealing with two closed systems, one a microcosm of the other, but rather because 'it is open upon a world, and the world, the universe, is itself the Open' (10; compare 1966: 105). If an instant is little more than an immobile section of movement, a snapshot of transition, then movement is a mobile section of duration. Movement is not without quality – an animal moves for a purpose, for example (to feed, to migrate) – and presupposes differences of potential. Movement implies that what takes place are changes in the state of a whole: for example, when the tortoise is overtaken by Achilles what changes is the state of the whole that encompasses the tortoise, Achilles, and the distance between them. Deleuze wishes to stress the importance of changes in qualities:

> . . . the fall of a body presupposes another one which attracts it, and expresses a change in the whole which encompasses them both. If we think of pure atoms, their movements, which testify to a reciprocal action of all the parts of the substance, necessarily express modifications, disturbances, changes of energy in the whole. What Bergson discovers beyond translation [beyond movement as simply translation in space] is vibration, radiation. Our error lies in believing that it is the any-element-whatevers, external to qualities which move. But the qualities themselves are pure vibrations, which change at the same time as the alleged elements move.
>
> (1986: 8–9)

Although there is a whole of duration this is a whole made up of relations; moreover, it is a whole in which time is precisely the power that prevents the whole from ever reaching closure and thus from ever being given. If one had to define the whole, says Deleuze, it would be in terms of the primacy of 'Relation'. For Deleuze empiricism is not to be conceived simply as the doctrine which asserts the primacy of the sensible, from which the intelligible is then derived (which is to posit an entirely abstract first principle that gives rise to sterile dualisms), but rather as a doctrine on the externality of relations.[28] This is to be taken neither as an abstract principle nor as a discovery simply about the operations of the mind (of what goes on in our heads); rather, it is a 'vital discovery' concerning the movement of life and the composition of the world. Indeed, Deleuze argues that thought must be forced to think this discovery as an experimentation which does violence to thinking. There is not only the world of being (of what something 'is': the sky 'is' blue, or God 'is . . .'), but also of 'extra-being' and 'inter-being' in which the 'And' by which relations between things are created is not simply a conjunction but that which subtends all relations, making relations shoot outside their terms and the set of these terms. This thinking in terms of the 'And' rather than the 'Is' is the 'secret' of empiricism.[29] It also provides us with another way of thinking multiplicity: as residing neither in the terms themselves nor in their set or totality. The multiple need not be merely adjectival, a predicate fixed of something that does not itself change (the subject of a predicate), but can be construed as a noun (a substantive itself which potentially inhabits each thing). Relation is not only not a property of objects or terms themselves but it is also inseparable from the 'Open' which never ceases to change. Deleuze insists that this whole and the wholes that form within it are not to be confused with sets (*ensembles*) since these are always subject to artificial closure. One (the sets) is in space, while the other (the whole and the wholes) is in duration. This is because while the objects of a set change their positions by movement in space, it is through relations that the whole is transformed and qualitative changes are brought about. Movement has two aspects: by changing qualitatively duration divides up in objects and the objects are 'united in duration' by losing their contours: 'We can therefore say that movement relates the objects of a closed system to open duration, and duration to the objects of the system which it forces to open up. Movement relates the objects between which it is established to the changing whole which it expresses, and vice versa' (11).

The novel aspect of Deleuze's commitment to the empiricist doctrine of Relation is that it approaches the issue in terms of a Bergsonism (time *qua* duration, the virtual multiplicity of an open whole) and not a logicism or simple associationism (discrete elements juxtaposed abstractly and mechanistically in space). By definition sets and closed systems are to be defined in terms of discernible objects and distinct parts. It is precisely this concentration on discernibility and distinctness that Bergsonism shows to be of limited empirical value since it is applicable to only one facet of the universe, a facet that our understanding concentrates its attention on. Hence the need within Bergsonism to appeal to a notion of the whole. Deleuze makes the key point:

> The whole is not a closed set, but on the contrary that by virtue of which the set is never absolutely closed, never completely sheltered, that which keeps it open somewhere as if by the finest thread which attaches it to the rest of the universe.
>
> (ibid.; on the thread compare Bergson 1983: 10–11)

Set theory can only think in terms of actual or spatial multiplicities; the innovation of Bergsonism is to think virtual multiplicities (Deleuze and Guattari 1994: 127). Moreover, Bergson's philosophy is able to provide an account of the possibility of set thinking by showing that it represents a specific extraction and abstraction from this virtual open whole or what Deleuze himself calls a 'plane of immanence'. Closed or finite sets are made possible through the exterior nature of the parts of this plane. But it itself is not a set and it escapes the contradiction that revolves around the problem and paradox of the 'set of all sets'. What the science of set theory cannot access is the open whole which cuts across the parts of systems and links up different systems, so preventing absolute closure.

> The plane of immanence is the movement (the facet of movement) which is established between the parts of each system and between one system and another, which crosses them all, stirs them all up together and subjects them all to the condition which prevents them from being absolutely closed. . . . This is not mechanism, it is machinism.
>
> (Deleuze 1986: 59)

The artificial division of a set or a closed system rests on a well-founded illusion. It is owing to the organization of matter itself that there are systems which are relatively closed, while our deployment of spatial habits makes them necessary for us. It is for this reason that Deleuze wishes to identify duration with the free movement of the open whole and not to locate it within the realm of any particular system.

Deleuze acknowledges that this notion of the plane of immanence might seem a long way from Bergson, but he maintains that he is being faithful to him (ibid.: note 11 p. 226). Some things Bergson discloses in a letter to William James (dated 25 March 1903) lend a degree of plausibility to Deleuze's bending of Bergson and his declaration of fidelity in doing so. In it Bergson speaks of the need to transcend 'a simple logic' and 'the methods of over-systematic philosophy which postulates the unity of the whole'. If a 'truly *positive* philosophy is possible', he adds, it 'can only be found there' (Bergson 1972: 589).[30] A 'positive' philosophy, I take it, is one that would be genuinely experimental in its conception of the whole. It would be the opposite of a closed system of metaphysics which one could decide to take or leave. Indeed, Bergson commits himself to the possibility of an open system of metaphysics that could 'progress indefinitely' (1972: 652).

The plane of immanence is bound up not with 'mechanism' but with a 'machinism'. Mechanism would be correct if there was only closed systems and if becomings could be rendered reducible to the self-directed movement of such systems. The recourse to 'machinism' is less obvious but it is clearly a reflection of Deleuze's desire to avoid approaching or constructing the 'whole' (of duration, of a creative evolution) in terms of a dialectical organicism. Indeed, machinism is simply an aspect of Deleuze's overriding commitment to empiricism and the doctrine of relations being external to their terms. Indeed, it is for empiricist and pluralist reasons that Deleuze will invoke this specific plane, a plane of immanence.[31] The plane of immanence is itself a mobile and temporal section and perspective, it is a 'bloc of space-time' in which the time of the movement at work within it is also a part of every time. But this monism does not prevent there from being an infinite series of such blocs and mobile sections, that is, a multiplicity of 'presentations of the plane' (1986: 59); on the contrary, the monism can only be properly and adequately approached in terms of such a pluralism. What makes the plane one of immanence is that the movement it gives expression to is the durational movement of the open whole: this whole never stops becoming and changing, there is nothing transcendent to it and it itself is not a force of transcendence. Conceived in these terms, then, immanence can only be immanent to itself, that is, to the movement of the open whole that is always becoming and changing (it is immanent neither to matter nor *esprit*). Something of this will be demonstrated in the two essays which now follow.

2

'A LIFE OF THE REAL' AND
A SINGLE TIME

Relativity and virtual multiplicity

> Time can affirm its formidable reality even to those who loudly
> proclaim its nothingness.
>
> (Schelling, *Ages of the World*, 1813)

> Aion is the past-future, which in an infinite subdivision of the
> abstract moment endlessly decomposes itself in both directions
> at once and forever sidesteps the present. For no present can be
> fixed in a Universe which is taken to be the system of all
> systems, or the abnormal set.
>
> (Deleuze 1990: 77)

> Bergson's philosophy triumphs in a cosmology where everything
> is a change in tension and nothing else.
>
> (Deleuze 1999: 59).

In this essay I wish to examine Bergson's thinking on duration in the context of his reading of the spatial habits of thought within ancient philosophy and modern science. This will provide a terrain on which we can better appreciate the nature of his encounter with Relativity, an encounter that reveals a great deal about the strengths and limitations of Bergsonian thinking. Before turning to Bergson, however, I want to first take a look at how Popper reads Einstein. The criticism that Relativity rests upon a spatialization of time is not peculiar to Bergson. And Popper, like Bergson before him, has recourse to ancient sources of thought in order to demonstrate this point. His question is a simple one: is Einstein a Parmenidean? We shall encounter the force of Popper's position in favour of the reality of change but the limits of his position will also manifest themselves. His thesis is worth examining because, like Bergson, it too claims that Relativity, for all its novel insights, has effected another spatialization of time.

A meeting between Bergson and Einstein actually took place at the Collège de France in Paris in April 1922, where the physicist and the philosopher attempted to exchange views on time. Einstein concluded the exchange by stating that there was an unbridgeable gulf between the time of the physicist and the time of the philosopher, the latter being a complete mystery to him. The gulf that divided them continues to inform the relation between philosophy and physics on the question of time.[1] Relativity dealt a fatal blow to any theory that presupposed a definite present instant in which all matter is simultaneously real (an absolute present).[2] The idea of a huge, instantaneous 'Now' spread transversally across the universe is well-entrenched in the human mind. But although Einstein did not believe in the reality of time, or the flow of time, he adhered to the fiction of the instant: the simultaneity of instants is what is relative. The question continues to persist: did Einstein spatialize time? Or, more precisely in the terms of Deleuze's Bergsonism does Relativity confuse the virtual and the actual? The physicist gives us space-time in which time has no independent meaning; but the philosopher holds that this space-time is really spatialized time and not time at all. The physicist then retorts that the time of the philosopher is merely phenomenological or psychological. Is there a way of thinking time beyond this impasse?

In this essay the task is twofold: to examine the charge of spatialization levelled at Relativity by both Popper and Bergson, and to clarify what impact, if any, the conception of time as a virtual multiplicity has on the claims of physics.[3] We wish to do justice to all sides.

Popper on Parmenides

We encounter a striking claim made at the start of essay six of Popper's posthumous collection *The World of Parmenides*: Western civilization is a civilization based on science, notably the science founded by Copernicus, Galileo, Kepler, and Newton, and *this science is a continuation of the Greeks*. And what can be said of Newton in this regard can be said of Einstein who in his thinking of space-time is a Parmenidean. The Presocratics were preoccupied with questions of cosmology – Thales, Heraclitus, etc. all offer variations on a theme (all is water, all is fire) – and with questions of a theory of knowledge and not ontology, Popper claims, since the primary problem for them was not the problem of being but the problem of change. The two are indissolubly linked in Greek thought. 'All science is cosmology', Popper writes in the opening essay of the volume (Wittgenstein's *Tractatus*, he says, is interesting as a cosmological treatise, not as an exercise in linguistic philosophy). What Popper ingeniously locates in Greek thinking on cosmology are the seeds of a critical rationalism.

For Popper there is no such thing as ontology, so for him the problem of change is not an ontological problem but a cosmological one: 'We can explain Parmenides's problem as the problem of whether our world is a changing universe or a dead block universe. And this is not a problem of being, or of the word "being", or of the copula "is", but a problem about

44

the character of our cosmos' (Popper 1998: 114). So, for Popper the nature of change or time is not restricted to a matter of psychology, of our consciousness, but concerns the universe. The question of time and change must be a question of cosmology and evolution. This refusal or repudiation of ontology in Popper is deeply rooted in his thinking and I cannot examine the reasons for it here; let us simply note that in the case of his engagement with Parmenidean rationalism the fact that he will not allow himself an ontology of becoming severely restricts the scope of his critical response.

Parmenides of Elea (515–445 BC) is for Popper a philosopher of nature, whose chief philosophical work may well have been called 'On Nature', alluding to his predecessors, the works of the Ionians such as Anaximander and Heraclitus. It takes the form of a poem in two main parts, 'The Way of Truth' and the 'Way of Opinion' (Doxa), in which the goddess Dike reveals to Parmenides the distinction between the true world and the apparent world.[4] The first world, the true one, is established by means of a rationalist and anti-sensualist epistemology, which then proceeds to a logical proof that culminates in the thesis that change is an illusion. The world consists of one huge and unmoving solid block of spherical shape in which nothing ever happens. There is no past or future. The world conceived as a world of becoming and change, of movement and development, of colourful contrasts (light and night, or growth and decay) is the world of ordinary mortals who are caught in the veils of illusion.

All the contemporaries of Parmenides think that his system amounts to a scandalous paradox (change is unreal), in the same way that Zeno's paradoxes, themselves inspired by Parmenidean thought, are scandals up to this day.[5] Obviously, there is a battle over what constitutes common sense: for Bergson common sense is represented in the Zenonist view that motion is an illusion; in the modern world it is the Heraclitean view which is the scandal since it goes beyond our deepest habits of representation. The recoil from sensualism on the part of Parmenides rests on the discovery that the observation that the Moon waxes and wanes during the course of time is false. The apparent changes of the Moon are illusions, so the conclusion is reached that the clear observation of change or motion is completely unreliable. The Moon is a globe that is always the same size and shape. Of course, this discovery could not have been made without another observation, namely that the Moon receives its light from the Sun. The apparent bodily change of the Moon turns out to be a mere play of shadows. So observation can imply the falsity of observation. However, what interests Popper is how none of this can be established except through logical reasoning, which is what he identifies as the mark of Parmenides's thinking.

Parmenides is led then to the conclusion that *all* change and motion is illusory. The proof that movement is impossible is established in *a priori* and strictly logical terms, and also in the form of a refutation. There is nothing empirical in the proof (Popper 1998: 86). It is hypothetico-deductive and anti-positivistic (126). He is in key aspects a critical rationalist practising science in terms of the art of making conjectures and refutations. Parmenides was the first to make epistemology the centre of philosophical thought and to announce a rationalist programme: 'Pure thought, critical logical argument, rather than common sense, plausibility, experience, and tradition' (159). But he was also wrong, wrong that change is an illusion. Change may be an illusion, says Popper, but it is a *real* illusion. Popper arrives at a tricky and ambiguous position. Illusions can be real of course, but the task is to examine how we configure change, whether we conceive the condition of time in terms of our subjectivity or whether we can show that this subjectivity is grounded or implicated in duration itself (in terms of specific tensions and contractions of matter). We could simply rest content with giving an account of how this illusion arises, or we could try and show that change is real and frozen immobility is the illusion, one produced by the inability of our intellect to think duration. This is clearly the move made by Bergson.

Popper confesses to being a critical rationalist and a realist. He holds that Parmenides has been the major influence on modern science from Newton to Einstein and Schrödinger. Part of his objections to the neo-Parmenidean tradition is that it sets limits to rationalism: namely, that science is limited to the search for invariants, for what does not change during change. His opposition to this restriction of science explains why for him it is necessary to recognize that there might be something valuable in the attacks on rationalism made by irrationalists : 'something important has been seen by those irrationalists who spoke of "creative" or "emergent" evolution' (154). This possibly disguised reference to Bergson is, however, more than a concession to so-called irrationalism on Popper's part.[6] It rests on the realization that the problem of change cannot be adequately approached from the perspective of Parmenidean rationalism. The problem that Popper has with irrationalist alternatives is that none of them, he thinks, has produced a serious theory of becoming, that is, one that could be rationally and critically discussed (172).

The problem of change

The problem of change can be staged as follows:

1   All change is change of something. There must be a *thing* that changes; and this thing must remain, while it changes, *identical with itself*. But, if it remains identical then how can it ever change? (change is a property of a thing, a substance, which, in fact, never changes.)

2   Heraclitus' solution is as follows: 'Everything is in flux, and nothing is at rest.' This denies that it is 'things' that change since there are no 'things', only changes or processes. This also applies to the self, as when

Heraclitus said 'I searched myself'. What he found was not a thing but processes and if the processes stop so do we. We are not things but burning fires or flames. Or, as Nietzsche epigramatically puts it in *Thus Spoke Zarathustra*, 'You must be ready to burn yourself in your own flame: how could you become new, if you had not first become ashes' ('Of the Way of the Creator'). We may also note again Bergson's challenge on the question of change, namely, the need to conceive of change without there being *things* that change and of a movement that does not imply or require a mobile (Bergson 1965: 147).

3   Parmenides tries to show that change is paradoxical but also logically impossible. The existence of change can be logically disproved. Nothingness cannot exist and what is full exists because what exists is full. There are two main claims in this position: the 'is' is all continuous and one (indivisible); and the existing is motionless, it is self-identical and remains where it is and does not move. So, if the existing is indivisible and all is full, then there is no space for movement. We have a motionless block universe.

This is an empirically testable conclusion Popper argues, and is, in fact, refuted by experience. One refutation – that of atomism – goes like this:

Motion is a fact; therefore motion is possible; therefore the world cannot be *one* full block. It must rather contain both many (divisible) blocks and be nothingness (empty space). The full blocks are *in* empty space. But, this is still Parmenidean: the blocks are unchangeable atoms moving about in the void. The conclusion is that all change, all qualitative change, is due to spatial movement and all change amounts to a mere rearrangement (the atoms never change). On this model, as Popper points out, there is no intrinsic change or novelty, but only a 'new rearrangement of what was intrinsically always the same thing' (this is strikingly similar to Bergson's argument; see his essay on 'The Possible and the Real', 1965: 91–107). It is this theory of change, claims Popper, which has remained the basis of theoretical physics for over two thousand years. In short, Western science has been dominated by Parmenidean rationalism and remains so. One example is the laws of the conservation of energy: one thing remains the same in spite of all changes taking place, namely, the amount and momentum of energy.

Popper on Einstein as a Parmenidean

For Parmenidean thinking then nothing happens and there is no intrinsic novelty: everything that happens or exists happened and has existed in some form or other in God as one of his perfections (the effect is always present or preformed in the cause). For Popper, as for Bergson, this is a doctrine which can be located, albeit in different guises, in all the modern rationalists (Descartes, Leibniz, and Spinoza). Popper argues that the idea of Parmenides reaches its 'highest fulfilment in the continuity theory of Einstein' (165). Popper mentions that he discussed this point with Einstein and that the characterization was accepted, although we have no independent corroboration of this claim. 'Einstein's deterministic cosmology is that of a four-dimensional Parmenidean block-universe.' This is to read the space-time continuum of General Relativity as a space or geometry that incorporates time. Objective, physical time gets assimilated to space co-ordinates. The result is that it is only our consciousness that experiences the flow of time, that is, as a historical process that goes forward in time. Thus, the world simply *is*, it does not *happen*. It is only to the gaze of my consciousness that a section of the world comes to life as a fleeting image in space which continuously changes in time. In the four-dimensional objective reality there is no change, this belongs to the world as experienced by mere mortals.

It has been established, Popper believes, that the problem of the reality of change is really the problem of the reality of time (the arrow or direction of time). The main question is whether the fundamental temporal relations of 'before and after' are objective or merely an illusion. Popper does not discuss Kant's thesis that time is *both* transcendentally ideal and empirically real. He clearly wants to argue that time is an objective feature of changes in the world and not simply objective for a transcendental subject. He is convinced, he says, that change and therefore time are objective and that no good arguments have been offered against this view (Gödel's time machine would be a strong argument, only if his premises for it were valid and it could be made to work). Even in the work of Boltzmann on the entropy law the suggestion, Popper points out, is that time does not have an objective direction. On the contrary, in Boltzmann one finds a geometrization or spatialization of time, which is not to say that there is no time left in the theory, but rather that it exists as a co-ordinate that is framed without any sense of an arrow or a direction. As Boltzmann himself insisted, just as in space there is no objective up and down, so in the universe as a whole the two directions of time are indistinguishable. Whenever there is some major fluctuation in some part of the world, then any living organism or observer will *experience* a direction of time and experience that the future lies in the direction of entropy increases. This explains the second law, but there is no suggestion that this is to reveal an arrow of time as some objective feature of the universe. For Popper Boltzmann's thinking on entropy still implies that 'change is an illusion', which amounts, he says, to a 'Parmenidean apology' (170).[7]

Let's make one point clear: Popper, like Bergson before him, argues that Relativity presents a serious blow to the common-sense view of time which has to be corrected in the light of the new critical findings: space and time do not exactly have the properties we naively assume (there is no one universal time; as we shall see, this does not rule out for Bergson the positing of a 'single time', which is a time, he will argue, even presupposed by the plural times of Relativity). Time is no longer separable from motion and this from space: space and time are linked together. There is no subjectivity or consciousness in the theory (the 'observer' in the theory is simply a recording device or instrument). However, Popper, like Bergson, argues that we still need to side with common sense: the future is not determined but indeterminate and the illusion of change is a real one since we do, in fact, experience change. The philosophical problem has become this: how do we account for this change in an objectively changeless universe? Popper suggests that even if there are changing illusions then there is change. For example, a cinema film exists all at once but in order to create the illusion of change it must run through a projector, that is, it has to move and change. His ultimate position is to claim that change cannot simply be an illusion of consciousness, even though consciousness plays a key role in having the experience of change; rather, consciousness must be *decoding* certain facts in the environment, one of which is change (176).

Before we examine how Bergson encounters Relativity and seek to clarify the idea of a single time (which has to be rendered compatible with the view that time is a virtual multiplicity), I want to present an account of Bergson's own thoughts on the links between ancient philosophy and modern science.

Bergson on the ancients and the moderns

Bergson contends that the mechanistic philosophy and science of the moderns remains bound, as if through so many invisible threads, to the 'ancient philosophy of Ideas'. As a praxis science is also a response to the requirements of our understanding. The first claim is a bold one. How does he seek to argue and demonstrate it?

To comprehend this we have to begin, however abstract the operation might seem, with Bergson's ontology of becoming. His argument is that our perception and understanding must presuppose as their basis a 'fluid' and moving 'continuity of the real'. This is a life of the real. The focus on this moving continuity as the primary basis of an ontology of things and their relations constitutes the Copernican Revolution of *Matter and Memory*. Everything that lives perceives, from simple beings that vibrate to complex beings that are able to contract trillions of vibrations and oscillations within a single perception. Indeed, for Bergson the primary and primal function of perception is to grasp a series of elementary changes (movements in the environment) under the form of a quality or a single state and to do this through a work of condensation. Within the moving continuity of the real we can posit and locate the boundaries of bodies that exist in varying degrees of individuation (again, from the contractions of a simple protoplasm to living systems with highly developed nervous systems). All these bodies change 'at every moment', resolving themselves into groups of qualities consisting of a succession of elementary movements (Bergson 1983:

302). The stability of a body lies in its instability – it never ceases changing and it changes qualities without ceasing to be or become what it is. It is such a body, conceived as a relatively closed system, that we are entitled to isolate within the continuity of matter. What is 'real' are two things: the moving continuity of the whole and the continual change of form within a living body. We need to note here that 'form' as such is only 'a snapshot view of a transition'. And what our perception does is to solidify the fluid continuity of the real or the open whole into discontinuous or discrete images. It does this *necessarily* as a condition of its evolution and adaptation. The changes taking place in the whole, however, are received by perceptual living systems as if on a surface. A system like ours, with its evolved habits of representation, either turns away from the movement of life or becomes interested only in the unmoveable part and plan of the movement rather than the movement itself. All kinds of acts are reduced to the image of simple movement or movement in general, and knowledge comes to bear on a state rather than a change. In short, we develop three kinds of representations that correspond to three categories of words: qualities (adjectives), forms of essences (substantives) and acts (verbs). While the first two are designed to capture states, the latter is related to movement and expresses something we find it hard to think (life *qua* the virtual or the infinitive).

Bergson argues that becoming is infinitely varied and yet we have fostered the habit of extracting from these variations in order to provide ourselves with an image of 'becoming *in general*'. He writes:

> An infinite multiplicity of becomings variously colored . . . passes before our eyes: we manage so that we see only differences of color, that is to say, differences of state, beneath which there is supposed to flow, hidden from our view, a becoming always and everywhere the same, invariably colorless.
>
> (1983: 304)

In short, we have cultivated for the purposes of social life and language a 'cinematographic' model of the real: which is to say, we reconstitute and compose the mobility of the real in terms of a series of juxtaposed and successive immobilities, and so generate for ourselves the illusion of continuity. The real moving continuity of the whole is concealed from us, therefore, by our very habits of representation, which are largely spatial. For us movement is something impersonal, mechanical, abstract and simple. There is a good reason for the congruence between our knowledge of the operations of nature and its practical effectiveness. This is because the 'cinematographical character of our knowledge of things is due to the kaleidoscopic character of our adaptation to them' (306). If our body is related to other bodies in terms of an arrangement that is like the pieces of glass in a kaleidoscope, we can say that each time the kaleidoscope is given a shake what we detect or decode is not the shake in and for itself but rather only the new picture that has emerged from the transformation. In short, it is owing to the practical character of our understanding and intellect that there is generated the illusion that change is an illusion. For us change is decomposable, almost at will, into states and out of this decomposition we produce a movement from out of a series of immobilities.

For Bergson it is necessary to begin with the Eleatics since it is this school, which included Zeno, that generates the illusions that continue to bedevil modern thought.[8] The division of the real into sensible and intelligible aspects is born of the effort to deny the reality of change: beneath the qualitative becoming, beneath an 'evolutionary becoming', there must be sought something which defies change, a form, an essence, and an end. This takes us to the Platonic philosophy of Forms or Ideas. The word *'eidos'*, Bergson suggests, has a threefold meaning, denoting a quality, a form or essence, or an end or design (in the sense of an intention which traces in advance an action to be accomplished). It is these three aspects which conform to the attributes of language, such as adjective, substantive, and verb. *Eidos* or 'idea' denotes the stable view taken of the instability of things, the quality which is a moment of becoming, or the form as a moment of evolution. The philosophy of Ideas can thus be shown to correspond fully to the cinematographical mechanism of the intellect and its relation to the real. By placing at the base of the moving continuity of the real the immutable Ideas or eternal Forms there is generated an entire physics, cosmology and theology. Bergson concedes that he is condensing in this view what is a highly complex movement within ancient thought. He maintains, however, that there is little that is accidental or contingent in the development of the tradition that stretches from Plato to Plotinus, and from Aristotle to the Stoics, since what we find here is a vision of the real obtained by the systematic intellect when it dwells in the immutable. Now, if thought begins with the immutable then it can only generate a notion of change in negative terms. Change will not be conceived as a positive reality that adds to the Ideas; rather the passage from the immutable to becoming can only take place in terms of a diminution or attenuation, such as Plato's 'non-being' or Aristotle's 'matter', 'a metaphysical zero which, joined to the Idea, like the arithmetical zero to unity, multiplies it in space and time' (1983: 317). Between the Ideas the mind sees an 'elusive nothing' that 'creates endless agitation, eternal disquiet, like a suspicion insinuated between two loving hearts' (ibid.). It is only in the contemplation of the immutable Ideas or Forms that the 'theoretical equilibrium of Being' can be maintained. Artificially cut off from the becoming that is their virtual-actual condition, the Forms withdraw into their own definition, the concept becomes reified, and thought now dwells in eternity. Posited as independent of time, Form cannot be anything found in perception but has to be a concept. Because the reality of the concept is both inextensive and outside of time, space and time themselves share the same origin and have the same value: 'The same diminution of being is expressed both by extension in space and detention in time' (318).

An inversion of the real is effected, then, whereby eternity no longer hovers over time as an abstraction but is posited as its underlying reality and the Forms come to represent the only positive aspects of becoming. Between eternity and time there is established 'the same relation as between a piece of gold and the small change – change so small that the payment goes on forever without the debt being paid off' (318). The debt, however, could be paid off with the single piece of gold, and this paying-off is expressed for Bergson in Plato's 'magnificent language' concerning God being unable to make the world eternal and so giving it time as a 'moving image of eternity'.[9] But this is an image of time as an always incomplete and inadequate reality, a real that has gone astray from itself, perpetually trying to catch up with itself and failing, and, we, as fallen creatures of time are condemned to Sisyphean labours:

> Move an imaginary pendulum, a mere mathematical point, from its position of equilibrium: a perpetual oscillation is started, along which points are placed next to points, and moments succeed moments. The space and time which thus arise have no more 'positivity' than movement itself. They represent the remoteness of the position artificially given to the pendulum from its normal position, *what it lacks* in order to regain its natural stability. Bring it back to its normal position: space, time, and motion shrink to a mathematical point. Just so, human reasonings are drawn out into an endless chain, but are at once swallowed up in the truth seized by intuition, for their extension in space and time is only the distance, so to speak, between thought and truth. So of extension and duration in relation to pure Forms or Ideas . . . What was extended in space is contracted into pure Form. And past, present, and future shrink into a single moment, which is eternity. This amounts to saying that physics is but logic spoiled . . .
>
> (319–20)

On this Platonic model the physical order, conceived as 'a degeneration of the logical order', represents the 'fall of the logical into space and time'. The philosopher who has made the ascent from percept to concept, however, discovers condensed in the logical all the positive reality that the physical can possess: *Being is grasped only so far as materiality has been disavowed.*

Bergson contends that Aristotle, in his refusal of an independent realm of Ideas, in no way reverses this priority of concept over percept, of the ideal over the real, of the immutable over the always changing. Aristotle's God is a *virtual* God in the sense that everything pours from it and does so as from an eminent power. The causality operative in the world is that of an *impulsion*, says Bergson of Aristotle's thought, one that is exercised by a prime motionless mover on the whole of the world. Bergson notes that Aristotle demonstrates the necessity of a prime mover not by arguing that the movement of things must have a beginning, but by pursuing the argument that such movement could have never have begun and can never come to an end. In short, if movement exists, and if the small change is being counted, then the piece of gold has to be located somewhere; moreover, if the counting is infinite, and never actually begins, then the 'single term that is *eminently* equivalent to it must be eternal' (1983: 325, my emphasis). The perpetuity of movement is established by the support of an eternity of immutability, 'which it unwinds in a chain without beginning or end'. We are, however, unable to follow the details of Bergson's reading of Aristotle here.[10] All we wish to note is that this critical account of Aristotle within *Creative Evolution* shows the need to dissociate Bergson's own conception of the original impulsion of life from the Aristotelian one. The immanent and *virtual* reality of the *élan vital* has to be of a different kind and it is necessary that the difference be ascertained and determined. A clue as to the nature of this difference can be found in the way Bergson describes Aristotle's account of the prime mover, namely, that its virtuality is of the nature of an *eminent* power. The difference, then, concerns whether the (simple) virtual is thought in terms of *eminence* or *immanence*.

The model of science arrived at in ancient thought has two main features: the physical is defined in terms of the logical and beneath the changing phenomena that appear to us as if being unrolled in a film or transparence there is a 'closed system of concepts subordinated to and coordinated with each other' (1983: 328). How does modern science build on this model and differ or depart from it? Although its form may be a speculative one, and although it is not motivated by immediate ends, science is informed by a practical utility and shares the same preoccupation with the extremities of the intervals of time, and not with what happens between them, that characterizes human intelligence and language. The difference between ancient and modern science consists in their attitude towards change; whereas the former attempts to know an object by isolating its privileged moments (the aim is to know the quintessence of a thing), the latter is able to consider an object at *any* moment whatsoever. The difference comes out well when one considers the approach adopted to a falling body by Aristotle and Galileo: Aristotle's finalism would mean that what is of interest is the final term or culminating point which is set up as the essential moment of a falling body (hence its preoccupation with the concepts 'high' and 'low', with spontaneous and forced displacements); in Galileo, however, there is no privileged instant or essential moment. This means that for modern science time has no 'natural articulations' and all moments count equally. The concern is now with quantitative variations of change, either with respect to a phenomenon itself or to its elementary parts. The greater precision aimed at by modern science accounts for its setting up of 'laws' that establish constant relations between variable magnitudes. For Bergson modern science is, in its essential aspects, the daughter of astronomy. Its prime concern is with calculating the positions of the objects or forces (planets, for example) of any material system and in which all moments are treated equally. Now, the key point for Bergson is that modern science aspires to treat *time* as an independent variable in its calculation of a system and to relate all other magnitudes to the magnitude of time. But, the question is, what is this 'time' of modern science? For Bergson it cannot be the time of duration, of a virtual qualitative multiplicity, which is characterized by a 'continuity of interpenetration' and not discreteness (1983: 341), simply because modern science treats all moments equally as 'virtual stopping-places' (336), that is, as immobilities in effect. Time can be divided at any moment and sliced or cut up as science pleases. What does not interest science is either the flux of time or the effect of this flux on a consciousness. Instead of intuiting or mapping out the flux, science deals with the counting of *simultaneities*. And for science the 'object' is always the simultaneity of *instants*, not that of fluxes (337–8). Modern physics deals with isolated systems, that is, with events and systems of events that have been detached from the whole, so that it counts 'simultaneities between the events that make up this time and the positions of the mobile T on its trajectory' (342). So while modern physics differs from ancient science in considering any moment of time, it still rests on a substitution of 'time-length' for 'time-invention'.

Modern science has no more to do with a becoming than bridges thrown across a stream have to do with following the water that flows under their arches. Contra modern science, then, Bergson wishes to claim that there is an actual succession within things and that this succession is more than a number and not equivalent to space. The law of entropy, regarded by Bergson as the most 'metaphysical' of the laws of physics, denotes only a tendency of matter-life, and cannot be read as a final end or posited as a teleology.[11] Moreover, he wishes to point out that the time that is given all at once, or that can run at any speed, is not real duration. As he asks, why is not the life of the universe given at once as on the film of the cinematograph? Why do things take (their) time and why do we, as beings of duration implicated in other durations, have to *learn* time? Now, if time is not given, if the future of living systems and forms cannot be read off from the present state of the material universe, then there has to be a time of 'invention' or 'creative evolution'. This is the time we shall explore in the next essay.

Bergson, it should be noted, does not deny the validity of modern science with respect to its calculation of time; rather, he wants to show how its 'image' of time still rests on a cinematographic model and to ask whether there can be any conciliation between the time of the physicist and the time of the philosopher. Taking a look at his encounter with Relativity affords us valuable insight into how we might expose both the real challenge and the limits of his thinking.

Bergson and relativity

Bergson tells us that he is convinced that Einstein has provided not only a new physics but new ways of thinking. But it is largely for the benefit of his own thinking that the encounter with Relativity is carried out. He wishes to find out the extent to which the notion of duration is compatible with Einstein's views on time (Bergson 1999: preface). Bergson, however, presents the encounter badly and confusedly. This is because he places the emphasis on the 'direct and immediate experience' of duration, rather than emphasizing what he has shown in texts such as *Matter and Memory* and *Creative Evolution*. In *Duration and Simultaneity* Bergson appears to be drawing mainly on arguments presented in his first book, *Time and Free Will*: that succession presupposes a consciousness able to synthesize the qualitative aspects of a duration (a 'before' and 'after'). Because of this it is quite easy for critics of Bergson to argue that in his engagement with Relativity he has misconceived the 'observer' issue by turning the observer into a phenomenological consciousness.[12] But the challenge Bergson presents to Relativity is not simply a phenomenological one. Indeed, there may be no need for a phenomenology of time to present *any* challenge to the cosmology of time. As Husserl pointed out, a phenomenology of time does not need to address the question of how the time that is posited in a time-consciousness (as phenomenologically objective) is related to 'real Objective time', including real temporal intervals, a concrete duration, world-time, etc. (Husserl 1964: 23). The 'immanent time' of the flow of consciousness does refer to an actual time and duration but only in the sense of their 'appearing' as 'absolute data'. What Husserlian phenomenology takes as phenomenological givens, Bergsonism does not and cannot simply because it conceives the philosophical project and task in a fundamentally different manner.

There is, I believe, a specific reason as to why Bergson presents his own case – the fact that he is posing something other than a phenomenological challenge to science (a challenge that does not need posing anyhow) – so poorly in *DS*. This is owing to him placing on his own thought and on modern physics a restrictive empiricism. This empiricism consists, in short, in the argument that any time we can conceive has to be perceived and lived, or capable of being so (so we get the equation: conceived time = perceived time = lived time) (1999: 33). This means that any time which we cannot perceive, that does not have the potential of being perceptible, is unreal and phantasmatic (as the multiple times of Relativity are, Bergson will go on to argue). Appearances are real, says Bergson, until they have been proven to rest on illusions. In the essay on 'The Perception of Change' (1911), however, he declares that philosophy is born from out of the *insufficiency* of our faculties of perception and insists that our experience and knowledge of the universe cannot be based on the claims of a natural perception (1965: 132, 135). Philosophy, he says, must learn how to think 'beyond the human condition'. With the position he adopts in *DS*, however, Bergson not only places severe and unwarranted limits on the praxis of science, he also places unnecessary limits on his own thinking (limits that in other writings he does not simply take as given). The problem with the argument of *DS* is that it returns us to the antinomies of *Time and Free Will*, in which outside us there is only 'the expression of simultaneity' or 'mutual externality without succession', and duration is solely a property or feature of what is 'within us', conceived as 'succession without mutual externality' (Bergson, 1960: 227).[13] In *DS* Bergson reinstates a distinction between actual lived time and spatialized time and relies heavily on it in order to challenge Relativity. He goes wrong in supposing that this exhausts the possibilities of thinking time.

Let me now move to dealing with some of the details of Bergson's encounter with Relativity. It should be noted that Bergson has no desire to resurrect pre-Relativistic physics. There is much in the theories of Relativity that he accepts and that he finds compatible with his own thinking: he accepts the mathematical expression of the constancy of the speed or velocity of light; he too rejects the idea of there being any absolute frame of reference and appreciates the need to jettison the idea of a motionless aether (as a kind of carrier of motion within which the speed of light would be relative and not absolute). Relativity is both a theoretical and empirical advance over earlier physics: the universe is not static and space is not absolute. The puzzling aspect of *DS*, however, resides in Bergson's claim (made in other texts too) that there is a 'single time' common to all times, including the multiple times of Relativity. How do we make sense of Bergson's notion of a single time? Is this not a simple refusal on his part to take seriously the claims of Relativity? The difficulty is twofold: first, reconciling the notion of virtual multiplicity with that of a single time; and, second, showing that the notion of a single time does not mean that everything that exists beats according to the same rhythm of time (in *Matter and Memory* Bergson had argued that there are multiple tensions of duration and that our duration is simply one of many). The error to be avoided is that of confusing the single time with the claim that in the universe there is only a single tension of duration.

As Einstein himself tells us, the revolution of Relativity consists in effecting certain transformations in our conception of *space* and its focus is on '*space-like concepts*' (Einstein 1999: 141). Indeed, as Einstein informs us, the general theory of Relativity is able to confirm in a 'roundabout way' the intuition of Descartes that there is no empty space (how can space exist independent of the material objects that fill and extend it?) (1999: 136). While Einstein concedes that the idea of a space independent of things is pre-scientific, he upholds the idea that there exists an infinite number of spaces in motion relative to one another. In short, there is a veritable multiplicity of space-time blocs and space-time events. And as Deleuze recognizes, the achievement of Relativity is to have pushed further than before 'spatialization' and to introduce into science the idea of there being a multiplicity of blocs of *space-time*. Bodies are contracted and times are dilated. From this it is concluded that there has taken place a dislocation of simultaneity. What is simultaneous in a fixed system ceases to be so in a system that is mobile. Einstein notes that the essential difference between classical and modern physics lies in how each conceives a four-dimensional continuous manifold. In classical physics an event is localized by four numbers, composed of three spatial co-ordinates and a single time co-ordinate, just as it is for the modern physics of Relativity. However, in the former the four-dimensional continuum *objectively* divides into one dimension of time and three-dimensional spatial sections and it is only in the dimensions of space that simultaneous events are contained. This resolution is then held to be the same for all inertial systems, in which the simultaneity of two events with reference to one inertial system involves the simultaneity of the same events for all inertial systems. It is in this way that we can declare time to be absolute and not relative on the model of classical mechanics. The special theory of Relativity changes this image of time completely. Although the 'sum total of events' that are held to be simultaneous with a selected event exist, this does not hold independently of the choice of the inertial system. In other words, the four-dimensional continuum can no longer be resolved into sections all containing simultaneous events on any *objective* basis. The 'now' loses all objective meaning for the spatially extended world. Moreover, it is because of this that space and time must be regarded as a four-dimensional continuum that is objectively unresolvable, if it is 'desired to express the purport of objective relations without any unnecessary conventional arbitrariness' (1999: 149). There is then no single, universal time spread out across the universe that is objectively valid for all systems; rather there are only a plurality of times with different speeds of flow, all equally real but each one peculiar to a system of reference. As Einstein points out, 'Every reference-body (co-ordinate system) has its own particular time', and if we are not told the reference-body to which a statement of time refers then we can attach no meaning to it with respect to the time of an event (Einstein 1999: 26). In short, there is no longer assumed within physics the idea that a statement of time has any absolute significance in which it would be independent of the state of motion of the body referred to.

There is one more important point to take cognizance of and again this concerns the reformulation of the question of space in Relativity. Einstein draws our attention to the shift involved in moving from the special to the general theory of Relativity on this question. He notes that in classical mechanics *and* in the special theory space or space-time has an existence independent of matter; in the general theory, however, space, as opposed to 'what fills space', held to be independent of co-ordinates, enjoys no separate existence. In the general theory space becomes implicated in a *field* of forces (such as a gravitational field) and 'space-time has no independent existence but exists 'only as a structural quality of the field' (1999: 155). This is how Einstein responds to the dilemma of Descartes noted above: there exists no space that is empty of *field*.

Given these points, what is the challenge presented to the thinking by Bergsonism? Deleuze is especially helpful here. He points out that the confrontation is, in part, necessitated by the fact that Relativity invokes similar concepts, such as expansion, contraction, tension and dilation in relation to space and time. Moreover, the confrontation does not come about abstractly or arbitrarily but is prepared by the notion of multiplicity. Bergson reworked Riemann's distinction between the two multiplicities in *TFW* and Einstein drew heavily on Riemann's new geometries (see Einstein 1999: 86, 108, 111, 154). Bergson's essential challenge emerges out of this common source: is time to be treated as a virtual and continuous multiplicity or an actual and discrete one? Moreover, does Relativity confuse the one with the other, namely, the virtual and the actual? Deleuze insists that the proper question to pose is not, 'is duration one or many?', but rather, 'what is the multiplicity that is specific and peculiar to it?'. Duration does not have to be construed as simply multiple; it can be a One but 'in conformity with *its* type of multiplicity' (1991: 85). Bergson's principal argument is that the fourth dimension of space-time serves the role of a 'supplementary dimension' in which the relativity of simultaneous instants can be fixed and placed. It is this which informs his criticism not of Relativity's preoccupation with spatialization as such (he acknowledges that this is the domain in which modern physics moves and makes its contribution), but with the specific spatialization of time that the theory effects.

Science, Bergson argues, works exclusively with measurements, and the measuring of time consists in counting simultaneities (1999: 40). In dealing with time the concern of physics is with the extremities of time and the illusion is generated that the extremities of an interval are identical with the interval itself. What takes place in the intervals – an actual duration – is neglected and lost sight of, and this means that the counting of simultaneities can only take the form of a counting of instants. Bergson goes further: it does not matter at what speed time runs, if the number of extremities is indefinitely increased, or if the intervals are indefinitely narrowed, these changes would have no great impact on the calculations of time carried out by the physicist:

The speed of unfolding of this external, mathematical time might become infinite, all the past, present, and future states of the universe might be found experienced at a stroke; in place of the unfolding there might be only the unfolded. The motion representative of time would then have become a line; to each of the divisions of this line there would correspond the same portion of the unfolded universe that corresponded to it before the unfolding universe; nothing would have changed in the eyes of science.

(41)

But everything would have changed in terms of a qualitative duration that does not admit of measurement, such as that belonging to a living system whose duration and spatio-temporal dynamics are bound up with the flow of things in nature and its environment. Bergson contends that the simultaneities of Relativity are instantaneities that have been artificially abstracted from a concrete duration and, moreover, are purely mental views and habits (42). Furthermore, he argues that the simultaneity of instants measured by the physicist is dependent upon a simultaneity of fluxes which it neglects as its condition (37). The simultaneity of the instant is needed in order to fix the simultaneity with a clock moment. However, Bergson contends that unless the simultaneity of two motions outside us which are taken to measure time are connected to the moments of an 'inner duration' we would not even be able to formulate an actual measurement of time. This leads Bergson to ask whether the 'real' of Relativity exists anywhere else than in the equations of the physicist.

In order to advance its theses Relativity, Bergson contends, is dependent on symbolical tricks and employs the conventional habits of the intellect. How real are the multiple times of Relativity? Can they be lived by any system? On one level, they clearly cannot simply because no living system can exist at one and the same time in more than one frame of reference. No observer can experience, therefore, the dilation of its local time. But does this mean, as it seems to do for Bergson, that the plural times of Relativity are merely imaginary or fictional times? (Bergson was of the view that the times do not admit of empirical verification, which has proven wrong.) Part of the difficulty in answering this question is that Bergson misunderstood a crucial aspect of the theory, one that did not become clearer until the advance of the general theory. This concerns the factor of acceleration. It is this factor that Bergson wrongly treats as relative and which leads him to pointing out the absurdity of the well-known twins paradox. If acceleration is relative and thus each co-ordinate system perfectly reciprocal then we have a genuine paradox since both of the twins will both age two years and two hundred years depending on which frame of reference we select (and the choice of system, whether it be the Earth or the projectile, is a purely arbitrary one on this model). The two clocks (the one on Earth, the one in the projectile) are both going slower and faster than each other. We thus have a veritable absurdity, as Bergson was keen to point out. However, the paradox disappears once acceleration is recognized to be absolute and not relative within this example, for then there is only one twin that ages two hundred years on Earth while the twin rocketing out to space and back will have aged only two years. It is only if we assume acceleration to be relative that we can declare the example to be fictional. By not appreciating the advance offered by the general theory on this issue (an error repeated in Deleuze's ingenious and judicious assessment of Bergson and Relativity in chapter 4 of his 1966 text), Bergson was led to upholding the view that the time experienced and lived by the two twins would be absolutely identical. It is this error which leads him to propound the view that it is only when we arbitrarily privilege one of the two systems that we get the paradoxical formulation of multiple times: these times are mere projections made from inside a selected system (1999: 56). It is after having made this point that Bergson then makes the fatal move of equating the idea of there being only a single time with the identical time lived by the two systems. All the time that Bergson is discussing the twins (named Paul and Peter) he is thinking in terms of what consciousness can actually live. If we want to know, he says, how long Paul has actually lived, as the twin who has travelled in the projectile, what we need to do is not to consult the image the other twin has of him but ask Paul himself as a living and conscious subject: 'As soon as we address ourselves to Paul, we are with him, we adopt his point of view' (1999: 54). And when we adopt this point of view, argues Bergson, we discover that the projectile has stopped and it is now the Earth which is the mobile system. The two systems are completely interchangeable. From this he concludes that in Relativity we are only ever dealing with 'attributed' and not 'lived' time. It is this lived time that he now takes to be the 'single real time' and all others are imaginary. In the case of the twins they are, in fact, he says, living one and the same time but simply *attributing* differing times to each other (56).

It could be argued that Bergson is not, in fact, advocating the view that the time actually lived in a system has to be the same for every system. Rather, his point is that each system treats, and can only treat, its system as an absolute one. As he points out: 'If all motion is relative and if there is no absolute point of reference, no privileged system, the observer inside a system will obviously have no way of knowing whether his system is in motion or at rest' (1999: 24). In other words, we are always inside a system, bounded by a specific perspective or horizon of space-time, and cannot freely move around different systems. As Robin Durie notes, Bergson is not suggesting that from the perspective of one observer the time lived by another is not real because it is different to that observer's lived time. His argument is rather that any time projected by one observer to another observer's system of reference is an imaginary time since it is not a time lived by any observer.[14] But is this not a platitude? Does it not completely miss the challenge of Relativity? For surely Relativity is not positing multiple times from the perspective of 'projection'? (it is clear from the text that Bergson refuses in the example of the twins to climb the ascent to the viewpoint of the physicist).[15] Is Bergson suggesting we cannot step outside our own system?

Milic Čapek has shown that Bergson reaches the position he does through quite spurious reasoning: from the insight that each observer can perceive only their own local time the inference is made that there has not in fact taken place any actual dilation of time (the dilation of time and contraction of lengths of duration are held to be unobservable in principle). By means of the Lorentz equations we compute that our own duration must appear dilated in any other system that is moving with respect to our own at a certain speed. But as soon as we enter another system this apparent dilation will vanish. This is why Bergson argues that as soon as we do this the modifications of time and length posited by Relativity will show themselves to be purely phantasmatic: they are not experienced by a concrete observer but are only 'attributed' to an external observer who is moving with respect to an 'attributing' observer. In other words, the illusion arises from the fact that an actual observer is mentally identifying him or herself with an external observer and imagining themselves to be perceiving the modifications of space-time that remain imaginary and disappear as soon as the first observer steps into the other system. For Bergson, therefore, within the multiple times of Relativity only *one* of them can ever turn out to be real. Whenever this one is selected the rest are exposed as 'mathematical fictions' (1999: 20). But while it is plausible to propose that no observer can experience the dilation of their own time as a dilation, it is illegitimate for Bergson to draw the conclusion that no observer can perceive anything going on outside their own system (Čapek 1970: 244). As Čapek points out, this is an almost solipsistic position to uphold and it is one that the texts of *MM* and *CE* do not adhere to (indeed, they seek to demonstrate the exact opposite). If we followed Bergson's logic it would mean that the relativistic increase of mass would be unobservable (each observer could only perceive the masses associated with their own system and all masses would remain constant). Thus the experiments, carried out *before* Bergson wrote *DS*, which demonstrated the increase in the mass of the electron would have been impossible. Bergson's thinking contra Relativity reduces the world to the perception of discrete and self-contained Leibnizan monads. As Čapek points out, it commits the fallacy of simple location and flies in the face of everything Bergson says about the importance of beginning our thinking with the universal continuity and interaction that characterizes the material universe.

What may strike the reader of Bergson's text as strange is his argument that duration, or lived time, is always *actual* while the time which the physicist experiments with is a 'virtual space-time' (Bergson 1999: 115). Lived time is always a perceived time. There is, therefore, no virtual time! Indeed, this is the main criticism he makes of Relativity: it puts the actual and the virtual on the same plane (see Bergson in Gunter 1969: 174). How, on this basis, can we uphold Bergson as a philosopher and an ontologist of the virtual? In delineating the virtual and actual in this way, however, Bergson is simply drawing a contrast between imaginary and real. Relativity disregards the nature of lived time – the durational time of living systems – and puts all times, including mathematical times, on the same plane. It is thus unable to tell us what time is. However, Bergson needs a virtual–actual distinction if his own thinking on time as a specific kind of multiplicity is to be sustained. Without it his thinking of time ends up positing an empty multiplicity of times (each one is relative but treats itself as absolute and all durational times have the same tension). If his thinking is to be saved from falling into incoherence it is necessary to revise the conception of a single time.

Čapek approaches the issue in terms of topology. He argues that without a time common to all mathematical times, 'what would it mean to say that they are *contemporary*, that they are contained in the same interval?' (1970: 248). Take the example of the paradox of twins who are living in the same moment of time when they are being separated and later again at the same moment when they are reunited. This moment refers not to metrical time since the time of the spaceship and that of the earth are metrically different. Yet the different metrical times are bounded by the same successive moments and are thus contemporary, meaning that they express two complementary aspects of one and the same stretch of universal duration:

> If we designate the moment of separation **A** and the moment of return **B**, then the succession of **B** after **A** remains a succession in *all* systems because of the causal dependence of **B** on **A**. Such succession is thus a *topological invariant* not affected by the effects of relative motion nor by the dynamic effects of acceleration. What is modified is the *rhythms* of local times, that is the local time units whose different degree of dilatation in different gravitational fields account for different measuring of time in two systems. But these metrical differences do not affect the irreversibility . . . of the underlying common duration.
>
> (Čapek 1970: 249)

In other words, the topological or non-metrical unity of time which underlies the diversity of relative terms is not affected. The unity of time immanent to all frames of reference needs to be understood in a non-metrical sense and the same stretch of duration can underlie discordant metrical temporal series. Čapek thus upholds the thesis that 'there are certain types of succession which remain successions in all the frames of reference' (232). Moreover, while the relativization of simultaneity conceived as a relativization of time is simply a relativization of juxtaposition, the irreversibility implicit in durational time is of 'absolute' significance or status and has a reality that is 'objective' in the sense that it is independent of our choice of system of reference (233). Bergson was, in fact, oblivious to his own fundamental error, which consists in confusing the unity of the (cosmic) duration that underlies metrically discordant times with *oneness in a metrical sense*.

The seeds of a more radical revision of Bergson's argument can be found in Deleuze's text of 1966 *Bergsonism*. The stress on the virtual multiplicity as a One that is peculiar to it is a unifying feature of the way Deleuze reads a number of the major texts of Bergson, notably *MM*, *CE*, and *DS*. In the case of his reading of *DS* he comes up with what we might call a 'strong' reading of the single time. This consists in the claim that the single time denotes not the duration that is common to all times (a continuity of interpenetration or a topological unity), but rather that it refers to a whole that is virtual. For Deleuze this is the single time that Relativity presupposes and confirms. Upholding this interpretation of the single time involves Deleuze producing a particular reading of some especially ambiguous passages in *DS* (notably 31–2, and 33–4). The importance of Deleuze's reading on the question of the single time is that it removes the consciousness problem from its attachment to the observer issue and seeks to show that it is bound up with a virtual whole of duration that refers to a 'universal and impersonal' time.

The relevant claims from Bergson's text itself are the following:

a   It is difficult, if not impossible, to speak of a reality that endures without inserting consciousness into it (including memory). Duration is 'essentially a continuation of what no longer exists into what does exist' and without an elementary memory to connect two moments there would only be one or the other, as well as no before and after and no succession, no time (Bergson 1999: 33).

b   But then, the question arises, what is this consciousness for Bergson? The interesting aspect of his argument is when he suggests that it is not necessary to take our own memory and transport it into the interior of something else in order to conceive of a thing that endures, but rather of following the opposite course. The duration of a consciousness can be placed 'at the heart of things for the very reason that we credit them with a time that endures' (ibid.).

c   This is to conceive of an impersonal and universal time, what Deleuze calls a 'monism of time', and although Bergson hesitates over its reality (34), Deleuze does not. On the one hand, Bergson contemplates the universe forming a 'single whole' in which duration is a feature of the whole physical world and not simply limited to the lived reality of our own body: 'if the part that is around us endures in our manner, the same must hold, we think, for that part by which it, in turn, is surrounded, and so on indefinitely. Thus is born the idea of a duration of the universe . . . an impersonal consciousness that is the link among all individual consciousnesses, as between these consciousnesses and the rest of nature' (31). On the other hand, and a few passages on, Bergson argues that although we can distinguish between higher and lower tensions among different kinds of consciousness, we have no good reason for extending this 'theory of the multiplicity of durations to the physical universe'. The apparent contradiction between these two passages disappears once we realize that the term 'physical universe' refers to something specific, namely to worlds that might exist outside our own universe (the universes of the multiverse if one wishes). This explains why he is able, in the very next sentence, to go on to commit himself to the hypothesis that there is a 'physical time' that is 'one and universal'. This is to entertain the idea of a 'single duration' that gathers up 'the events of the whole physical world along its way' (32).

The real difficulty with Bergson's presentation, which exposes a problematic aspect of his thinking in *DS* that has already been treated, concerns whether or not in his conception of the single time and duration of the whole he supposes that there is only the one reality of time *qua* duration (all consciousnesses and all modes of being experience the same tension of *durée*). In spite of it being unclear in the text itself (see 32–3), I wish to maintain that Bergson is not committed to this view. My duration has the power to disclose and encompass durations that are different to it ('inferior' and 'superior') and different in kind. It cannot be the case that other durations are the same as or identical with my own. It is in Deleuze's 1966 reading that we find the alternative conception we are seeking.

Deleuze insists that duration is not simply the indivisible but rather 'that which has a very special style of division' (1991: 81). It is at the level of the virtual where no divisions have been carried out that the single time is to be located. As a virtual multiplicity duration divides into elements and lines that differ in kind (the flux of Achilles and the flux of the tortoise as well as the different steps of the two different fluxes). These differences in kind take us back to differences of tension, of contraction and relaxation, and these latter differences exist in the virtuality that encompasses them and that is actualized in them (82). He reaches the conclusion that implicated in the one time (monism) we find an infinity of actual fluxes (a generalized pluralism) that participate in the same virtual whole (a limited pluralism). The latter refers to the fact that a duration cannot disclose itself but can only be disclosed through other durations and all durations are unfolded in relation to a whole that is always virtual.

Following Deleuze on this issue is, I appreciate, extremely difficult. The reason for this is that it unleashes a whole series of questions regarding the reality of the virtual. What is this virtual that Deleuze is utilizing? Does it pre-exist everything that actually exists? Or is such a question caught up in a badly analysed composite (in this case, time and space)? How do we (actually!) think the virtual and its actualization? The task of addressing these questions and helping to answer them begins in the next essay.

Popper encounters Bergson

We saw in our treatment of the essays which make up *The World of Parmenides* that Popper openly acknowledges that critical rationalism needs to draw on the resources of 'irrationalism' with respect to the issue of a creative evolution (change is something real and not merely part of a phenomenological presentation of the real). The only problem, he contends, is that no theory of becoming has yet proven worthy of discussion. Perhaps our reading of Bergson is able to put this to the test. It would be a test carried out on a number of levels and we would need to convince the Popperian rationalist that intuition is not a method of irrationalism but a positive way out of the limitations of the intellect. We cannot undertake this task here; further insight into Bergson on intuition will have to be deferred until essay five which examines Bergson's response to Kant. There we shall see the extent to which the elaboration of a philosophy of intuition is, in a certain key aspect, Bergson's response to *Kant's* critical rationalism. For now, I wish to note some other important points about Bergsonism.

It is interesting to note that both Bergson and Popper approach the issue of the spatialization of time in Relativity by seeking to trace a genealogy from classical sources of ancient thought – essentially Parmenidean rationalism and the Platonic theory of Forms – to modern variations. Bergson shows that the break between the ancients and moderns lies in that for the latter there is no privileged moment of time; instead the focus is on any moment of time whatsoever. This 'any' instant, however, remains subject to spatialized conceptions of time. In Platonist thinking time is a 'moving image *of* eternity' (time belongs to eternity – if there is a utilization of this image in Deleuze this consists in a reversal in which eternity is shown to dwell in the virtuality of time). In this image time is a deprivation of eternity and hence something negative. In modern thinking time is treated as an invariable magnitude that measures the relative simultaneity of two instants. Outside of this mapping of closed systems time does not endure, indeed, duration has no meaning in physics. This is why, for all his confusions about Relativity, Bergson is absolutely right when he says that unless the 'philosophical meaning' of the theory is clarified we run the risk of 'giving a 'mathematical representation the status of a *transcendent* reality' (114; my emphasis). To avoid this it is necessary to develop a theory of systems (closed and open, artificial and natural), and to bring both philosophy and science into contact with the study of life and of living systems.

Bergson's achievement, which goes further than anything we find in Popper, is to clarify the notion of time *qua* duration: a virtual multiplicity that involves a continuity of interpenetration. No doubt Popper would consider such a notion to be the expression of an irrationalist metaphysics. Those inspired by Bergson, however, must reject such a tag simply because it is 'irrational' to accept the definition of knowledge and of metaphysics offered by the rationalist tradition. If Bergson is right then there is nothing natural or given about our intellect and its spatialized habits of representation; on the contrary, such habits are deeply rooted in the conditions of (evolutionary) life and thus there is needed a genesis of the intellect. It is the understanding, Bergson insists, that 'treats duration as a deficiency, a pure negation' (112). Restoring a wholly positive reality to time does *not* mean creating a 'metaphysical construction' (111).

I have argued that the single time cannot name what Bergson thinks it names: a real time that is lived or able to be lived and which then allows us to declare that the times of Relativity are all imaginary. The single time common to all times is the time of duration, where duration is conceived as a virtual multiplicity (a multiplicity that has a One that is peculiar to it). This is the 'philosopher's time' that Einstein denies has any existence or reality. My claim is that this time is not simply the time of the philosopher. It is also the time of life. This is why it is important that duration *qua* a virtual multiplicity is not restricted to the solely psychological or phenomenological but also encompasses the vibrating rhythms of matter. In *MM* Bergson argues that these vibrations are not instantaneous, in which the time of nature and of matter would simply be one of the succession of discrete instants (1991: 269). Moreover, Einstein's theory of Relativity is so myopically formulated it is unable to appreciate the extent to which it ultimately requires the philosopher's time to render it coherent and consistent. This point has been astutely noted by Philip Turetzky:

> The theory of relativity pictures the whole of time laid out in Riemannian space. But even this does not entirely spatialize time. For the formula for space-time separations between two events marks a qualitative difference between spatial and temporal components by the sign of the temporal component. In its analysis the theory of relativity attempts to represent time fully actualized. It analyzes qualitative into quantitative multiplicity, treating the universe as entirely actual, already complete. By restoring the unfolding of the virtual in its actualization, this near spatialization becomes compatible with Bergsonian *durée*.
>
> (Turetzky 1998: 210)

Within Bergson's thinking there is the possibility of forging a new alliance between the philosopher's time and the mappings of the physicist. In *DS* Bergson will refer again to the need to begin with a continuity of material extension and insist that beginning with such a continuity indicates nothing 'of the artificial, conventional, merely human' (1999: 25). This is a point that echoes a position he had outlined in *MM*. Such an extensity is filled with qualities of contracted and relaxed matter, making for a 'qualified and qualitatively modified continuity'. For example, the visual perception of a body by a living system, such as ours, is the result of dividing up a coloured extension and cutting it out of the continuity of extension. Although colours would appear differently to our eyes if they were differently formed there would, nevertheless, be something real which physics would resolve into elementary vibrations (the colour and the vibrations are different but both are real; colour is not simply something in our head).[16] The fragmentation of the continuity of extension is executed differently by different species of animal. Both philosophical analysis and physics provide us with insights into continuity *and* discontinuity. For example, on the one hand physics dissolves a body into a virtually infinite number of elementary particles, and, on the other hand, it shows how a body is linked to other bodies by numerous reciprocal actions and reactions.

This stress on the continuity of material extensity is relevant to our appreciation of Relativity because, as was intimated at in the preceding discussion, a key aspect of Einstein's transvaluation of space is the emphasis placed on the notion of field. As Einstein himself notes, the appearance of this concept initially had nothing to do with the problem of space-time (Einstein 1999: 144). It comes eventually, however, to have everything to do with it in his thinking. For a start it replaces the dubious notion of the aether as the incarnated space at rest in which space-time happens. But more than this the notion of field replaces the idea of there being particles conceived as material points. If the idea of a space without field is an illusion, then this can only mean that space-time, as a 'structural quality of the field', must be thought in relation to the dynamics of such a field. Such a thinking of blocs of space-time within a dynamic field of forces potentially gives us back the whole in the dimension of its moving continuity. Atoms become unthinkable apart from their implication in intra-atomic influences in which there is fusion and interpenetration between them. It is only artificially that we can abstract atoms, conceived as discrete corpuscles of matter, from their existence in a field of force. As Bergson notes:

> We see force more and more materialized, the atom more and more idealized, the two terms converging toward a common limit and the universe thus recovering its continuity. We may still speak of atoms; the atom may retain its individuality for the mind which isolates it, but the solidity and the inertia of the atom dissolve either into

movements or into lines of force whose reciprocal solidarity brings back to us universal continuity.

(1991: 200)

Conclusion: towards the time of life

In reflecting on time and space in an essay on 'Idealism and Realism' Max Scheler argues that we should not start with space as some *a priori* form of sensibility; rather we should begin with the phenomena of variation, movement, and alteration as the primary phenomena and then define spatiality in relation to them (Scheler 1973: 339). This means that the objects of experience are not forced to accommodate themselves to any geometry of the intellect or imagination, such as Euclidean geometry. Instead the choice of geometry will accommodate itself to the 'laws of observable movements'. The further question as to whether this objectification of a capacity for movement represents a unification of only our possible experiences, or whether it touches upon 'things themselves', depends on whether one assumes for Scheler a 'single, supra-individual "life"' or rules out such a notion as metaphysical. Either way one can maintain the 'existential relativity of spatiality to life in general'. But what of time, is this existentially relative too?

Scheler argues that the most primitive experience of time common to many living systems is the future. Here the future denotes the self-modification of the animal: '*The future is the possibility of spontaneous self-becoming through spontaneous self-modification*' (341). It is only when this spontaneous vital behaviour is cast aside that thinking is led to positing and privileging a solely 'theoretical time' as the actual form in which events take place. Because in 'physical time' the dimensions of past, present, and future are treated as existentially relative to certain living systems, it must deprive time of both structure and rhythm. All temporal determinations of events are now held to be entirely relative to one another, they do not exist outside of the relations between mobile and fixed systems. Scheler notes: 'Duration is here assumed from the start to be something merely specious' (348). The physical time is a time of 'spatial determinations', in which the only things that can be said to endure are measurable units. It is a time of the 'present' in which there is a continual sequence of 'nows' that are independent of any peculiarity of the creature or form of life whose 'now' these points are: 'There can be "happenings" in physical time but no "history"' (348). This is because it is of the nature of a history that a past remains active at every moment and 'that the contents of this past are variously brought into relief by the tasks belonging to the future' (ibid.). In physical time, by contrast, it is conceived that one and the same event can recur and since the arrangement of time depends wholly on the arrangements of events in space, this means that when the same state of the world recurs (the same configuration of forces), time itself will run back into itself (this is how, at least on one possible reading, Nietzsche presents the doctrine of eternal recurrence in section 1066 of *The Will to Power*).[17]

Physical time reaches its limits when the notion of 'life' is introduced. The evolution of life is bound up with a history (although not a teleologically conceived one). Physical time, Scheler suggests, is unique to the theory of Relativity. Although he does not accept the idea of there being anything we could call an 'absolute space' he does think it possible to conceive of an 'absolute time', and this would be the time of life. The time of life is absolute in the sense that the dimensions of past, present and future are not simply relative to a particular form or life or living creature. It suggests rather that the *evolution of life* is a unique, irreversible process. This 'life' is one in which the whole history of the universe participates, and the same events could only recur 'in artificially isolated systems' (350). The cosmos is not given but becomes, and the universe does not simply 'have' a history, *it is its history*. The temporality of time conceived as the process of life in its unique, irreversible becoming cannot be existentially relative to life since it is 'the form of the process of life itself'.

So, what does it mean to ascribe a 'positive reality' to time? If we take seriously the delay of duration at instantaneity we allow for a 'creative' evolution and not simply a mechanical one in which time would simply be given and things would exist as preformed possibles awaiting realization. With this 'delay' or reserve of duration we are able to conceive of a 'hesitation' and an 'indetermination' which, while vague and nebulous, are wholly positive aspects of time and becoming.

3

DURATION AND EVOLUTION

The time of life

... if we see that mathematical calculation of change does not explain but tends to deny change, we shall discredit the implications of necessity and determination implied in a phrase like 'contained in', and see that mathematical causation argues the present is contained in the past only because it wrongly spatialises change. If we regard time as real, we cannot regard the present as contained in the past, we must recognise the emergence of what is new, recognise that there is creation.

(Lindsay 1911: 42)

... against this pan-logical civilization Bergsonism brings to bear an inestimable message. It perceives the essential – if one can say – of psychism in change, in an unceasing passage to the other which does not stop at any identity; it teaches us time in primordial change, not as a 'mobile image of immobile eternity' – what it has been in the whole history of Western thought: simply the forfeiture of the permanence of being, a privation of eternity – but as the original excellence and the very superiority of *esprit*.

(Levinas 1987: 129)

How should the new be thought? This question remains at the forefront of philosophical disputation and, interestingly, has once again taken the form of an encounter between Bergsonism and its critics, with the agon between Alain Badiou and Gilles Deleuze echoing the complaints made in the 1930s by Bachelard contra Bergson. In contesting Deleuze's Bergsonism, for example, Badiou has argued in favour of the 'founding break' over 'creative continuity' and of the 'stellar separation of the event' over the 'flux'. If in the occurrence of an event there is a creative excess then, for Badiou, this creativity comes not from the inexhaustible fullness of the world but rather from the event not being attached to it *and* 'in the absence of continuity' (it comes from its being separated and interrupted) (Badiou 1994; 65). And exactly like the foremost critic of Bergsonism of a previous generation,

Bachelard, Badiou has recourse to set theory and its selection of actual multiples as a way of contesting the reliance on virtual multiplicities. The dispute is not, it perhaps needs to be noted, over the reality of the new but precisely how the production or creation of the new is to be thought. For Bachelard and Badiou the new is, almost by definition, that which exceeds prior conditions and which cannot be explained in terms of them. The quarrel with Bergsonism appears to rest on the claim that the new cannot be genuinely new if it is bound up with, in however complicated a fashion, the past. Bachelard, for example, sought to reject completely Bergson's attachment to continuity because, it appeared to him, this meant that the present was always inscribed in the past: the 'solidarity of past and future' and the 'viscosity of duration' mean, he argues, that 'the present instant is never anything other than the phenomenon of the past' (Bachelard 2000: 24). For Badiou the event has no relation to duration, it is a punctuation in the order of being and time (if it can be given a temporality it is only of a retroactive kind).

For Bergson, and Deleuze following him, however, the new is bound up with a creative evolution[1] (a notion that becomes a highly complicated one in certain of Deleuze's texts).[2] It cannot be conceived outside of duration. Contra Badiou, Deleuze argues that to think the new, or the event, otherwise is to reintroduce *transcendence* into philosophy and to talk of the production of the new in terms of an interruption or founding break is to render it mysterious and almost inexplicable. In this essay I want to demonstrate, contra the criticisms made of Bergsonism from Bachelard to Badiou, how it is possible to conceive duration as a condition of novelty. My focus will be on *Creative Evolution*, the text in which Bergson does not restrict duration to a phenomenological provenance. It cannot be a question of reducing the present to the status of being little more than a mere brute repetition of the past – if it were, it would be difficult to see how time could be given in Bergson's conception of a creative evolution (there would be nothing creative about it and there would not even be a phenomenon we could describe as evolution), but rather of thinking a duration 'in which each form flows out of previous forms, while adding to them something new, and is explained by them as much as it explains them . . .'. (Bergson 1983: 362).

Life as a virtual multiplicity

As we have seen, for Deleuze one of the most important innovations of Bergson's philosophy is to be found in the way he thinks duration as a multiplicity. As he notes, multiplicity is not part of the traditional vocabulary of philosophy when denoting a continuum (Deleuze 1991: 38). The distinction between a discrete or actual multiplicity and a continuous or virtual one marks a difference between thinking objects and things discretely, whereby the relations between them are ones of juxtaposition and exteriority, and thinking the components of a system in terms of fusion and inter-penetration. This notion of a virtual multiplicity becomes important for thinking evolution since it serves to show that we do not have to oppose heterogeneity and continuity. Duration is not a simple indivisible which admits of no division; it is rather that it changes in kind in the very process of getting divided up. This is why Deleuze treats it as a nonnumerical multiplicity 'where we can speak of "indivisibles" at each stage of the division' (42) (as in the run of Achilles; there is number but only potentially). But what is it, in the case of evolution, that is getting divided up? The answer to this lies in Bergson's conception of the vital impetus as a virtual 'whole', the nature of which is to proceed via dissociation and which is inseparable from an actualization. In the case of evolution, then, there is clearly heterogeneity (divergent lines such as plant and animal), but there is also continuity (something of the impetus of life persists across the divergent lines and continues to be explicated).

The notion of the virtual is opposed to that of possibility. An application of the notion of possibility is to be delimited to closed systems; however, in the case of an open system, such as the evolution of life, the notion of a virtual multiplicity is required in order to bring to light its characteristic features. Why is a thinking of evolution that focuses on the realization of the possible so inadequate? The simple answer to this is that it deprives evolution of any inventiveness or creativity. If the products of evolution are given in advance, in the form of pre-existent possibles, then the actual process of evolution is being treated as a pure mechanism that simply adds existence to something that already had being in the form of a possible. In effect, there is no difference between the possible and the real since the real is simply an image of the possible and indistinguishable from it. If the real merely resembles the possible then we are providing ourselves with a real that is ready-made (preformed) and that comes into existence by a series of successive limitations. In the case of the virtual, however, the situation is quite different, for here the process of differentiation does not proceed in terms of resemblance or limitation but rather in terms of divergent lines that require a process of invention. But there is another aspect to our construction of the possible and the real, one, as we shall see, that plays a crucial role in Bergson's attempt to expose the operations involved when we think events in terms of space and not time (duration): it is not simply the case that the real comes to resemble or mirror the possible but rather the other way round (the possible resembles the real). This is because our notion of the possible is arrived at by abstracting from the real once it has been made and then projected backwards.

To what extent can we produce a coherent conception of *evolution* if we construe it solely and strictly in terms of a set or series of discrete mechanisms (including discrete informational units), ones, it is alleged, that will automatically produce successful adaptations solely through the exogenous workings of natural selection? (Let us note that it is selection that is doing all the work of finality in the theory.) Some key points are perhaps worth stressing at the outset:

1   The claim is not that the scientist has no right to deal with closed systems. Bergson's concern is with what happens when this focus on closed systems, systems from which duration has been artificially extracted, is extended to an explanation of life. His contention is that the focus on closed systems is itself the result of certain intellectual tendencies that have become dominant in the history of our evolution, leading to the ironic result that the human intellect, on account of its spatial habits, and which are highly useful for manipulating and regulating matter, is unable to adequately understand its own conditions of existence, that is, unable to comprehend its own creative evolution. Bergson does not deny that there are closed systems. Rather he wishes to point out that isolable systems that can be treated geometrically are the result of a certain tendency of matter itself but that this tendency is never fully actualized or reaches a point of completion. If science does isolate a system completely this is for convenience of study, it must still be recognized that a so-called isolated system remains subject to external influences.

2   There is a role for calculation and computability (aspects of the present can be calculable as functions of the past), such as in the realm of organic destruction, but this cannot be extended uncritically to all domains, such as organic creation and other evolutionary phenomena which elude mathematical treatment.

3   It is necessary to distinguish between artificial and natural systems, or between the dead and the living. In the case of the living body of an organism the present moment cannot be explained by a preceding moment since the whole past of an organism needs referring to. An artificial system is one in which time is reduced to a series of discrete instants. But the idea of the immediately preceding instant is a fiction and an abstraction. In effect it denotes that which is connected with a present instant by the interval dt: 'All that you mean to say is that the present state of the system is defined by the equations into which differential coefficients enter, such as $de\backslash dt$, $dv\backslash dt$, that is to say, *present* velocities and *present* accelerations' (Bergson 1983: 22). In short, in such systems we are only ever dealing with an instantaneous present, one that carries with it a tendency but which it treats as a number (in Bergson a tendency has number *only potentially*): 'In short, *the world the mathematican deals with is a world that dies and is reborn at every instant – the world which Descartes was thinking of when he spoke of a continued creation*' (ibid). For Bergson the variation of evolution is being produced continuously and insensibly at every moment, although,

of course, it is only within specific conditions and under specific circumstances that it gives rise to a new species. No amount of knowledge of elementary causes will suffice to foretell the evolution of a new life form.

4 Contrary to a widespread misconception which has persisted from Bachelard onwards, Bergson's thinking of creative evolution places a notion of contingency at the centre of its concerns and conceives duration precisely in terms of an interruption and discontinuity: duration involves 'incommensurability between what goes before and what follows . . .' (ibid.: 29). Indeed, it is only by thinking of time as duration that the features of rupture and discontinuity can be rendered intelligible. There is a common prejudice running from Bachelard to Badiou that Bergson cannot think discontinuity. Such an assumption fails to recognize that Bergsonism provides an account of continuity *and* discontinuity.

The possible and the real

Mechanism is not wholly illegitimate or simply false in Bergson's view. It is a reflection of our evolved habits of representation rather than an adequate reflection of nature itself. These are habits that conform in large measure to certain tendencies of matter. Mechanism gives us only a partial view of reality and neglects other crucial aspects such as duration. Mechanism is often blind to its own mechanisms and ignorant of the fact that it is the product of a certain kind of impulse, namely, one towards utility. This impulse exposes itself when it is situated in the context of an understanding of how human intelligence has evolved and works. It is intelligence which demands the masking of duration. The intellect is the product of a natural evolution and has evolved as an instrument of praxis or action. Action exerts itself on fixed points. Intelligence, for example, does not consider transition, but prefers instead to conceive movement as a movement through space, as a series of positions in which one point is reached, followed by another, and so on. Even if something happens between the points the understanding intercalates new positions, an act that can go on *ad infinitum*. As a result of this reduction of movement to points in space, duration gets broken up into distinct moments that correspond to each of the positions (this is what we can call a discrete or actual multiplicity). Bergson writes:

In short, the time that is envisaged is little more than an ideal space where it is supposed that all past, present, and future events can be set out along a line, and in addition, as something which prevents them from appearing in a single perception: the unrolling in duration (*le déroulement en durée*) would be this very incompletion (*inachèvement*), the addition of a negative quantity. Such, consciously or unconsciously, is the thought of most philosophers, in con-

74

formity with the exigencies of the understanding, the necessities of language and the symbolism of science. *Not one of them has sought positive attributes in time.*

(1965: 95)

The difference to be thought is between an 'evolution', in which continuous phases interpenetrate, and an 'unfurling' in which distinct parts are juxtaposed with each other. In the former case rhythm and tempo are constitutive of the kind of movement in play, so that a retardation or an acceleration are internal modifications in which content and duration are one and the same thing. Throughout his writings Bergson is insistent that states of consciousness and material systems can both be treated in this way. If we say that time merely 'glides over' these systems then we are speaking of simple systems that have been constituted as such only artificially through the operations of our own intellect. Such systems can be calculated ahead of time since they are being posited as existing prior to their realization in the form of possibles (when a possible is realized it simply gets existence added to it, its fundamental nature has not changed). The successive states of this kind of system can be conceived as moving at any speed, rather like the unrolling of a film: it does not matter at what speed the shots run an 'evolution' is not being depicted. The reality here is more complex, however, but the complexity is concealed. An unrolling film, for example, remains attached to consciousness that has its own duration and which regulates its movement. If we pay attention to any closed system, such as a glass of sugared water where one has to wait for the sugar to dissolve, we discover that when we cut out from the universe systems for which time is an abstraction, a relation, or a number, the universe itself continues to evolve as an open system:

> If we could grasp it in its entirety, inorganic but interwoven with organic beings, we should see it ceaselessly taking on forms as new, as original, as unforeseeable as our states of consciousness.
>
> (1965: 21)

One of the difficulties we have in accepting this conception of duration as the invention of the new is due to the way in which we think of evolution as the domain of the realization of the possible. We have difficulty in thinking that an event – whether a work of art or a work of nature – could have taken place unless it were not already capable of happening. For something to become it must have been possible all along (a conception of logical – spatial – possibility). As Bergson points out, the word 'possibility' can signify at least two different things and often we waver between the two senses. From the negative sense of the word, such as pointing out that there was no known insurmountable obstacle to an event or a thing's coming into being, we pass

75

quickly onto the positive sense of it, in which we hold that any event could have been foreseen in advance of its happening by a mind with adequate information. In the form of an idea this is to suppose that an event was pre-existent to its eventual realization. Even if it is argued that an event, such as the composition of a symphony or a painting, was not conceived in advance, the prejudice still holds sway that such an event *could have been*, and this is to suppose that there exists a transcendent realm of pre-existing possibles.

This reduction of the real, and of real complexity, to mathematical calculability or computation – the very type of reduction which, as we shall see, Daniel Dennett seeks to perform on evolution – is one that Bergson locates in both nineteenth-century physics and biology. He quotes the following passage from Du Bois-Reymond's *Über die Grenzen des Naturerkennens* of 1892:

> We can imagine the knowledge of nature arrived at a point where the universal process of the world might be represented by a single mathematical formula, by one immense system of differential equations, from which could be deduced, for each moment, the position, direction, and velocity of every atom of the world.
>
> (1983: 38)

And this longer citation, highly pertinent to our concerns, from a work of T. H. Huxley's:

> If the fundamental proposition of evolution is true, that the entire world of the living and not living, is the result of mutual interaction, according to definite laws, of the forces possessed by the molecules of which the primitive nebulosity of the universe was composed, it is no less than that the existing world lay, potentially, in the cosmic vapour, and that a sufficient intellect could, from a knowledge of the properties of the molecules of that vapour, have predicted, say the state of the Fauna of Great Britain in 1869, with as much certainty as one can say what will happen to the vapour of the breath on a cold winter's day.
>
> (ibid.)

Bergson seeks to expose the error of this way of thinking an event or a creative evolution in his essay 'The Possible and the Real'. The error he investigates and exposes is not, as we shall see, restricted to nineteenth-century articulations but also lies at the heart of much current thinking about evolution. Once I have examined further how Bergson addresses the key issues at stake, I shall proceed to show how this same error influences the way Daniel Dennett has recently construed evolution by natural selection. The aim is not to refute or discredit the thesis of natural selection; rather, we are concerned solely with how an account like Dennett's exemplifies the extent to which any mechanistic approach to evolution produces a spatialized conception of it.

In his essay on 'The Possible and Real' Bergson argues that whether we are thinking of the unrolling of our inner lives or that of the universe as an open whole, in both cases we are dealing with 'the continuous creation of unforeseeable novelty' (1965: 105). The first obstacle we have to overcome is that which would posit an opposition between matter and consciousness, or the inert and the living, in which repetition is attributed to the first aspect of the pair, while the qualities of being original and unique are only attributed to the latter. Bergson points out that our focus on the inert is only an abstraction, often serving the need to calculate and map what is solid and simple (matter does have a tendency to inertness but it is only a tendency, one that is never fully completed). The life of consciousness – growth, ageing, in short, duration – is by no means the preserve of animal life, but can be identified in vegetable life. Moreover, the repetitions of the inorganic world constitute the *rhythms* of creative conscious life and measure their duration. It is owing to the fact that time can be conceived as a 'searching' and a 'hesitation' that there is a creative evolution in any event or becoming.

The 'searching' and 'hesitation' do not name anything substantive. Rather, they categorize the general directions, movements, and tendencies of life that are always inventive but in which the products of invention are never given in advance. The notion that there is a 'searching' process of duration within evolution is not peculiar to Bergson. It has most recently been articulated by Manfred Eigen, Nobel prize-winning scientist and Darwinian, in his *Steps Towards Life: A Perspective on Evolution*. Eigen argues that selection 'does not work blindly, and neither is it the blind sieve that, since Darwin, it has been assumed to be' (Eigen 1992: 123). The problem with Eigen's account, however, is that it treats the active searching feedback mechanism of selection solely in terms of an over-arching tendency that is always given – with natural selection one always knows what is going to be produced in advance as a general law of evolution (survival of the fittest and successful adaptations). The key aspect of time for Bergson is that it introduces *indetermination* into the very essence of life (this indetermination does become materially embodied: a nervous system, for example, can be regarded as a 'veritable reservoir of indetermination' in that its neurons 'open up multiple paths for responding to manifold questions' posed by an environment, 1983: 125). However, our natural or instinctive bent is always to construe this indetermination in terms of a completion of pre-existent possibilities. This is because we are subject to habits of thinking that have evolved from conditions of evolutionary life, which are conditions of utility and adaptation. Bergson provides the example of how perception works:

Perception seizes upon the infinitely repeated shocks which are light or heat . . . and contracts them into relatively invariable sensations: trillions of external vibrations are what the vision of a colour condenses in our eyes in the fraction of a second . . . To form a general idea is to abstract from varied and changing things a common aspect which does not change or at least offers an invariable hold to our action. The invariability of our attitude, the identity of our eventual or virtual reaction to the multiplicity and variability of the objects represented is what first marks and delineates the generality of the idea.

(1965: 95)

The intellect, which has evolved as an organ of utility, has a need for stability and reliability. It thus seeks connections and establishes stable and regular relations between transitory facts. It also develops laws to map these connections and regularities. This operation is held to be more perfect the more the law in question becomes more mathematical. From this disposition of the intellect emerges the specific conceptions of matter that have characterized a great deal of Western metaphysics and science. Intelligence, for example, conceives the origin and evolution of the universe as an arrangement and rearrangement of parts which simply shift from one place to another. This is what Bergson calls the Laplacean dogma that has informed a great deal of modern enquiry, leading to a determinism and a mechanism in which by positing a definite number of stable elements all possible combinations can be deduced without regard for the reality of duration (1983: 38).

Many of the anxieties of metaphysics concern problems that have been badly posed. In the essay 'The Possible and the Real' Bergson reduces these problems to the way in which we construe a negative as containing less than its positive opposite, such as is found in the pairs 'nothing/being', 'disorder/ order', and 'possible/real' (in this essay he is building on the analysis of the opening part of chapter 4 of *CE*, where he had sought to expose the illusions contained in our thinking of nothingness and the void). These evaluations, however, reflect the habits of our intellect. Bergson ingeniously shows that there is, in fact, more intellectual content contained in the negative ideas than in the positive ones. This is because they draw on several orders and several existences in order to make themselves intelligible. For example, what does saying that the universe is 'disordered' exactly mean? What is the status of the appellation 'disorder' in this case? Here the idea of disorder is posited on the basis of a conception of order we already have, which leads us to positing this disorder in relation to an order we expect to find but do not. In the intriguing case of the 'possible' our guiding habit is to suppose that there is less contained in the possible than in what is actually real and, consequently, we hold that the existence of things is preceded by their possibility. Bergson once again shows that the reverse is in fact the case. If we take the example of living things 'we find that there is more and not less in the possibility of each successive state than in their reality'. This is because the possible only precedes the real through an intellectual act that conceals its own illusion with regard to the issue. Bergson expresses the key insight, puzzling on first encounter, as follows, '. . . the possible is only the real with the addition of an act of mind which throws its image back into the past, once it has been enacted'. What does this mean? If we accept that reality is implicated in duration, and that this duration involves the creation of the new in the sense of something that is unforeseeable and incalculable, then we arrive at the insight that we ought not to say that the possible precedes its own reality but rather than it will have preceded it once the reality has appeared. An event happens, a work of nature or a work of art is created or comes into being, and we then construe its possibility in terms of a mirage of the present in the past. Owing to our construction of time as a linear succession of stages and instants we know in advance that every future will ultimately constitute a present, every present will become a past, and so on. It is by way of such illusions that we regulate our individual and social lives. The illusion is real, and what Bergson is concerned with is bringing out the genuinely creative aspects of the living that it misses and overlooks.

The possible is only posited from the vantage point of the real or when something has become actual. In other words, it works in a contrary fashion to the way we habitually suppose. Of course, Bergson does not deny that we can construct closed systems in which the relation between the possible and the real would conform to our intellectual expectations. But this is because such systems have been artificially carved out, made subject to the regularity of mathematical or physical laws, and rendered isolable because duration has been left outside the system. If, however, we understand the illusion of the possible and show how it is generated, we come to appreciate that evolution involves something quite different than the realization of a programme. The point is an important one for Bergson since it reveals to him that the 'gates of the future' are open. There is indetermination in life owing to the fact that the universe is an open system. This indetermination is not to be confused with a competition between pre-existent possibles. Darwinism is well able to explain the sinuosities of the movement of evolution, Bergson argues, but as for the movement itself it has no conception.

Dennett on Darwin's dangerous idea

Bergson is not an anti-Darwinian thinker. His own thinking is neither possible nor intelligible without an appreciation of the import of Darwinism. The language of 'transformism' (as Bergson calls natural selection) now forces itself, he says, upon all philosophy and science, making it impossible to speak any longer of life as an abstraction. 'Life' is a continuity of genetic energy that cuts across the bodies 'it has organized one after another, passing from generation to generation, [and that] has become divided among species and distributed amongst individuals without losing anything of its force, rather intensifying in proportion to its advance' (Bergson 1983: 26). Bergson is, in fact, open to the different accounts of evolutionism that modern thought provides. He holds, for example, that the whole issue of the transmission of acquired characteristics cannot be settled either by making an appeal to vague generalities about evolution or by closing it down through some *a priori* conception of the nature of evolution and of what is and is not possible; rather, it has to be open to further empirical inquiry and experimentation (ibid.: 78).[3]

In exposing the limits of mechanism Bergson does not go on to embrace a finalist position. He argues that finalism is merely an inverted mechanism which also reduces time to a process of realization. In the doctrine of teleology, for example, evolution is construed as the realization of a programme previously arranged and ordered. Again succession and movement remain mere appearances, and the attraction of the future is substituted for the impulsion of the past (hence the inversion). In Leibniz time is reduced to a confused perception that is entirely relative to the human standpoint. For a mind seated at the centre of things there would be no time and the confused perception would vanish. The only notion of finality Bergson will permit, contra Leibniz and Kant, is a strictly *external* finality. However, while conceding that actual change is something accidental he insists that the *tendency to change* is not (85). If there were no such tendency it is difficult to see how the idea of an evolution could be made intelligible. In short, Bergson argues that the evolution of life cannot be treated either simply in terms of adaptations to accidental circumstances or as the realization of a plan or programme.

In Bergson's conception of creative evolution the notion of tendency serves an important function. He first introduces the word in the opening argument of the book where it denotes the directions of life and serves to counter the idea that there is a single universal biological law that can be applied automatically to every living thing and the assumption that evolution can ever be made up of *completed* realities. Evolution for him is marked by different and conflictual tendencies: for example, life reveals a tendency towards individuation and a tendency towards reproduction. The notion of tendency is also designed to suggest that the study of life can be approached in terms of problems that are *immanent* to an evolutionary process or movement. The directionality and movement of life are not, however, to be understood in terms of a simple mechanical realization of pre-existing goals. Rather, the problems of life are general ones, evolving within a virtual field that is responded to in terms of specific solutions (an example to illustrate this would be cases of convergent evolution, such as the eye, representing solutions to general problems that are common to different phylogenetic lineages, in this case that of light and the tendency 'to see', or vision, and which involve a heterogeneity in the mechanisms actually involved). Bergson is struck by the fact that evolution has taken place in terms of a *dissociation* of tendencies and through divergent lines that have not ceased to radiate new paths. The evolution of life becomes intelligible when it is viewed in terms of the *continuation* of this impetus that has split up into *divergent* lines. On Bergson's model no dominant tendency within evolution can be identified and neither can the different forms of life be construed in terms of the development of one and the same tendency.

The aim is not one of simply attacking mechanism but rather trying to determine the precise character of the mechanisms of life and the nature of adaptation. What is the notion of mechanism we are thinking with? Dennett insists on approaching natural selection as an entirely mechanistic process based on algorithmic designs. Natural selection aims to show how a non-intelligent – that is, robotic and mindless – artificer is able over periods of time to produce successful adaptations. According to Dennett, Darwin's celebrated 'one long argument' is composed of two demonstrations, a logical one which claims that a 'certain *sort* of process would necessarily have a certain outcome' and an 'empirical' one that aims to show that the 'requisite conditions' for such a process can, in fact, be identified in nature (Dennett 1995: 49). The two demonstrations come together when it is shown, Dennett claims, that at the heart of Darwin's discovery is the power of an algorithm. This he defines as 'a certain sort formal process that can be counted on – logically – to yield a certain sort of result whenever it is "run" or instanti-ated' (50). In other words, evolution is a programme and in its actualizations it simply instantiates. It has a design, albeit that of a nonintelligent and mindless artificer, which is able to be instantiated to produce certain results whenever it is programmed to run. An algorithmic 'process' has several features, but one of the most salient ones is that it is made up of constituent steps. These are mindless steps which produce 'brilliant results'. Any 'dutiful idiot' or straightforward mechanical device could perform these to make the machine of selection yield the necessary results (successful adaptations).

Now, Dennett does *not* want to claim that results generated within evolution are conceived in advance. He writes, for example, 'Evolution is not a process that was designed to produce us, but it does not follow from this that evolution is not an algorithmic process that has in fact produced us' (56). Conceived as an algorithmic process natural selection is not about what it will inevitably produce but what it may or is most likely to produce and what it will 'tend' to yield.

> Here, then, is Darwin's dangerous idea: the algorithmic level *is* the level that best accounts for the speed of the antelope, the wing of the eagle, the shape of the orchid, the diversity of species, and all the other occasions for wonder in the world of nature. It is hard to

81

believe that something as mindless and mechanical as an algorithm could produce such wonderful things. No matter how impressive the products of an algorithm, the underlying process always consists of nothing but a set of individually mindless steps succeeding each other without the help of any intelligent supervision; they are 'automatic' by definition: the workings of an automaton.

(59)

The object of Dennett's attack is, of course, any nonnaturalistic account of evolution. However, Bergson's quarrel with Darwinism is not over an anti-naturalism versus a naturalism, in which a mindless mechanism would be replaced with something mindful. Bergson's conception of a creative evolution is, in fact, working against the idea of there being some transcendent mind – which he thinks is modelled on the habits of our intellect anyhow – that would be able to design evolution in advance. Evolution for him remains creative even in its adaptations. In other words, natural selection, as one key component in evolution, is a creative not a mechanical process. The fact remains, however, that Dennett can only think evolution in terms of logical possibility. For Dennett, Darwinism is all about evolution by design, and it just happens that this takes place via mindless, mechanistic means.

Throughout his text Dennett persists in positing spurious oppositions, a key one being that between a 'crane' and a 'skyhook', in which the former refers to the discrete stages that characterise an algorithmic process, while the latter corresponds to the failure of nerve that characterises any approach that has recourse to some kind of *deus ex machina* to explain the origins and development of something. But this limits the routes available to theoretical and empirical enquiry far too narrowly. The choice is far too simple-minded: *either* the algorithms of natural selection *or* some appeal to divine or special creation. In Dennett's terms everything from Nietzsche's 'will to power' to Bergson's *élan vital* would be readily dismissed as conforming to the latter strategy. The problem here is that he has no serious philosophical appreciation of why these thinkers felt compelled to introduce such notions into their accounts of evolution (chiefly because of their appreciation of the limits placed on our conception of life by the stress on adaptation to external circumstances).

Let me now show how Dennett is restricted in his conception of evolution on account of his attachment to thinking it largely in terms of the possible. Indeed, there is a whole chapter in his book, the title of which takes its inspiration from a work by Francois Jacob, called 'The Possible and the Actual'. At the heart of his conception is the idea of a 'design space'. Such an idea corresponds exactly to Bergson's exposition of how the intellect – an organ for manipulating matter and manufacturing tools and implements – reduces time to space. Dennett claims: 'There is a single Design Space in which the processes of both biological and human creativity make their tracks, using similar methods' (123).

The famous Tree of Life is to be thought in terms of this design space, meaning that the actual trajectories and tracks of evolution are to be understood as 'zigzagging' through a vast multidimensional space, 'branching and blooming with virtually unimaginable fecundity', while managing only to fill 'a Vanishingly small portion of that space of the Possible with Actual Designs' (143). What is meant exactly here by the 'possible' and the 'actual'? This comes out clearest in the idea Dennett develops of a 'library of Mendel', which he offers as a variant of Borges' library of Babel and which he develops as a way of answering 'difficult questions about the scope of biological possibility'. In Borges' library there lies a potential infinity of possible books that could be written. Not only do we find *Moby Dick* in there but also a million 'impostors', each one of which differs from the real one by a single typographical error. All these books, and billions more besides, exist in the library of some virtual or possible but stupendously vast logical space. The problem is how to search, locate and find the book we might want to actualize, such as the biography of one's life (which may exist in multiple forms). The 'Library of Mendel' is constructed as a biological variant of this logical space of all possible books, containing all possible genomes or DNA sequences. Possible genomes and sequences refer here, of course, to what we know of life on planet Earth, so just as Borges' library ignored books composed of other alphabets (Chinese, for example), so the library of Mendel excludes genetic codes not yet known to us. Of course, the analogy between the two libraries does not strictly hold. Dennett, for example, reflects on the chemical stability of his library, noting that all the permutations of the sequences of DNA (adenine, cytosine, thymine and quanine) enjoy this stability and that all could conceivably be constructed in principle in a gene-splicing laboratory. But then he notes that not every sequence in this library corresponds to a 'viable organism', simply because many if not most DNA sequences are 'gibberish' – 'recipes for nothing living at all' (113). Of course, in the library of Babel one can well imagine that the vast majority of books would be of this type – the gibberish of *Finnegans Wake*, for example. Of course, we need to ask, not only whether this is an 'original' book or a mere impostor, but also, to complicate things dramatically, by considering whether the so-called 'original' text might not itself be the impostor. Such examples could be readily multiplied but none of these books would for this reason be considered a lesser book – as in a failed adaptation – as a result of being composed of 'gibberish'. Indeed, what this example shows is that natural selection fails to acknowledge its own reliance on an over-arching tendency to explain the actual movement of evolution, one that the theory runs the risk of positing as a substantive transcendent principle, namely, survival of the fittest. Does not such thinking run the risk of turning the mechanism of selection itself into a *deus ex machina*? As one contribution to thinking 'beyond natural selection' notes, the evolution of certain traits can be viewed not simply as adaptations but rather as the fulfilment of certain tendencies or potentials (e.g. the height of the giraffe, which is clearly useful) (Wesson 1991: 193).

All the time that Dennett thinks about logical genetic possibility and actual evolution he is thinking spatially. This explains why, for example, he is able to hold to the position that tigers were, all along, a logical possibility in this design space of the library of Mendel. But what is the logical sense of this view? In truth, Dennett's speculation on the possibility of tigers conforms precisely to Bergson's insight that the construction of the possible takes place only in terms of retrospection. Dennett, for example, writes: 'With hindsight, we can say that tigers were in fact possible all along, if distant and extremely improbable' (Dennett 1995: 119). But could we not say this, with the benefit of hindsight, of anything that now exists (that it was in fact possible all along if somewhat improbable)? What is the empirical weight of such a claim? Dennett's insistence that he is concerned not with what is possible in principle in this library of Mendel but with what is 'practically possible' makes no difference to the force of our objection to his construal of a mechanical evolution. Dennett's argument appears to be deeply metaphysical and empirically worthless. As G. Adamson points out in a recent wide-ranging article on Bergson and evolution, Dennett's conceptions of probability and possibility 'hide some fairly extravagant epistemological assumptions'. However, it is not that Dennett denies 'Darwin's basic intuition that forms are created', as Adamson claims, but that he construes such creativity in terms of the instantiation of an algorithmic procedure (Adamson 1999: 144).

If any further proof were needed that Dennett reduces the time of evolution to the space of logical genetic possibility, consider his treatment of why certain non-actual possibles didn't in fact happen, such as all your non-actual brothers and sisters. The answer he gives is the intelligibly straightforward one that your parents didn't have the time, desire or energy, and ultimately no reason can be given for this unfortunate or fortunate state of affairs. But read carefully the way he argues this:

> As the actual genomes that *did* happen to happen began to move away from the locations in Design Space of near misses, their probability of ever happening grew smaller. They were so close to becoming actual, and then their moment passed! Will they get another chance? It is possible, but Vastly improbable, given the Vast size of the space in which they reside.
>
> (Dennett 1995: 125)

One wants to ask, not only what is the 'space' being spoken of in this passage, but also: what does it mean to posit 'near misses' that never came into existence and that probably never will, and to talk of things being close to 'becoming actual'? How are these conceptions actually constructed by our intellect? For surely what Dennett is saying in this bizarre passage reveals far more about the nature of the intellect than it does about the actual nature of evolution. I'd like to quote a fairly long passage from Bergson, which contains genuine insight coupled with his customary clarity. The passage captures both the confused working of the logic of the possible, to which, as the preceding passage makes clear, Dennett is committed; but also precisely how Bergson's notion of a creative evolution enables a genuine thinking of novelty:

> Our ordinary logic is a logic of retrospection. It cannot help throwing present realities, reduced to possibilities or virtualities, back into the past, so that what is compounded now must, in its eyes, always have been so. It does not admit that a simple state can, in remaining what it is, become a compound state solely because evolution will have created new viewpoints from which to consider it. . . . Our logic will not believe that if these elements had sprung forth as realities they would not have existed before that as possibilities, the possibility of a thing never being (except where that thing is a purely mechanical arrangement of pre-existing elements) more than the mirage, in that indefinite past, of reality that has come into being. If this logic we are accustomed to pushes the reality that springs forth in the present back into the past in the form of a possible, it is precisely because it will not admit that anything does spring up, that something is created and that time is efficacious. It sees in a new form or quality only a rearrangement of the old and nothing absolutely new. For it, all multiplicity resolves itself into a definite number of unities. It does not accept the idea of an indistinct and even undivided multiplicity, purely intensive or qualitative, which, while remaining what it is, will comprise an indefinitely increasing number of elements, as the new points of view for considering it appear in the world. To be sure, it is not a question of giving up that logic or of revolting against it. But we must extend it, make it suppler, adapt it to a duration in which novelty is constantly springing forth and evolution is creative.
>
> (Bergson 1965: 26)

Dennett himself raises a key question in this chapter of the book when he asks, is it possible to measure Design, albeit imperfectly? This, he then goes on to say, involves dealing with the question of whether Darwinian mechanisms are powerful and efficient enough to have done all the necessary work in the time required. He poses the issue in terms of the error of analysing genomes – and allied phenomena such as random drift, etc. – in isolation from the organisms they create. In order to get any serious purchase on the issue it is necessary, he argues, 'to look at the whole organism, in its environment' (Dennett 1995: 127). Now this is a good Bergsonian move to make, since it complicates massively the algorithmic picture we have so far been blackmailed into accepting (if you do not believe in evolution as an algorithmic process we will 'out' you as a closet skyhooker). Of course, Dennett believes he can speak in terms of the vast possible and the finite actual because he has a correct appreciation of the material facts and details of evolution. However, this means that he is wedded to some unempirical ideas about the nature of open systems. It is only artificially that he can put back together the pieces of the jigsaw which he has separated by an act of abstraction (genes, organisms, the environment, time, etc.).

According to Dennett, the key lesson to be learned from Darwin's revolution is this: Paley was right in holding Design to be not only a wonderful thing but also to involve intelligence. Darwin's contribution was to show that this intelligence could be broken up into 'bits so tiny and stupid that they didn't count as intelligence at all, and then distributed through space and time in a gigantic, connected network of algorithmic process' (133). He insists that there is only one Design space and everything from the biological to the social and technological evolves from it and, moreover, that everything actual in this space is united with everything else (135). As both designed and as designers we ourselves manufacture products in terms of the non-miraculous logical power of the algorithm and always in accordance with the blind and mechanical process of selection. Dennett asks us to reflect on the following 'problem' as a genuinely serious problem:

> How many cranes-on-top-of-cranes does it take to get away from the early design explorations of prokaryotic lineages to the mathematical investigations of Oxford dons? That is the question posed by Darwinian thinking.
>
> (136)

If *this* is the question that lies at the heart of Darwinian thinking, the difficulty is not in determining what is dangerous or radical about it but rather why we should take it seriously. It is not sufficient for Dennett to proclaim that anyone who cannot recognize this as a serious question is someone who cannot, perhaps on account of deeply rooted existential resistances and traumas, come to terms with the fact that they and their consciousness are the product of mindless robots and purely mechanical processes. Positing a Manichean world of craners and skyhookers is a neat but unsubtle way of considering the complex questions at issue and the difficult problems at stake, which are in need of a less simple-minded approach than is on offer in his work. Dennett's exposition of Darwin's dangerous idea is, I believe, an instructive example of the extent to which much contemporary thinking about evolution remains in the grip of spatialized habits.

Bachelard on Bergsonism

Bergson insists that he does not depart from the fundamental axiom of scientific mechanism, namely, that there is an identity between inert matter and organized matter. Instead he shifts the ground of the question by asking whether the natural systems of living beings are to be assimilated to the artificial systems that science cuts out within inert matter. If there is a mechanism of life this is a mechanism of the 'real whole', and not simply that of parts artificially isolated within this whole (Bergson 1983: 31). The isolable systems that are cut out of this indivisible continuity are not actually parts at all but rather '*partial views*' of this whole. Chemistry and physics are unable to provide us with the key to life because they simply put these partial views end to end. No reconstruction of the whole is possible on this basis, which would be like multiplying photographs of an object in an infinite number of aspects in a vain effort to reproduce the object. The isolable or closed systems that the intellect carves out from the real are, of course, not mere fictions; rather they correspond to actual tendencies of matter itself, notably entropic ones.

Bergson's argument that movement is irreducible has already been encountered. Movement cannot be reconstituted from either positions in space or instants in time. If it is said that we do this by adding to the positions or instants the idea of a succession, it is not being recognized that this move is equally abstract since it consists of a time that is mechanical and homogeneous, one that has been copied from space and that is valid for all movements. It is his adherence to the irreducible character of movement which informs Bergson's contention that life is not reducible to its physico-chemical basis. Just as we may legitimately ask whether a curve is composed of straight lines, so we can ask whether 'evolution' is made up of discrete stages and isolable systems. For Bergson evolution can be thought in terms of a 'single indivisible history' (1983: 37). Mechanism errs in focusing attention only on those isolable systems that it has detached from the whole. A mechanical explanation is only possible through such an artificial extraction. It is with this conception of the whole that it is possible to show the limits of the criticism that has been levelled at Bergsonism from Bachelard to Badiou.

Bachelard declares that he accepts 'everything' of Bergsonism except the thesis on continuity. He turns to sets as an example where *discontinuity* is established and which decides the nature of the continuum:

> We do not feel we have the right to impose a continuum when we always and everywhere observe discontinuity; we refuse to postulate the fullness of substance since any one of its characteristics makes its appearance on the dotted line of diversity. Whatever the series of events being studied, we observe that these events are bordered by a time in which nothing happens. You can add together as many series

as you like but nothing proves that you will attain the continuum of duration. It is rash to postulate this continuum, especially when one remembers the existence of mathematical sets which, while being discontinuous, have the power of a continuum. Discontinuous sets such as these can in many respects replace one that is continuous.

(Bachelard 2000: 46)

In response to this passage it should be noted that Bergson does have a notion of discontinuity. It is not that all – the whole – is a continuous pleni-tude. We say this not simply because Bergson construes the organism in terms of a discontinuity within the flow of genetic energy that characterizes life, but rather that discontinuity – in the form of the dissociation of tendencies and the divergency of lines of evolution – is an integral and essential part of his conception of the continuity of life. This will be demon-strated in more detail in the next essay.

In declaring that he accepted everything of Bergsonism except continuity, Bachelard was drawing attention to the need to show that continuities can never be regarded as complete, solid and constant. Rather, they 'have to be constructed' (Bachelard 2000: 29). This means for Bachelard that the continuity of duration cannot be an immediate datum of consciousness but has to be conceived as a problem. As we have seen, however, this is precisely how Bergson comes to construe duration in *Creative Evolution*, as a problem of relatively isolable systems and the threads that connect these systems, including the invisible bonds that maintain a solidarity and a communic-ation between diverse forms of life, to the rest of the universe. Where Bachelard goes wrong is in supposing that we have to choose between continuity and discontinuity, that we can only have sets and parts at the expense of the whole and wholes, and that in order to allow for the new we have to sacrifice duration. What he fails to appreciate in Bergson is this innovative way of thinking systems in both their actual and virtual com-plexity. In arguing for the need to see a 'fundamental heterogeneity at the very heart of lived, active, creative duration' (2000: 29), he failed to see that such heterogeneity is already at the heart of a Bergsonian appreciation of duration. His assertion that 'Bergson no doubt had to ignore accidents when writing his epic account of evolution' reveals a similar naïve appreciation of the details of Bergson's arguments in *CE* (see Bachelard 2000: 71). It both disregards the important role Bergson ascribes to contingency within evolution and fails to engage with his examination of the inadequacy of Darwinism as a theory of evolution.[4] Evolution cannot simply be made explicable in terms of a mechanical adjustment to external conditions or circumstances. Bergson argues, for example, that the theory of mechanism cannot adequately explain a crucial element in the evolution of the eye, namely, 'correlation'. On the one hand we have a complex organ, and on the other we have a unity and simplicity of function. It is this contrast, says

Bergson, which should make us pause for thought. If vision is 'one simple fact' how is it possible to account for its organization and operation in purely exogenous terms and in terms of chance modifications (Bergson 1983: 88)? If we are to take seriously the idea that a complex organ like the eye was the result of a gradual formation, as well as of a process of highly complex correlation (which Bergson does believe), then it becomes necessary to attribute to organized matter the power of constructing complicated machines able to utilize the excitations that it undergoes (72). Bergson makes it clear, in responding to a critical point on utility which would argue that the eye is not made to see but that creatures see because they have eyes, that he is not simply referring to an eye that has the capacity to see when speaking of an eye that 'makes use of' light. Rather, he is saying that what needs paying attention to are the precise relations existing between the organ and the apparatus of locomotion. In other words, the problem is not that of a discrete organ, such as the eye, but the complexity of its evolution in relation to other systems of an organism.[5]

Bergson is not tied to the idea that there are no accidents or contingencies in evolution, or that we have to posit evolution in terms of a linear and direct process destined to attain a specific goal; on the contrary, for Bergson there is a process characterized by frequent dead ends, numerous aborted lines, and lines that have failed to evolve. On the other hand, however, 'the failures and the deviations of the transformist mechanisms have not arrested the increase in either anatomical or psychic complexity'. Evolution has developed along a plurality of lines and if the universe as a whole is carrying out a plan, then this is something which can never admit of an empirical demonstration. What we do know is that nature 'sets living beings at discord with one another' and 'everywhere presents disorder alongside of order, retrogression alongside of progress' (1983: 40). One of the reasons why vitalism is such an intangible position to hold is because of its crucial claim, at least as articulated in Bergson, that in nature there exists neither purely internal finality nor absolutely distinct individuality:

> The biologist who proceeds as a geometrician is too ready to take advantage here of our inability to give a precise and general definition of individuality. A perfect definition applies only to a *completed* reality; now, vital properties are never entirely realized, though always on the way to become so; they are not so much *states* as *tendencies*.
>
> (12–13)

Some problems

In seeking to demonstrate the limits of one way of thinking evolution we have thrown up problems regarding our own. We must now endeavour to clarify the notion of the virtual and the role it is playing in a thinking of the time of evolution. Does the notion of virtual multiplicity mean that life is a 'whole' and that this whole is a 'One' (even the power of a One)? We saw in the previous essay how Deleuze utilizes such a conception of virtual multiplicity in the case of the single time. I propose to defer a proper treatment of the question of the One until the next essay. Here I shall restrict the questioning to Bergson's presentation in *CE*. What kind of whole is the virtual and in what sense is it ever given? Before attending to this question I wish to tackle some critical points with respect to the notion of the *élan vital*. This will place us in a better position for tackling the notion of the virtual and the complex role it is playing in Bergson's *CE*.

Bergson's reliance on the notion of a vital impetus to account, in part, for the creativity of evolution is, without doubt, the most speculative aspect of his text and its encounter with Darwinism. It faces a number of important criticisms, which I now wish to unravel.

1   First, what kind of force is it and can it escape the biting criticism made of the notion of a life-force by Schelling in his own treatment of the philosophy of nature, for whom such a notion is self-contradictory? This is because a force can only be thought as something finite; no force is finite unless it is limited by another force (Schelling 1988: 37). Should we, then, understand the play between the tendencies of life and the tendencies of matter in Bergson's conception of creative evolution as a play of conflictual forces?

2   Second, what kind of power is the *élan vital*? Is it a simple power of immanence or does it have the power of eminence? This question, as we shall see in the next essay, becomes a crucial one for negotiating a response to Badiou's critique of Deleuze and of Bergsonism. The relevance of the question for this account of Bergson comes out when we consider a point made by Merleau-Ponty. He notes that Bergson, 'like Kant and Schelling', sought to describe the operation of a natural production in terms of a movement from a whole to parts but which would owe nothing 'to the premeditation of the concept and admit of no teleological explanation' (1988: 146). This is why, Merleau-Ponty suggests, Bergson's description of life in the opening chapters of *CE* is so 'scrupulously honest', hiding nothing of its hesitations and even failures. However, in speaking of it as 'simple act' is Bergson not assigning to the *élan*, he suggests, a reality 'in advance of its effects as a cause which contains them *pre-eminently*' and so contradicting his own concrete analyses? (my emphasis). Should we perhaps ask: how eminent is 'pre-eminent'?[6]

3   Third, and finally: Bergson will not hesitate to stake out the novelty of his approach for tackling some of the central problems within modern evolutionary thinking, such as the issue of convergent evolution. It is

here that the thesis of an *élan vital* is rendered highly vulnerable. He has posed the question whether an entirely accidential process of selection – a series of accidents added together with selection preserving them – can account for two entirely different evolutions arriving at similar results (for example, highly different lines of evolution, such as molluscs and vertebrates, coming up with eyes as a solution to the problem of light). It is worth citing him in his own words on this issue:

> . . . such similarity of the two products would be natural . . . on a hypothesis like ours: even in the latest channel there would be something of the impulsion received at the source. *Pure mechanism, then, would be refutable, and finality, in the special sense in which we understand it, would be demonstrable in a certain aspect, if it could be proved that life may manufacture the like apparatus, by unlike means, on divergent lines of evolution; and the strength of the proof would be proportional both to the divergency between the lines of evolution thus chosen and to the complexity of the similar structures found in them.*
>
> (Bergson 1983: 54–5)

Bergson has himself, then, raised the stakes incredibly high. A great deal of Bergson's criticism of mechanism could be readily accepted by many evolutionary biologists without them feeling the need to invoke a vital impetus which persists across different lines of evolution as a simple virtual. Let's stick for now with this third criticism, one I am raising myself. We shall then return to the other two.

Bergson's claim is that the initial impulse of life continues to abide in the parts, and it is this persistence that can, again only in part, explain the evolution of identical organs in very different forms of life. It is, for example, owing to this common impetus that he holds it is possible to explain the different solutions that divergent lines of evolution, such as plant and animal, come up with in response to problems of storing and transforming energy: 'the same impetus that has led the animal to give itself nerves and nerve centres must have ended, in the plant, in the chlorophyllian function' (1983: 114). Bergson is contesting the claim that complexity in evolution can be explained simply in mechanistic terms as the mere accumulation of a discrete series of accidents added to one another and preserved through selection. Of course, he is aware of the argument that would insist that resemblances of structure across very different organisms are the result of a similarity in the general conditions under which life has evolved. The weakness of this argument for him is that it suggests that external conditions alone are sufficient to bring about a precise adjustment of an organism to its environmental circumstances (and his claim is that in natural selection adaptation is equivalent to 'mechanical adjustment'). Hence his question and problem: 'How can accidental causes, occurring in an accidental order, be supposed to have repeatedly come to the same result, the same causes being infinitely numerous and the effect infinitely complicated?' (1983: 56). As he points out, that two walkers commencing from different points and wandering at random should finally meet is not a great wonder. However, what is surprising is that throughout their perambulations both walkers should describe two identical curves that are superposable upon each other. Furthermore, Bergson is more than willing to concede that the first rudiments of the eye can be found in the pigment-spot of lower organisms and that this was probably produced purely physically by the mere action of light, and that between this simple pigment and the complicated eye of a vertebrate there are a great number of intermediaries. But, as he then points out, 'from the fact that we pass from one thing to another by degrees, it does not follow that the two things are of the same nature' (70). In short, what is missing in the mechanistic conception of adaptation is any sense that in certain life forms the evolution of organs cannot simply be explained in terms of the passive adaptation of inert matter submitting to the influence of an environment. The simple influence of light cannot be held to be the cause of the formation of the various systems (nervous, muscular, osseous) that are continuous with the apparatus of vision in vertebrate organisms (71).

While Bergson's point about the irreducible complexity of the eye remains pertinent to the concerns of contemporary accounts of evolution, it is his hypothesis on cases of convergent evolution being explicable in terms of the vital impetus that is highly problematic.[7] The are numerous instances of convergency within evolution that can be explained without recourse to an initial impulsion of life. As one contributor to current debates points out, it may simply be that there are a limited number of ways, mechanical and physiological, by which potentials can be accomplished: 'One assumes that the octopus eye resembles the vertebrate eye because there are not many ways to make a cameralike apparatus' (Wesson 1991: 189). Similarly, the reason why both birds and mammals improved upon reptilian metabolism might be because there is only the one way to make the improvement. Is it necessary to appeal to a vital impetus to account for the similarity in the shapes of sharks and porpoises? It is important to note, however, that while Bergson's thesis may be weak with respect to convergency, this does not mean we ought to simply jettison the idea that evolution can be approached in terms of tendencies and potentials, directions and trends (orthogenesis is not so much the problem, what matters is how we think the directionalities of evolutionary life).

The claim that cases of convergent evolution are to be explained in terms of an initial impulse of life that has persisted across divergent lines can only remain highly speculative. In this respect one might credit it with the power of reflective judgement that Kant ascribes to a teleological judgement, that is, such a hypothesis cannot disclose to us what life really is; rather, it serves only to guide our investigations into nature beyond mechanistic assumptions. Even if this is conceded it is still possible to maintain a distinction between life and matter, and between the virtual and the actual (for example, on the level of tendencies and the progression of unactualized potentials). It is still even possible to retain a notion resembling the *élan vital*; what remains problematic is the claim that empirical phenomena of evolution, such as cases of convergent evolution, can be explained in terms of an original impulsion at source.

A fruitful way of dealing with the first two criticisms enumerated above is by attending in more precise terms to Bergson's notions of matter and life than we have hitherto. The fact that this distinction can assume the form of a dualism in Bergson's thinking is not the principal problem. Such a dualism is common to a great deal of thinking about evolution. Eigen, for example, maintains that 'Life is *not* an inherent property of matter' (Eigen 1992: 3), while in their study of complexity Coveney and Highfield suggest that if life is a process then it is the 'form' of this process and not its 'matter' that 'is the essence of life' (1995: 17). However, in the case of Bergson's text it is vital we appreciate that evolution is being addressed in terms of a necessary implication between tendencies of life and tendencies of matter. Evolution is both tension and de-tension (the contraction and relaxation of matter). Bergson's philosophy is often wrongly accused of producing a 'subjective idealism' in which matter is taken to be unreal and life necessarily gets reified (see, for example, Collingwood 1945: 136–41).[8] A creative evolution, however, presupposes and requires matter, it does not negate its reality. Bergson argues that life enters into habits of matter and draws it little by little onto different tracks. He appears to be positing a separation between the physico-chemical and the vital, and it is this separation which many have taken issue with and which appears to consign Bergson to an outmoded vitalism.[9] However, Bergson has no simple or single conception of matter. Instead one finds in his work an attention to kinds and types of matter (inert, organized, ossified, etc.) and even to types of life (organized and unorganized, virtual and actual, etc.). Conceived as a tendency, the role of life is to introduce an element of indetermination into matter. Left to itself matter would lead to entropic states. Nevertheless, Bergson does not hesitate to define the 'vital activity' of life in terms of 'the growing materialization of the immaterial' (1920: 230).

The force that is 'evolving throughout the organized world' is for Bergson a limited one (1983: 126). This is owing to the conflictual tendencies between life and matter. The force would like to transcend itself and create all at once (to be a 'pure creative activity', 245). It is, ironically, owing to the nature of matter that this cannot happen. Life insinuates itself into the habits and repetitions of matter – it becomes like matter, one might suggest – but it does not become contained by materiality. The force of life is not to be conceived in terms of entelechy simply because, while it is deeply implicated in the habits of matter, it is not identical to matter: it is not in the organism in the sense that the organism can determine its nature; rather, the force of life is a transversal one that cuts cross the bodies and the organisms that provide it with a materiality. If the impetus is to persist across divergent lines then there has to be a mechanism of transmission. Bergson appreciates this point, which explains why he is led to posit a relation between the vital impetus and something as biologically specific as Weismann's germ-plasm: '. . . *life is like a current passing from germ to germ through the medium of a developed organism*' (1983: 27; see also pp. 78–9). But life also serves to 'engraft' indetermination on the physico-chemical elements of the organism, so making it possible for evolutionary change to take place. Each species of life would like to treat itself as if it was an end-point of evolution. It should be noted that the effort of life, which is not that of an individual effort (Lamarckism, as Bergson conceives it) cannot result in the creation of energy; rather it secures and utilizes an accumulation of potential energy from matter (114–15). Animal life is said to consist in the procuring of a supply of energy and its expenditure in variable and unforeseen directions and via the means of a supple matter (253).

Now, the question emerges: does not this dualism of life and matter produce a reification of a force that acts and forces that are acted upon? The question appears to be a legitimate and trenchant one to ask of Bergson's thinking of creative evolution. But there is something amiss in its formulation. What it overlooks is the extent to which throughout the text Bergson is insistent that we render the idea of creation obscure to the extent that we think of *things* being created and a *thing* that creates. He maintains that there 'are no things, there are only actions' (248). The positing of a thing creating and created things is for him an illusion rooted in the nature of our intellect and its utilitarian bias. Creative evolution is not to be thought on the order of an external cause that 'plasters' a 'contrived organization' upon materiality. In other words, the cause of a creative evolution has to be conceived as an *immanent* one. Life and matter are opposing movements, but it is only in terms of an act of intellectual abstraction that they can be rendered separate and one (life) considered to the external designer of the other (matter). Bergson insists that to view evolution in terms of a hylomorphic schema, in which form is imposed on materiality from outside, is nothing more than an accustomed habit of our intellect which has been formed to 'act on matter from without' (250).

For Bergson the unity of life is to be explained in terms of a common impulsion and not a common aspiration. His thinking of evolution entails both continuity (of genetic energy) and discontinuity (divergent lines, individuated organisms, and different species). He is insistent that life proceeds by dissociation and division. The question that needs to be returned to now is this: does the virtual multiplicity of tendencies pre-eminently contain all that will actually be created within evolution? If this were so, it would surely mean that Bergson's position becomes indistinguishable from a preformist account of pre-existent possibles. It is only possible to defend Bergsonism from the demanding and potentially damaging criticism made of it by Merleau-Ponty by grappling with the complex relationship between the virtual tendencies and the actualized divergent lines of evolution. I will offer some insight into this relationship in the concluding section and then examine it in detail in the next essay.

Conclusion

Bergson's position on the virtual is a complicated one to negotiate and get a critical purchase on unless we realize that there are, in fact, two different presentations of the 'whole' in the text: the whole of a simple virtual and the whole of an open. Both are at work in his conception of creative evolution.[10] What is the relation between these two wholes? On the one hand, there are only the lines of actualization. This is because the whole, *qua* a virtual whole, *only exists in terms of its divisions and differentiations*. It is this which explains Deleuze's insistence that the whole is never *given* (1991: 104). To regard it as ever given would be to treat it in terms of space and not time; and there is only ever the time of creation and differentiation (time enjoys an entirely 'positive reality', says Bergson). On the other hand, however, the initial impulsion of life *is* given but only in terms of a simplicity; this is the simplicity of a limited force that becomes divided and differentiated when it comes into contact with materiality. It is given, then, in the sense of a limited force; evolution itself, however, can never be said to be given.

It is only in artificial terms that the whole, as virtual, can be thought in abstraction from its actual divisions and movements (by turning time into space). This is important, since it shows that the actualization of the virtual is not to be conceived in terms of a Platonism – the actual forms of life created are not degraded forms of some transcendent and immutable being. The virtual, then, is neither a Platonic form or Idea of evolution nor is it a supplementary dimension existing in some given realm that would be transcendent to an actual evolution. The virtual is *not* a fourth dimension of space. It is only if we conceive it in terms of space that it assumes the appearance of such a dimension. Admittedly, it is difficult to think the virtual in this way, but the difficulty demonstrates, I would suggest, the tremendous efforts required of us to think non-spatially. The appeal to the virtual, then, is made in order to account for evolution understood as a genuine creation of positive acts and an invention of lines of actualization conceived as lines of differentiation. At the same time, however, it is vital that we cognize the double nature of Bergsonism on the question of virtual life: an *irreducible* pluralism (the actualized lines of differentiation) is completely affirmed.

In conceiving evolution in terms of the two terms, the virtual and the actual, we cannot reach the conclusion that Bergson has fallen back onto preformism simply because of the tremendous difference that has to be assumed between the tendencies existing in an intensive state of a virtual manifold and the actualized lines of evolution in which these tendencies manifest themselves in specific adaptive life-forms. It is as if Bergson is asking us to think evolution on two different planes, equally real, at one and the same time: on the plane of a pure virtual in which the tendencies of life have not yet been actualized and so exist in terms of an intensive fold (a monism); and on the plane of an actualization in which there are only divergent lines with forms of life, such as animal and plant, becoming closed on themselves, constituting an unlimited pluralism. As Deleuze says: 'Each line of differentiation or actualization thus constitutes a "plane (*plan*) of nature" that takes up again in its own way a virtual section or level' (1991: 133).[11] This virtual whole is given but only in the sense that it is a limited force or power in need of actualization: it is given as a simple virtual (of tendencies) but never given as a virtual whole that is always being actualized. As an original impulsion it must be finite though capable of potentially infinite transformation. Here the infinite is to be thought not in terms of space, as the realization of infinite possibilities, but in terms of positive time, an infinity of potentialities within finity. The finite and infinite are not being conceived numerically (as the one and the many), but rather in terms of limited and unlimited, neither of which are given in advance and once and for all.[12]

4

THE SIMPLE VIRTUAL

A renewed thinking of the One

A static and immobile being is not the first principle; *what we must start from* is contraction itself, the duration whose inversion is relaxation.

(Deleuze, 'Bergson's Conception of Difference', 1956)

Our starting point is a unity, a simplicity, a virtual totality.

(Deleuze, *Bergsonism,* 1966)

All life begins with contraction . . .

(Schelling, *Ages of the World,* 1813)

Introduction

Alain Badiou has described the virtual as the principal name of Being in Deleuze and claims that his thinking amounts to a *Platonism* of the virtual. Badiou argues that in Deleuze the virtual is presented as 'the ground of the actual', and moreover, that it is *the ground of itself* as the 'being of virtualities'. Badiou likes to speak of the virtual as that which lies 'beneath' as in '"beneath" the simulacra of the world' (Badiou 2000a: 46). This explains why he has such problems with any talk in Deleuze of the virtual in terms of an *image*. Is not the 'image' the status only of the actual? How can the virtual, conceived by Badiou as the 'power proper to the One', be a simulacrum? No doubt, he says, 'the virtual can give rise to images but it is difficult to determine how an image can be given of it or how it can itself be an image' (52). There is a Berkeleyean dimension to Badiou's point which serves to disclose the somewhat peculiar nature of his question. In his *Principles of Human Knowledge* Berkeley poses a problem with regard to soul or spirit in terms that bear a strikingly similarity to the way Badiou has posed the problem of the virtual qua image. If spirit is One, that is, simple and undivided, and if it is the primary 'active' being, how can an 'idea' or image be formed of it since inert ideas/images cannot represent to us that which acts? (Berkeley 1962: 77). The incorporeal and immaterial substance cannot be represented, cannot itself be an idea or image, since it is the causal ground of them.

Badiou is adamant that Deleuze is a classical thinker whose project is primarily and essentially an ontological one. In Deleuze the task is to think the real of the One: 'Deleuze's fundamental problem is most certainly not to liberate the multiple but to submit thinking to a renewed concept of the One' (2000a: 10). This means that the multiple is to be conceived 'integrally' and in terms of the 'production of simulacra'. Badiou is aware that notions of the ground (*fondement*) and of foundation are taken to task in contemporary thought and that Deleuze's work can be construed as at the forefront of these developments – he does, after all, speak in *DR* of a 'universal un-grounding' (Deleuze 1994: 67). Nevertheless Badiou persists with his reading, establishing the notion of ground in Platonist terms by speaking of it as the 'eternal share' of beings (Badiou 2000a: 45). It is because Deleuze thinks the virtual in terms of this eternal share that his thinking demands 'that Being be rigorously determined as One' (ibid.). 'Ground', therefore, is being identified not with the (Kantian) noumenon but with the Platonist notion of participation. Deleuze, as we shall see, opens chapter 11 of his 1968 book on Spinoza by addressing this very issue of participation.

Badiou opposes Deleuze on account of his deployment of the two terms, the virtual and the actual. He wishes to discredit the appeal to the virtual and desires that we speak instead of '*the univocity of the actual* as a pure multiple' (my emphasis) (52). The multiple of multiples has to be affirmed, it cannot be posited in terms of the power of a One. The One, and along with it Life, has to be sacrificed. The two 'classicisms', says Badiou, are irreconcilable.

Badiou has, without doubt, raised a number of important questions concerning Deleuze's project. To deal satisfactorily with the issues they raise, however, I believe we need more precision. What kind of Platonism of the virtual might be stake in an encounter with Deleuze and with Bergsonism? Is Deleuze a thinker of the One or is he not a thinker of virtual multiplicity that has gone beyond the opposition of the one and the many? Badiou knows this, of course, but persists in reading Deleuze as a thinker of the one and not the multiple. I will argue that Deleuze's thinking of the virtual does have a link with an important (neo-) Platonist source and that it is legitimate to describe him as a thinker of the One. However, the reading I offer here of Bergsonism's renewed thinking of the One produces a quite different image of Deleuze's thought. Badiou's curious affirmation of the *univocity of the actual* (as pure multiple) shows that he has inadequately understood the role of the virtual in Deleuze and discloses a fundamental incoherence in his own thinking.

The One of pluralism: Bergson and Deleuze on Plotinus

When we think the virtual in terms of the question of the One – as the One that is peculiar to a virtual multiplicity – we encounter all kinds of philosophical conundrums. As Hegel notes in his treatment of the One in Plotinus – and it is a Plotinian reference we need in order to determine the nature of both Bergson's and Deleuze's Platonism – the principal difficulty, 'known and recognized many years ago', is 'the comprehension of how the One came to the decision to determine itself' (Hegel 1995: 416). As Deleuze acknowledges in his 1966 reading of Bergson, we are led inevitably to the question of how the One, 'the original identity', has the power to be differentiated' (Deleuze 1991: 100).

Almost everything at stake in this thinking of the One would seem to turn on what kind or nature of power is assigned to it: is it eminent or simple? In *Bergsonism* it is neither accidental nor incidental that Deleuze should repeatedly speak of the virtual as a *simple* virtual (1991: 95, 96, 100). This is a 'simplicity' he had already outlined in his 1956 reading of Bergson as a philosopher of (internal) difference (1999: 51, 53). Gerson has argued against a straightforward creationist or emanationist reading of the Plotinian One, and his argument is worth citing since it brings to light the reasons for Deleuze's designation of the virtual as a simple power:

> . . . Aquinas must say that God is not just virtually all things but eminently all things as well. That is, every predicate that belongs to complexes belongs to their simple cause in a higher mode of being . . . By contrast, Plotinus is less concerned with preserving omnipotence than he is with preserving the unqualified simplicity of the first ἀρχή . . . by refusing to accept that virtuality in being entails eminence in being, Plotinus' negative theology constrains itself in a way that Aquinas' negative theology does not. Plotinus cannot just infer that the One is eminently whatever its effects are in an inferior way. To do so would compromise the simplicity of the One.
>
> (Gerson 1994: 32)

Now, although this indicates to us some of the reasons as to why philosophy might have a desire to appeal to the One *qua* simplicity, it does not follow that Deleuze's conception of the simplicity of the virtual is the same as Plotinus' insistence that there 'must be something simple before all things' (Enneads V, 4). The difference from Plotinus can be articulated as follows: in Plotinus the simplicity of the virtual is thought in strictly negative terms (we cannot say what it is, only what it is not) (see Bussanich 1996: 40–1); moreover, it is a power that always withholds from expressing itself in the beings that irradiate from it, which explains why Plotinus insists that this simple must be completely other to all the things that come after it and exist by itself, 'not mixed with the things which derive from it' (ibid.). In Deleuze, by contrast, the simplicity of the virtual denotes the pure positivity of being as a power of self-differentiation which, in differentiating itself, ceases to be what it is 'all the while keeping something of its origin' (Deleuze 1999: 55). In other words, the virtual both ceases to be and continues to persist.

Admittedly, this is all very paradoxical. On Deleuze's conception of differ-ence, however, the asymmetry between the virtual and the actual must be maintained in order to allow for a thinking of the *immanence* of Being, of Being as univocal. To proclaim a univocity of the actual, as Badiou does, is to render one's thinking incoherent: the univocity of Being cannot be upheld by predicating it of actual beings, since such beings are beings already constituted or individuated. The power of the simple virtual cannot be transformed into an eminent one without sacrificing immanence. As a way of warding off such a move Plotinus adopted a rigorously negative (and ecstatic) approach to the One.[1] The result is a negative theology.

The importance of Plotinus for Bergson has been noted and examined in the literature.[2] The fact that Bergson lectured regularly on Plotinus is not surprising given the central preoccupations of his thinking (time, free will, matter, creativity, etc.).[3] In his Gifford lectures of 1914 on 'Personality' Bergson goes so far as to claim that modern metaphysics (Leibniz, Spinoza) is a repetition of Plotinus but in a weaker form (Bergson, 1972: 1058; see also remarks Bergson makes on Plotinus and the modern likes of Spinoza, Kant and Schopenhauer in a lecture course of 1907 on 'Theories of the Will', 1972: 716–17). The starting point of Plotinus' philosophy, which is also its essence for Bergson, is the attempt to rediscover a unity that has become lost in time. 'The philosophy of Plotinus', he writes, 'may be taken as the very type of the Metaphysics which we are eventually led to when we look upon internal time as pulverised into separate moments, and yet believe in the reality and the unity of the Person' (1972: 1056). In other words, we are two modes of existence, a *de jure* one in which we exist outside time, and a *de facto* one in which we evolve 'in' time. Considered in *de jure* terms we are Ideas (eternal essences), 'pure contemplation', in contrast to the life of the sensible world in which praxis takes place. But if the *de facto* existence is a diminution or degradation of the eternal then to act or to desire is to have need of something and thus, consequently, to be incomplete. Evolving in time 'is to add unceasingly to what is'. However, because the one mode of existence is a distension or dilution of the other, in which an original unity has broken up into a multiplicity, our actual existence can be little more than that of a 'dispersed multiplicity' always 'indefinitely striving to produce an imitation of unity in Time' (ibid.). So where Plato construes time as a 'moving image of eternity' in terms of the figure of resemblance, Plotinus construes it in terms of an imitation. Bergson insists that if the original element is posited as unity then it is insufficient to say that in Plotinus' system there is a return to the 'multiplicity which is One'; rather the return has to go further back to 'a Unity which is unity only' (1057). This is how he reads the theory of the three hypostases in Plotinus (God, the Intelligibles, and Minds with bodies), in which the movement consists in the Mind that is in body returning to the Intelligible. So although 'matter' entails division and 'unrolling', Bergson notes, it is the movement of immateriality as *a move-*

ment of return to the immaterial which is the *telos* of this mode of thinking the One, unity and multiplicity. The immaterial is conceived as an original unity that is without number potentially *or* actually, it has no multiplicity to it whether virtual or actual.[4]

What are we trying to learn from this brief consideration of Bergson on Plotinus? It is clear that Bergson's ambitions are not (neo-) Platonist ones. Plotinus stands out among the ancients for Bergson because he considers him to be a 'profound psychologist' and what must be extracted from his system are its purely psychological elements (1058). The actual edifice of this system, however, is fragile. It remains instructive in that it brings out an important aspect of later metaphysical systems but which is only implicit, chiefly, the idea that movement is *less* than immobility and that duration is divided indefinitely. This means that to find 'substantiality' it becomes necessary to place ourselves outside time. Modern metaphysics is a repetition of this view up to and, even after, Kant, Bergson claims.[5] Bergson wishes us to know that he holds the opposite to be the case (there is no fall into time and time is not an imitation of eternity) and that, while it is important to give full weight to certain aspects of Plotinus' doctrine it also has to be *inverted* (ibid.). Badiou does not comment on Bergson's attempted inversion of Plotinus, and there is no reason why he should other than perhaps for the purposes of lending greater precision to his claim that Bergsonism ultimately amounts to a Platonism of the virtual. But as we shall see, against all the indicated signs in Bergson and Deleuze's texts he will argue that they are thinkers not of time but of eternity (the eternity of the One *qua* virtual) and that the mobile is ultimately grounded in the immobile: *for Deleuze* the being and the truth of time are 'immobile' (Badiou 2000a: 61).

Let us now turn to Deleuze on Plotinus. Important references to Plotinus can be found in *DR* (1994: 75) and *WP?* (1994: 212) (in both it is the notion of 'contemplation' that is put into effect). The most relevant treatment for our purposes is to be found in the 1968 book on Spinoza and expressionism. In this work Deleuze also speaks of Aquinas as a thinker of eminence and in the context of a discussion of how the method of analogy seeks to avoid anthropomorphism. In Aquinas the qualities that are attributed to God do not imply a community of form between divine substance and finite creatures but only an analogy, 'a "congruence" of proportion or proportionality' (1992: 46). Deleuze's contention is that Spinozism effects an inversion of the problem:

> Whenever we proceed by analogy we borrow from creatures certain characteristics in order to attribute them to God either equivocally or eminently. Thus God has Will, Understanding, Goodness, Wisdom, and so on, but has them equivocally or eminently. Analogy cannot do without equivocation or eminence, and hence contains a subtle anthropomorphism, just as dangerous as the naïve variety.
>
> (ibid.)

101

For Deleuze the significance of Spinoza's philosophy resides in its struggle against the equivocal, the eminent, and the analogical. He belongs to the 'great tradition of univocity'. This is the thesis that 'being is predicated in the same sense of everything that is, whether infinite or finite, albeit not in the same "modality"' (63). This means that although there is a difference between *natura naturans* (substance) and *natura naturata* (attributes) they are not in a relation of hierarchy in which the former enjoys a power of eminence over the latter. In his Bergsonism of 1956 and 1966 Deleuze will insist on the need to treat duration as both 'substance and subject'; indeed, duration is likened to a 'naturing nature' and matter to a 'natured nature' (1991: 93).[6] Moreover, as a power of the virtual, duration is pure immanence (that which does divide but as a division that always changes in kind). And we need to recall Bergson's own insistence that we err in our thinking of the immanence of a creative evolution when we think of a thing that creates and of things that are created (1983: 248). Moreover, Bergson insists that the divergent creations of evolution are to be treated not as 'presenting analogies' but rather as 'mutually complementary' (ibid.: 97). For Deleuze 'the essential in univocity is not that Being is said in a single and same sense, but that it is said in a single and same sense *of* all its individuating differences and intrinsic modalities' (Deleuze 1994: 36). The thesis of univocity contests the view of Parmenides that there are two paths; rather the single 'voice' of Being includes all its diverse, varied, and most differenciated modes.

The key chapter from Deleuze's 1968 book on Spinoza is chapter 11 entitled 'Immanence and the Historical Components of Expression'. We cannot examine the full details of this reading here. Instead, let us note some key points.

For Deleuze the idea of an 'expressive immanence', the idea by which the univocity of being is to be thought, can be traced back to the Platonist problem of participation (see Plotinus IV, II on the participation of each member in the 'All-Soul'). In Plato we find different schemes of participation, such as 'being a part', imitating, and even being the recipient of something from a demon. Deleuze notes that in spite of these different schemes the principle of participation is always sought on the side of what participates. In all cases the sensible is forced to reproduce the terms of the intelligible, while also 'forcing the Idea to allow itself to be participated by something foreign to its nature' (1992: 170). The attempt to invert the problem is what defines the Postplatonic task. This is done by locating the principle of participation within the perspective of the participated itself: 'Plotinus reproaches Plato for having seen participation from its lesser side' (ibid.). In Plotinus participation does not take the form of a violence, in which it supervenes as a force from the outside which is then suffered by the participated, but rather as a 'gift': 'causality by donation, but by productive donation'. It is *emanation* that is this cause and gift: 'participation occurs only through what it gives, and in what it gives' (171). This explains why in

Plotinus the One is held to be beyond or above Being, since it is above its gifts: 'it gives what does not belong to it, or is not what it gives' (ibid.).[7] The One cannot have anything in common with the things that come from it. This is a thought of emanation in which an emanative cause is not only superior to its effect but also to what gives the effect.[8] For Deleuze this 'One-above-Being' is inseparable from a negative theology *and* from a method of analogy 'that respects the eminence of principle or cause' (172).

For Deleuze it is only on the basis of the kind of movement of thought we find in Spinozism or Bergsonism that the 'emanative transcendence of the One' can be transformed into an expressive immanence of univocal Being. The univocity of Being requires the power of the virtual be a simple one. Indeed, although Plotinus thinks the virtuality of being *qua* a simplicity this power remains emanative or eminent for Deleuze (as for other commentators, such as Jaspers for example).[9] The One remains above and outside what is explicated since it does not explicate itself: 'the One above Being does of course contain all things virtually: *it is explicated* but does not *explicate itself*' (p. 177; here we could readily substitute actualization for explication). With the univocity of Being there is also entailed the equality of Being in the sense that not only is 'being equal in itself, but it is seen to be equally present in all beings' (173). Causation is no longer 'remote' or eminent but truly immanent: 'Immanence is opposed to any eminence of the cause, any negative theology, any method of analogy, any hierarchical conception of the world' (ibid.). Once the hierarchy of hypostases is substituted by an equality of being this means that participation must now be thought in a completely positive manner and not on the basis of an eminent gift (say of Being to beings, of the virtual to actuals).

In describing Deleuze as thinker of the One Badiou took many readers by surprise. But although Deleuze does indeed intend to think beyond the opposition of the one and the many this does not, as we saw in essay two, rule out the possibility of speaking of the virtual multiplicity in terms of a One that is peculiar to it. Throughout the 1966 text Deleuze will insist on the need to posit virtual multiplicity as a single time, and the co-existence of all of the degrees and levels of Being is said to be virtual and 'only virtual' (1991: 93). It is precisely because the point of unification is said to be virtual that Bergsonism is led for Deleuze to the realization that it has an affinity with 'the One-Whole of the Platonists': 'All the levels of expansion and contraction coexist in a single Time and form a totality; but this Whole, this One, are pure virtuality' (ibid.) (if such a Whole has number it is only potentially). Badiou's reading of Deleuze's alleged 'Platonism of the virtual' does not persuade, however, for a number of reasons. It does not adequately comprehend the nature of the commitment to univocity or what is at stake in thinking a simplicity of the virtual. On Badiou's reading the actual becomes a mere simulacrum of the virtual and, as such, represents little more than a degraded, and even expendable, expression of an eminent power. Badiou's reading also fails to distinguish between the different presentations of the virtual in Deleuze. At the end of the last essay I argued that there are, in fact, two presentations of the virtual whole in Bergson: a first one that is to be understood in terms of a simple virtual of the vital impetus and a second one which refers not to a point of origin or an initial impulsion but rather to the ceaseless invention of forms to be thought on the level of the open whole of evolution. This is the whole that Bergson argues science extracts from when it isolates closed systems for diagrammatic study. It is this latter conception of the virtual whole that Deleuze brings to the fore in *Cinema 1* when he speaks of a 'plane of immanence' in terms of a 'machinism' as opposed to a mechanism.

After making his point about the One never being given in its totality Badiou then uses a citation from *Cinema 1* which speaks of the whole only in terms of the second conception (the open whole in which duration is said to be immanent to the universe).[10] Badiou then argues unconvincingly that because the real of the virtual is not given in its totality this means that the real 'consists precisely in the perpetual actualizing of new virtualities' (2000a: 49). This is a very odd construction of Deleuze's thinking of the virtual. It makes little sense of Bergson's conception of creative evolution and its uptake in Deleuze's texts of 1956 and 1966 where the movement is from the virtual to 'actuals' (the pluralization is Deleuze's) and where this movement involves the self-differentiation of a simple virtual in accordance with divergent lines of actualization. Badiou has completely reified the power of the virtual.

Badiou's neglect of the first whole must surely explain how and why he is able to turn Deleuze's virtual into a power of eminence. Let me make it clear: the simple virtual refers to the virtual of the vital impetus and is given not in the sense that it is given once and for all (time as space), but rather in the sense that it is given as a limited force (it requires contact with matter in order to divide and differentiate). It is, then, given as a limited force but not given with respect to actualization and differentiation. And what makes it 'simple' is that it exists as confused, inchoate, and undetermined – the contrast is between the tendencies in one mode of being (fusion and interpenetration) and in another mode (dissociation and divergency in which the tendencies acquire a more and more specific stress and dominant articulation). Deleuze's affirmation of the non-givenness of the open whole should not be overlooked or downplayed. It is, in fact, the principal feature of his Bergsonism in both the 1966 text and *Cinema 1*. As virtual this open whole cannot assemble its actual parts that are external to each other. But the assembling or reassembling of a whole is never the issue for Deleuze simply because of the asymmetry that exists between the virtual and the actual: the actual does not come to resemble the virtual because actualization does not proceed by rules of resemblance or limitation. So, while it may indeed be odd for Deleuze to describe the virtual as an image, it is equally strange to describe the actual in terms of a projected or produced image *of* the virtual, since this is precisely how the relation between the real and the possible is to be defined, and as a way of highlighting the creative character of the lines of differentiation that characterize an actualization: 'For, in order to be actualized, the virtual cannot proceed by elimination or limitation, but *must* create its own lines of actualization in positive acts . . . For while the real is in the image and likeness of the possible that it realizes, the actual, on the other hand does *not* resemble the virtuality that it embodies' (1991: 97). In the actual, says Deleuze, there reigns an irreducible pluralism. This is a pluralism that fills him with delight (104).

Deleuze on the difference of life

In order to demonstrate in more precise terms the nature of Deleuze's dual commitment to the One and to pluralism (the One of pluralism) I want to give a fairly close and exacting reading of the 1956 and 1966 essays on Bergsonism. Before we commence the analysis of Deleuze's texts let us consider the following key citation from Bergson's *CE*:

> While, in its contact with matter, life is comparable to an impulsion or an impetus, regarded in itself it is an immensity of potentiality (*virtualité*), a mutual encroachment of thousands and thousands of tendencies which nevertheless are 'thousands and thousands' only once regarded as outside each other, that is, when spatialized. Contact with matter is what determines this dissociation. *Matter divides actually what was but virtually multiple*; and, in this sense, individuation is in part the work of matter, in part the result of life's own inclination.
> (Bergson 1983: 258; my emphasis and translation modified)

Again we encounter the dual manner in which Bergson approaches the real: life regarded in itself is a pure virtual and in terms of its contact with matter it is a virtual with divisions. I cite this passage not simply because it is only the example we have in Bergson's text of the description of life in terms of a virtual multiplicity, but rather because it signals an issue that is crucial to decide upon, even though there is a certain undecidable element to it. The problem is this: Deleuze, as we shall see, credits the virtual with the power of self-differentiation. In this passage, however, it would seem that what is crucial for Bergson is 'matter': 'matter divides actually what was but virtually multiple'. Do we have a fundamental difference here between Bergson and Deleuze's Bergsonism? Might it mean that Deleuze has, in some sense, reified the virtual by positing it in terms of an independent, albeit simple, power? To respond at all adequately to these questions we must follow the details of Deleuze's reading extremely carefully. The turns of Deleuze's thinking in both the 1956 essay and the 1966 text are remarkably nuanced and subtly unfolded.

The 1956 essay begins by stating that conceived as a philosophy of difference – the difference between differences in degree and differences in kind or nature, the difference between the virtual and the actual, the difference of Being itself *qua* self-differentiation – Bergsonism operates on two levels, a methodological one and an ontological one. The differences between things lies, ultimately, in their differences of nature, and it is the task of thinking to demonstrate this and determine these differences. It is not immediately self-evident to thinking what this difference is (the difference of nature) simply because the natural bent of the intellect is to think in terms of differences of degree (positing the differential relations between things in terms of 'more' or 'less'). The task is to show that the differences of nature are neither things nor their states but rather tendencies. This methodological problem, which can only be resolved via the method of intuition (Deleuze 1991: chapter 1), turns into an ontological one when we realize that these differences of nature suppose the difference 'of' Being itself. Consideration of differences of nature leads us to thinking about the nature of difference (1999: 42). It is clear that for Deleuze the relation between the two, between Being and beings, will not be construed as one of emanation or analogically: everything is an expression of difference but, in turn, each thing expresses its own internal difference. The difference 'of' Being resides in the differences of beings.

Deleuze conceives duration as that which '*differs from itself*'. He then goes on to treat matter as the domain of repetition (it does not differ from itself), a distinction between difference and repetition that is complicated by Bergson in texts such as *MM* and especially *CE*, and which Deleuze goes on to complicate in this essay and also in the 1966 text. Psychical life is taken as an example of the difference of nature in which there is always 'otherness' without there being 'number' or 'several'. If movement is qualitative change and vice versa – movement has to involve alteration if it is to amount to real change (see Socrates in *Theaetetus* 182c) – then this suggests that duration is a movement of self-differentiation: 'Duration, tendency is the difference of self from self; and what differs from itself is *immediately* the unity of substance and subject' (1999: 48). Duration then becomes Bergsonism's unconventional designation for the traditional notion of substance. Contra what he regards as the essential movement of Hegelianism, Deleuze insists that the difference of nature is an essential aspect of the internal logic of difference itself; it is not, therefore, external to Being – being does not have to become or 'decide' to become since it is already characterized by an internal difference as a power of self-differentiation: '*Difference of nature has itself become a nature.* Moreover, it was so from the beginning' (49). This is un-Hegelian for Deleuze simply because it means that we do not have to go to the level of contradiction and negation to account for the productive power of difference:

The originality of the Bergsonian conception is in showing that internal difference does not go and must not go to the point of contradiction, to alterity, to the negative, because these three notions are in fact less profound than it or are merely external views of this internal difference. To think internal difference as such, as pure internal difference, to reach the pure concept of difference, to raise difference to the absolute, such is the direction of Bergson's effort. . . . In Bergson and thanks to the notion of the virtual, the thing differs from itself *in the first place, immediately*. According to Hegel, the thing differs from itself in the first place from all that it is not, such that difference goes to the point of contradiction.[11]

(49, 53)

We have, no doubt, entered into the deepest waters of Deleuze's Bergsonism. These waters, however, are not necessarily murky. Let's seek to swim in them. How exactly are we to think the virtual and to conceive of this originary difference of Being? Deleuze's answer is: through a thinking of Life.

'Life is the process of difference' (1999: 50). Deleuze refers not simply to the differentiations of embryology but more to the differences of evolution, such as the production of species: 'With Darwin the problems of difference and life come to be identified in this idea of evolution, even though Darwin himself has a false conception of vital difference' (ibid.). The vital difference is not a simple determination but rather an indetermination. The difference is crucial for Deleuze since only by recognizing the unpredictable character of living forms is it possible to construe the true nature of evolution, namely that the *élan vital* is not a determination but a differentiation. And if life is not simply the result of a subsisting exteriority – the external mechanism of selection – then it is necessary to think this as a *self*-differentiation. It is here that we can now return to the citation from Bergson's *CE* concerning matter dividing actually what was potentially manifold.

Deleuze is not blind to the role of matter within a creative evolution. He is, in fact, giving a *reading* of Bergson's text which does not itself ever make explicit or clear the precise nature of this relation between the virtual multiplicity of tendencies and the actualizations of materiality. The passage from Bergson seems to suggest that it is matter that makes actual what is virtual. This seems to stand in contrast to Deleuze for whom differentiation comes about as the result of the resistance life encounters in matter but, first and foremost, 'from the internal explosive force that life carries in itself' (1999: 51, compare 1991: 94). The indetermination of evolutionary life, therefore, is a necessary and not an accidental feature of it. How do we square this emphasis on a *necessary* indetermination with Bergson's stress on the enormous role played by contingency within evolution? Strictly speaking, Bergson notes, it is possible to conceive of the evolution of life taking place either 'in one single individual by means of a series of transformations spread over thousands of ages' or in any number of individuals succeeding each other in a unilinear series. In both cases evolution would have taken place in only the one dimension (Bergson 1983: 53). But in actual terms we know that evolution has involved millions of individuals spread across divergent lines. Is such divergency entirely contingent? The list of contingencies within evolution is of quite a scale in Bergson's conception of evolution; they include the forms of life invented, the dissociation of the 'primordial tendency' into complementary tendencies that create divergent lines and relative to the obstacles that are encountered in a given place and at a given time, and also the adaptations, arrests and 'set-backs' that characterize it. Only two things are necessary for evolution to take place he suggests, (a) a gradual accumulation of energy and (b) an elastic canalization of this energy in variable and indeterminable directions. Moreover, although both of these conditions have been met on our planet in a particular way it was 'not necessary that life should fix its choice mainly upon the carbon of carbonic acid' (ibid.: 255). We can imagine life evolving in terms of a different chemical substratum. Now although the 'impulsion' would remain the same it is highly conceivable that it would split up very differently to the way it has on our planet which has specific physical conditions (257).

In the 1956 essay on Bergson and difference Deleuze writes: 'Self-differentiation is the movement of a virtuality which actualises itself' (1999: 51). In the 1966 text differentiation is said to take place as an actualization because it presupposes the unity and 'primordial totality' of a virtual that is dissociated according to lines of differentiation but which continues to show 'its subsisting unity and totality in each line' (1991: 95). For example, life becomes divided into plant and animal, the animal becomes divided into instinct and intelligence, but each side of the division 'carries the whole with it' (ibid).[12] Deleuze likens this persistence of this whole to an 'accompanying nebulosity', speaking of a 'halo' of instinct in intelligence, a 'nebula' of intelligence in instinct, and a 'hint' of the animate in plants. Now, could we not recommend eliminating these vague appeals to halos and nebulae and simply recognize that what we have here is an actual multiplicity of life which does not require a virtuality in order to account for it? As Badiou asks, is virtuality 'any better' than the finality it is designed to replace? (2000a: 53).

On the Bergsonian conception of creative evolution, however, life cannot be adequately conceived outside of the terms of an indivisible and uniquely historical continuity (one that more than allows for divergence and heterogeneity). In addition, Deleuze's point about the *élan vital* needs confronting: although evolution is littered with accidents, abortions and arrests it would be very strange to say that the impulsion of life and towards life, supposing we are committed to such a hypothesis, is itself something entirely accidental. This would indeed be to sacrifice everything to exteriority, to an external causality. As Bergson himself notes, the impulsion would remain what it is whatever the conditions of life. The problem is determining just what is and what is not contingent in this conception of creative evolution. The impulsion is not contingent and neither it seems is the dissociation; what is contingent is the particular form this dissociation takes within an actual historical evolution and the kind of divergency that takes place. Bergson speaks of a 'primordial tendency' of life dissociating itself into divergent lines which, while divergent, also have to be seen as complementary (simply because they are the dissociated products of a simple virtual whole). Moreover, if we think about the 'great scission' of life into the two major kingdoms of vegetable and animal and the way in which the two forms of life have sought to utilize and transform energy, it is possible to see, Bergson holds, that the evolution of life into these two main forms is not simply the result of 'external intervention' but rather can be seen as 'the effect of the duality of the tendency involved in the original impetus and of the resistance opposed by matter to this impetus' (1983: 254). The primordial tendency, then, has duality built into it and from this scission there has followed many others. Claims such as this do not negate the need to assign a role to contingency but rather clarify how we might more precisely configure it. The contingent character of evolution continues to be upheld in Deleuze: 'Indetermination, unpredictability, contingency, liberty always signify an independence in relation to causes: it is in this sense that Bergson credits the *élan vital* with many contingencies' (1999: 62).

If the chemico-physical conditions of a planet were different to our own, and their consistency sufficient to generate life, we do not know in any *a priori* terms what particular forms and lines of life would evolve; but what we do know, according to Bergson, is that the initial impulsion would be the same, an impulse characterized by a duality, even a multiplicity, of tendencies (of association, individuation, etc.). The problem here, which is perhaps also the problem of the virtual, is of speaking of an impulse of life in advance of any actual evolution and which supposes a separation of the vital from the physico-chemical. It is also the same problem we face when we try to conceive of tendencies, such as those of instinct and intelligence and as manifested in forms of plant and animal life, in advance of the actual emergence of particular plants and animals (see Bergson 1983: 135–6). Nevertheless, and as will become clear, this is precisely what Deleuze's philosophy of difference commits itself to: the difference of Being or of life is *at the beginning*,[13] and only a notion like the virtual, with its stress on an enfolded multiplicity of interpenetrating tendencies, can make this clear.

The problems we have with this thinking of virtual life are perhaps of our own making, the result of our peculiar intellectual habits, such as thinking the virtual, as well as the relation between the virtual and its actualization, in terms of space and not time. It is only when we engage in these habits that the virtual gets reified. As I noted in essay three, to think the virtual as a matter of time and not of space is extremely difficult. Bergson insists that 'division' is what characterizes life, it is not a mere appearance. Matter plays the crucial role in effecting this division (Bergson 1977: 114). Indeed, it is by studying the directionality of the great lines of evolution, which run alongside paths that have reached a dead end, that we are able to formulate the conjecture and hypothesis of a vital impetus that began by possessing the essential characteristics of these main lines 'in a state of reciprocal implication', such as instinct and intelligence 'which reach their culminating point at the extremities of the two principal lines of animal evolution' (115). Such tendencies are not to be abstractly combined into one but rather taken as given 'in the beginning' and as interpenetrating aspects of the 'simple reality'. The tendencies are given then not in the state of their actual evolution but in their simple virtuality. They cannot be 'given' in any other way if we are to take seriously the conception of a *creative* evolution, in which 'duration is invention or it is nothing at all' and in which hesitation and indetermination are its positive features. Of any 'original tendency' we might take and think about it is difficult to speak of its actual 'content' simply because we cannot tell in advance what will issue from it (297). Bergson insists that it is impossible to forecast the actual forms that will emerge 'by discontinuous leaps' and all along the lines of evolution (ibid.). A more unequivocal affirmation of the discontinuity entailed by actuality and materiality could not be found. Later in this book, his final text, Bergson will insist that the *materialization* of tendencies only comes about through a process of dichotomy. So although we can posit an 'undivided primitive tendency' it is equally essential that such a tendency is not reified and viewed independently of the actual divisions that have taken place: 'we will call *law of dichotomy* that law which brings about a materialization, by a mere splitting up, of tendencies which began by being two photographic views, so to speak, of one and the same tendency' (ibid.: 296). To neglect the different aspects of this 'image' of the vital impetus is, Bergson argues taking a stab at Schopenhauer, to be left with an 'empty concept', like the 'will to life', and presented with a 'barren theory of metaphysics'. We will examine the nature of this image of thought in the next essay.

The fundamental reason why Bergson is not a hylozoist is because he insists upon maintaining a distinction between matter and life conceived as different tendencies. Matter admits of relaxation, showing a 'certain elasticity', and on account of which its tendency towards inertia, geometry and determinism is never complete (Bergson 1920: 17–18). Bergson insists that there is a 'becoming of matter' (1983: 273). Duration is the most contracted degree of matter, while matter is the most expanded degree of duration (Deleuze 1991: 93). On this scheme there is no duality of homogeneous quantity and heterogeneous quality but rather a continuous movement from one to the other: 'quality is nothing other than contracted quantity' (ibid.: 74; see also p. 86). Matter is not geometrical solely as a result of our representation of it, it has this feature itself as a tendency (which explains why Bergson insists on coming up with a double genesis of matter and intellect).

In the 1956 essay Deleuze argues that the virtuality of the vital tendency of life 'exists in such a way that it realises itself in dissociating itself' and that 'it is forced to dissociate itself in order to realise itself' (1999: 51). Deleuze would seem to be arguing, therefore, that the dissociation of the vital tendency into divergent lines is not something accidental. Perhaps this point enables us to address the question of how the virtual can be said to 'differ *from itself*' (my emphasis) when it becomes actualized. The only answer that can be given is: because it is realizing itself and realizing itself in becoming something other than itself in its very persistence or endurance. As a movement of actualization evolution is an actualization of the virtual, not the brute eruption into being of either preformed or fully formed actuals. But then we need to ask: what is the character of its simplicity? This is, in effect, the same kind of issue: self-differentiation is a necessary characteristic of the simple virtual; its simplicity consists in the fact that it is operating on the level of inchoate and undetermined tendencies and although actual species of life evolve in and out of existence the tendencies they are implicated in persist and continue to be expressed in new forms of life, new kinds of animal and new kinds of plants for example.

The virtual defines 'an absolutely positive mode of existence' (1999: 55). Things differ and differ from themselves (in 'the first place' and 'immediately') on account of the positivity of this simple power. This is because it is a simplicity of tendencies that split up and diverge and that do not follow or conform to a logic of negation and supersession in which the tendencies could be said to enjoy a hierarchical development (relations of negation and supercession between plant and animal, and between animal and man, or a single line of development from the vegetal to the instinctual and the rational, for example). When one term is negated by another we have, in fact, 'only the positive realisation of a virtuality which contained both terms at once' (53). We have seen that duration is defined as that which differs from itself. Deleuze clarifies this by adding that if this is the case then 'that from which it differs is still duration'. So duration persists in its difference from itself since what differs from duration is still duration. Can the same be said of the virtual? Deleuze will describe the virtual in terms identical to the way duration was described, namely, as that which differs from itself. Differentiation is the expression of this essential difference of the virtual with respect to itself: 'What differentiates itself is *first* what differs with itself, which is to say the virtual. Differentiation is not the concept, but the production of objects which find their reason in the concept' (54).

The difficulties we encounter in trying to think the virtual can only be resolved by allying it with duration.[14] As the 'pure concept of difference' (1999: 55) the virtual entails the coexistence of all the degrees, nuances, and levels of being. The virtual can only be said to be a positive mode of existence if it is implicated in duration. If 'duration is the virtual' (55), then this means that it is capable of different expressions or articulations. The 'psychological' will be one such articulation or degree of duration. Deleuze defines the virtual as the mode of the 'non-active', which in differentiating itself also ceases to be itself, 'all the while keeping something of its origin' (55). So the virtual has a curious modality of being to it: it is both an original identity or simple totality (in its intensive state of inter-penetration) and it is also constantly dividing itself and thus becoming what it is. As the mode of *'what is'* it is the unity of being and becoming (or of substance and subject as Deleuze puts it).

In his major study of Spinoza of 1968 Deleuze's innovation was to pay careful attention to the notion of expression and to show that while there are traces of emanationist thinking in Spinoza the notion of emanation cannot help us to understand the theory of expression (it is on this point that Deleuze breaks with Hegel's reading of Spinoza's substance as a version of oriental emanation). It is the move to immanence that proves decisive for Deleuze. Expression is marked by two terms that are not to be construed as opposites: these are explication and implication. Expression is an explication in the sense that it is an unfolding of the One expressing itself in the Many (substance in attributes and attributes in modes). Because the One remains involved in what expresses it and immanent in whatever manifests it, we can also speak of an involution at the same time as we speak of an evolution (Deleuze 1992: 16). A crucial point concerning the theory of expression is that the One does not denote a number. For Deleuze a numerical distinction is never a real distinction and a real distinction is never numerical. Spinoza's substance cannot be identified, therefore, with either the number one or with infinity. A radical reading of Spinoza would be one that took its inspiration from Bergsonism, and this is what Deleuze in effect does in his major study. As Michael Hardt has noted of Deleuze: 'He presents the proofs of the existence of God and the singularity of substance as an extended meditation on the positive nature of difference and the real foundation of being' (Hardt 1993: 60). In both Bergson and Spinoza the stress is placed on a philosophy of difference in which primacy is accorded to internal causality and an immanent production of being. Number cannot have the nature of this substance simply because it involves a limitation and is dependent on an external cause. It is Deleuze's Bergsonism and his preoccupation with the two multiplicities that informs his entire reading of Spinoza and advocacy of Spinozism as a theory of expression and not emanation.

It is imperative that the difference between treating the virtual as a simple power and an eminent one be appreciated. If Deleuze's virtual is treated eminently then the distinction that he insists upon between the two quite different processes of the 'possible and the real', in which an actual existence is added to something that already existed in a nascent form, and the 'virtual and the actual', in which there is genuine invention and production, is lost and a thinking of creative evolution becomes indistinguishable from preformism.

Conclusion

'To do philosophy', Deleuze writes, '*is precisely to start with difference*' (1999: 62). This is a truly radical philosophy of difference simply because difference is said to be there 'from the beginning' as the very difference of Being. Moreover, in its most primordial reality this difference entails the differences of beings. These latter differences are internal ones because they are implicated in the simple and positive virtual which remains in them while, at the same time, they themselves are the givers of their own unique differences.

It is clear that Deleuze, in addition to transforming Bergson's project into a radical philosophy of difference, has ontologized the conception of creative evolution. This is evident in the way he establishes a 'rigorous' link between *MM* and *CE* (1991: 100). Moreover, it is the case for him that while the lines of differentiation are 'truly creative' the forms of physical, vital, and psychical life they create amount to embodiments of different *ontological* levels of the virtual. Matter and duration are the two extreme levels of relaxation and contraction. This introduces us to the idea of life being construed in terms of a cone of virtual memory. 'The Bergsonian schema which unites *CE* and *MM*', Deleuze writes in *DR*,

> begins with the account of a gigantic memory, a multiplicity formed by the virtual coexistence of all the sections of the 'cone', each section being the repetition of all the others and being distinguished from them only by the order of the relations and the distribution of singular points.
>
> (1994: 212)

If the virtual has its own peculiar reality, one that can be 'extended to the whole universe', this is because it has one that consists in all the degrees of expansion and contraction that never cease to coexist. What is different and has to remain different are the differences of level (singular points of contraction, etc.). The levels and degrees of being

> belong to a single Time; they coexist in a Unity; they are enclosed in a Simplicity; they form the potential parts of a Whole that is itself virtual. They are *the reality of this virtual*. This was the sense of the theory of virtual multiplicities that inspired Bergsonism from the start.
>
> (ibid.)

We have to approach the real and its articulations on two main levels at one and the same time. From the perspective of the lines of differentiation that diverge there is no longer any coexisting whole but merely lines of successive and simultaneous actualization. However, each one of these lines can be said to correspond to one of the degrees that coexist in the virtual totality. Obviously, it is only on the level of the virtual that the coexistence of levels and degrees can be posited. Each line retains something of the whole 'from a certain perspective, from a certain point of view' (Deleuze 1991: 101). The role of creativity in all of this should not be neglected: the lines of differentiation do *not* simply trace the levels or degrees of the virtual, 'reproducing them by simple resemblance' (ibid.).

While we can concur with Badiou that the virtual is the principal name of Being in Deleuze's thinking we also wish to stress the importance of thinking this virtual in neither emanationist nor eminentist terms. Badiou, it seems to me, is guilty of doing just this. He is right to point out that the nominal pair of virtual and actual 'exhausts the deployment of univocal Being' (2000a: 43). Two names are required only in order to 'test that the ontological univocity designated by the pair proceeds from a single one of these names'. In other words, on his reading the actual is reduced to being nothing more than the 'function of its virtuality' (ibid.). Badiou has successfully drawn our attention to the importance of a renewed thinking of the One in Deleuze; what he neglects, however, is the unequivocal commitment to pluralism. It is not that Badiou simply downplays this commitment to pluralism in Deleuze; it is rather that he fails to comprehend it and fails precisely because of the way in which he has configured the virtual in Deleuze's thinking and trans- formed it into a power of eminence (pluralism can only be incoherently established on the basis of a univocity of the actual). We agree with Badiou: Deleuze *is* a thinker of the One. But he is also a pluralist and an immanently qualified one. There are good reasons for positively hesitating in describing Deleuze as a Platonist of the virtual.

5

THE *ÉLAN VITAL* AS AN IMAGE OF THOUGHT

Bergson and Kant on finality

> Philosophy, as we define it, has not yet become completely conscious of itself. Physics understands its role when it pushes matter in the direction of spatiality; but has metaphysics understood its role when it has simply trodden in the steps of physics, in the chimerical hope of going further in the same direction? Should not its own task be, on the contrary, to remount the incline that physics descends, to bring back matter to its origins, and to build up progressively a cosmology which would be, so to speak, a reversed psychology?
>
> (Bergson 1983: 208)

> One can foresee that the more the sciences of life develop, the more they will feel the necessity for reintegrating thought into the heart of nature.
>
> (Bergson 1965: 238)

As a way of exploring the status of the *élan vital* in some of its hypothetical aspects I want to situate Bergson's thinking in the context of Kant's critique of teleological judgement, with its determination of finality in terms of a peculiar kind of judgement, the reflective judgement, and its stress on the regulative character of knowledge that might proceed on the basis of this kind of judgement. In this essay I want to show how Bergson has an affinity with Kant but also how his position is in key respects not a Kantian one.

Introduction

In a letter to Christian Garve of September 1798 Kant discloses that the origins of his critique lay in his consideration of the antinomies of pure reason, antinomies that arise when reason oversteps the bounds of sense and understanding and freely speculates on issues it is not equipped to adequately deal with and that generate so many contradictions, such as: 'The world has a beginning in time; the world does not have a beginning in time', or 'Man has complete freedom' pitted against the opposite and rival claim that 'There is no freedom since everything operates in accordance with natural necessity'. Bergson holds that Kant's philosophy 'lives and dies' by these antinomies.[1] His claim is that it is possible to think outside of their terms but to do this requires opening up the possibilities of thinking. Once we are able to think in terms of duration the antinomies dissolve, Bergson maintains, since they only ensnare the mind when it thinks time in terms of space.[2] The thesis and antithesis of an antinomy suppose the 'perfect coincidence of matter with geometrical space', and they vanish once 'we cease to extend to matter what is true only of pure space', that is, when we think matter in terms other than parts that are absolutely external to one another (Bergson 1983: 205).

Bergson goes much further than this in refusing to accept the terms under which the Critique has been laid down and put forward. He does not accept the thesis that knowledge is relative to our faculties of knowing and he does not accept that metaphysics is impossible on the grounds that there can be no knowledge outside of science or that science has correctly determined the bounds of metaphysics. In short, Bergson does not accept Kant's delimitation of metaphysics, bounded as it is by the privileging of Newtonian mechanism. A new relation between philosophy and science is called for and knowledge of the absolute is to be restored (Bergson 1965: 65). Bergson speaks of his new method of thinking as follows:

> This method claims to escape from the objections which Kant had formulated against metaphysics in general, and its principal object is to remove (*de lever*) the opposition established by Kant between metaphysics and science, by taking account of the new conditions in which science works. If you read the *Critique of Pure Reason* you see that Kant has criticized not reason in general, but a reason fashioned to the habits and exigencies of the Cartesian mechanism or the Newtonian physic . . . The doctrine that I defend aims to rebuild the bridge (broken down since Kant) between metaphysics and science . . .
>
> (Bergson 1972: 493–4)[3]

Bergson makes two major claims contra Kant: the first is that the mind cannot be restricted to the intellect since it 'overflows' it; and second, that duration has to be granted an 'absolute existence', which requires thinking time on a different plane to space. According to Bergson, Kant considered only three possibilities for a theory of knowledge: (i) the mind is determined by external things; (ii) things are determined by the mind itself; (iii) between the mind and things we have to suppose a mysterious agreement or pre-established harmony. In contrast to these three options Bergson seeks to demonstrate the need for a double genesis of matter and the intellect. It is not that matter has determined the form of the intellect or that the intellect simply imposes its own form upon matter, or even that there is some curious harmony between the two we can never explain, but rather that the two have, in the course of evolution, 'progressively adapted themselves one to the other' and so attained a 'common form' (Bergson 1983: 206). At the centre of Bergson's *Creative Evolution* is a generative account of the intellect as that aspect of the mind which is always turned towards inert matter. This explains why the elaboration of a philosophy of life comes to assume such a central role in Bergson's thinking on issues of knowledge. He insists that it 'is not enough to determine, by careful analysis, the categories of thought; we must engender them' (207). A 'theory of knowledge' and a 'theory of life' are to be viewed as inseparable since if our critique of knowledge is not accompanied by a thinking of life we will blindly accept the concepts – of matter, of life, of time, etc. – that the understanding has placed at our disposal. We will not generate a thinking of life but simply enclose the facts within a set of pre-existing frames. Thus, in order to think beyond the human condition it is necessary to provide a generative account of that condition. Once the understanding is situated within the evolutionary conditions of life it is possible to show how the frames of knowledge have been constructed and how they can be enlarged and gone beyond.

Bergson accepts Kant's demonstration that time and space, understood as homogeneous media and situated on the plane of action, cannot be viewed as properties of things themselves, since this leads to the 'insurmountable difficulties of metaphysical dogmatism'. However, instead of resting content with this critique of the dogmatic tendency of metaphysics, and uncritically privileging Newtonian mechanism, the effort should be made to recover the mind's contact with the real. This requires providing a generative account of the understanding (the abstract intellect), which would serve to show that homogeneous space and time are neither properties of things *nor* essential conditions of our faculty of knowing these things; rather their homogeneous character expresses 'the double work of solidification and division which we effect on the moving continuity of the real in order to obtain there a fulcrum for our action, in order to fix within it starting points for our operation, in short, to introduce into it real changes' (Bergson 1991: 211). In other words, Kant's conception of space and time as forms of sensibility is shown to have an 'interest', one that is 'vital' and not merely 'speculative'.[4] Instead of ending up with a split between appearance and reality, or between phenomenon and noumenon, we approach epistemological issues in terms of the relation between parts (our partial perspective on the real in accordance with our vital needs of adaptation) and a mobile whole (the moving continuity of the real). The sensible intuition of a homogenous time and space presupposes for Bergson a 'real duration' and a 'real extensity': the former are stretched out beneath the latter in order that the moving continuity can be divided and a becoming can be fixed. There arises at this point the need for another way of thinking, another kind of intuition.

Kant himself entertains the possibility of such an intuition but denies that we, as human beings, can have access to it. The first part of the *Critique of Pure Reason*, the transcendental aesthetic, draws to a close with a series of general observations. The most relevant one for our purposes is the claim Kant makes that, given our finitude, our mode of intuition can only be of a derivative kind and not an original one. By this he means that we have no access to an *intellectual* intuition. Kant allows for the fact that the way the human being intuits time and space may not be peculiar to it alone but may be something to be found among all finite beings that have a capacity of self-representation. But what he will not allow for is the possibility that we could overstep the bounds of our finitude and attain a higher intuition such as an intellectual one. This can only belong to the 'primordial being' (B 72). This issue is returned to repeatedly in Kant's text (for example, B 307–9, A 286–7/B 343), and it receives an important determination in the appendix that comes at the end of the transcendental analytic. This is in the context of a treatment of matter which, Kant says, we can know only in terms of its outer relations: the inward nature of matter, that is matter as it would be conceived by the pure understanding independently of sensuous intuition, is a 'phantom'. The most we can do is to posit a 'transcendental object' (*Objekt*) which may be the ground of the appearance we call matter, but this is an object without quantity or substance, it is 'a mere something of which we should not understand what it is, even if someone were in a position to tell us' (A 277/B 333). To be able to intuit things without the aid of our senses would mean that we could have knowledge 'altogether different from the human, and this not only in degree but as regards intuition likewise in kind' (A 278/ B 334). But of such non-human beings we do not know them to be possible or how they would be constituted. Kant does not deny that through observation and analysis it is possible that we can penetrate into 'nature's recesses', but he insists that this is nature conceived only in the aspect or dimension of its *appearance*: 'with all this knowledge, and even if the whole of nature were revealed to us, we should still never be able to answer those transcendental questions which go beyond nature', that is, beyond nature *qua* appearance (ibid.).

Perhaps it is strange that Kant should in this passage speak of the recesses of nature if all we can ever develop knowledge of is of nature as appearance (this whole issue is bound up with his preference for laying out the field of experience and knowledge in terms of the image of a sphere and not a plane, A 762/B 790). Ultimately, Kant is led to positing a *problematic* noumenon, which is not the concept of any determinate object but rather bound up with the limitation of human sensibility. This provides a 'place' for speculation with regard to there being objects outside of our specific field of intuition, objects 'other and different' to what we are able to intuit through our particular *a priori* intuitions of time and space, but of their existence nothing can either be denied or asserted (A 288/B 344).[5]

The possibility of a supra-sensuous intuition is treated again by Kant in the critique of teleological judgement, which I shall inquire into in the next section. Its importance for an appreciation of Bergson needs to be noted. It is perhaps readily apparent from the presentation so far not only that Bergson will contest the restriction of intuition to a sensuous mode – as we shall see his position is actually developed in a more nuanced fashion than this – but that given the centrality of intuition to this thinking of duration it is imperative that he wrestles with Kant in order to demonstrate precisely how it is possible to think 'beyond the human condition'. Now, this does not mean turning ourselves into God or the primordial being, but it does entail beginning at a different place and showing that neither experience nor thinking are limited to or by subjective conditions. If Bergson were to accept the territory on which Kant has established his Critique, then the ambition of thinking beyond the human condition, and bringing our duration into communication with durations that are 'inferior' and 'superior' to it, would be a vain and hopeless one.

As Lindsay noted in his fine early study, in addressing the question of time in relation to the question of life Bergson is devoting special attention to a problem that Kant raised but did not adequately resolve. In his first Critique Kant set out to show that metaphysics could not fulfil the conditions of the mathematical sciences and was thus discredited as a form of knowledge. However, he also acknowledged the existence of inquiries which cannot be given an *a priori* treatment, and in the third Critique he is concerned not with the constitutive principles of *a priori* forms of knowledge but with the postulates of empirical inquiry. This accounts for his preoccupation with the teleological estimation of nature that goes beyond the limitations of the mathematical and mechanical sciences. There is thus opened up in the third Critique the possibility of an empirical move but one that is not pursued by Kant beyond the limits he has established in the first Critique (mechanism is still accorded an uncritical primacy). In the transcendental deduction and schematism of the first Critique Kant is not concerned with the soundness of mathematical reasoning but rather with the validity of its application to reality as presented in perception. Kant's philosophy in the first Critique is essentially a philosophy of *form*. In his treatment of an intensive magnitude, for example, he makes it clear that the actual *quality* of sensation is always something empirical; thus, what we 'anticipate' in our perceptions, once we have grounded them in terms of transcendental conditions of possible experience, is simply that sensations will have magnitude (degrees of intensity): 'Consequently, though all sensations as such are given *a posteriori*, their property of possessing a degree can be known *a priori*' (*CPR*: A 176/B 218). All that we know *a priori* with regard to experience in terms of its magnitudinal aspect is that it has only the single quality of continuity and that of the quality of any given magnitude (heat, colour, etc.) we can know in *a priori* terms only its intensive *quantity* (that the colour or the heat will have a certain degree with respect to the continuity of many possible intermediate sensations).

Similarly, in the case of change it is impossible to have *a priori* knowledge of how one state in a given moment is followed by another in a subsequent moment, since this requires knowledge of 'actual forces' which can only be given empirically says Kant (the successive appearance of moving forces). What we do know *a priori*, apart from all question of the content of any actual alteration, is 'the form of every alteration', in which 'the succession of the states themselves (the happening), can still be considered *a priori* according to the law of causality and the conditions of time' (*CPR*: A 207/B 252). Kant thus posits a 'law of the continuity of all alteration', whose 'ground' is that 'neither time nor appearance in time consists of parts that are the smallest, and that, nevertheless, the state of a thing passes in its alteration through all these parts, as elements, to its second state' (A 209/ B 254). There cannot be a smallest time simply because the differences of time are on the order of differences of degree (magnitude). Kant argues that between any two instants there must be a time and that between any two instants there is a difference which has magnitude. Transition from one state to another takes place, therefore, 'in a time which is contained between two instants'. There is, then, a 'whole time' in which alteration takes place but the alteration 'does not consist of these moments, but is generated by them as their effect' (ibid.). While such a presentation may be perfectly legitimate with respect to a transcendental account of the formal structures of experience it cannot dogmatically inform a philosophy of nature and life. Kant cannot pursue the route taken by Bergson simply because he holds that 'every increase in empirical knowledge, and every advance of perception', amounts only to an extension of the determination of phenomenological time (the time of inner sense). Time can only be thought, therefore, in terms of the differences of degree (a degree zero scale) that constitutes a magnitude. With time 'we are merely anticipating our own apprehension' (A 210/B 256).

The problem Bergson has with Kant's presentation of time is that it introduces into the domains of experience and of knowledge a mathematical time. Mathematics involves the synthesis of the homogeneous, in which the synthesis is one of discrete elements (the work of the understanding). It is this principle of synthesis that is at work in the presentation of time in the schematism. Here time is treated by Kant as a homogeneous order: *the relations between the parts of time could not be anticipated unless this homogeneity was supposed.* As Lindsay notes, 'the principles involved in such a homogeneous order can be applied to reality in so far as real things appear in time' (Lindsay 1911: 14). Kant encounters a problem when he comes to treat causation simply because causation is a synthesis of the heterogeneous and so cannot be anticipated. How does he respond to this problem? By proposing that there can be an *a priori* principle of causation to the extent that things can be regarded as points within a time series:

> Causation is the relation, in a continuous change, between one point taken by us and another point also taken by us. We have made the discretion, and hence the synthesis is of a series the points of which are of our distinguishing.
>
> (15)

Kant makes it clear that the mathematical sciences are valid of phenomena only. An *a priori* law of causation can be deduced because causation is a time relation with respect to the formal determinations and anticipations of our experience of the real. However, *particular laws* of causation cannot be derived from the general nature of time but only from a study of real events that take place in time. This explains why in the third Critique we cannot remain on the phenomenological level of the 'anticipations of perception'. The notion of teleology is required in order to guide the empirical investigation into the individuality and distinct nature of different things. Although it is a notion with no relation to the *a priori* principles of the understanding, it becomes important when the concern is with a 'superior' empiricism in which we go beyond a synthesis of points within the field of appearance and attempt to discover the 'real articulation and individuality of things' (16).

Let us now examine Kant's position, and how Bergson responds to its inadequacy, in more detail. We need to appreciate that Bergson's conception of metaphysics is not the same as Kant's since it does not suppose that there is a completed task of knowledge but one which is necessarily incomplete and open.

Kant: the problem of teleology

For Kant teleology belongs to reflective judgement, which is to say, the concept we have of a thing as intrinsically a natural end or purpose (*Naturzweck*) cannot be a constitutive conception of either the understanding or of reason; rather, its conception is purely *regulative* in the sense that it aids the investigation of objects in terms of an analogy with 'our own causality according to ends generally', so providing 'a basis of reflection upon their supreme source' (Kant 1952: section 65, 24). It is organisms as beings of nature that can be conceived as ends in this way, and in this respect they supply natural science with the basis for a teleology. To judge objects, such as organisms, in this manner is to introduce into science a special principle of estimation that in any other terms is absolutely unjustifiable. What is this special principle? It is that which defines an organism in a specific way, namely, as *'an organized product of nature . . . in which every part is reciprocally both end and means*. In such a product nothing is in vain, without an end or purpose (*zwecklos*), or to be ascribed to a blind mechanism of nature' (section 66: 24–5). Kant concedes that although the occasion for adhering to such a principle has to have some basis in experience and observation, it must have some underlying *a priori* character owing to the fact that it has a universality and necessity. But then he insists, once again, that this principle is solely regulative in application in which the 'ends' in question may only reside 'in the idea of the person forming the estimate and not in any efficient cause whatever'. Such a principle thus provides a *'maxim* for estimating the intrinsic finality (or purposiveness) (*Zweckmässigkeit*) of organisms', although such intrinsic finality does not say anything actual about real bodies or organisms but only refers to how we are trying to conceive them (25). In other words, the finality we ascribe to nature is one that is *relative* to our comprehension ('man's power of judgement being what it is', Introduction, 3). The judgement we make of a purposive organism, or of a purposive nature, is an *analogical* judgement, and in this specific sense: when we bring a teleological estimate to bear on the investigation of nature and its products, and as a way of aiding scientific observation and research, we do so by analogy to a certain kind of causality that we identify with our own noumenal self, namely, a self-determining one, that is, one that sets ends or purposes (*Zwecken*) for itself. Kant insists that this is an estimate of the reflective and not the determinant judgement since no pretence is being made to *explain* anything on a constitutive or empirical level.

It is important to grasp precisely the concept of the organism Kant says we are entitled to deploy in terms of the reflective judgement. An organism is a being that can be thought not simply in terms of efficient causes (in which the series of causes and effects is invariably progressive), but rather in terms of a final cause (in which we have a series that involves regressive as well as progressive dependency). Kant then stipulates that the first requisite condition of a physical end is that the parts are 'only possible by their relation to the whole'. This is because the thing is itself an end, it is its own end. So far, however, there has been merely a determination of a thing as a work of art, in the sense that it is being considered as the product of an intelligent cause that is distinct from matter. In order to conceive a thing as a product of nature it is necessary to add a second condition, which is that 'the parts of the thing combine of themselves into the unity of a whole by being reciprocally cause and effect of their form' (section 65: 21). However, in order to think a natural product as more than 'an instrument of art' it is necessary not only to conceive of every part as owing its existence to the agency of all the other parts, and of existing for the sake of these parts and of the whole, but also to think the part as a productive 'organ', that is, as *'producing* the other parts – each, consequently, reciprocally producing the others'. In short, the product has to be not only an organized being, but, more decisively, one capable of *self-organization* (22). The difference, as is well known, is between a mere machine that enjoys only 'motive force' (*bewegende Kraft*) (a watch is the example given by Kant) and an organism that, by contrast, enjoys a 'self-propagating, formative force' (*sich fortpflan-zende bildende Kraft*). This latter is a power or force (*Kraft*) that cannot be explained in terms of mechanism.

The introduction into science of a new causality – that of beings acting 'technically' as opposed to obeying a mere blind mechanism – is one that we borrow from ourselves and apply to other beings but not in any constitutive sense, in which it would assume the form of a determinate judgement. The deployment of regulative principles is 'immanent' for Kant in the sense that they are 'adapted to the human point of view' (section 76: 58). Indeed, were it not for the fact of our kind of understanding 'we should find no distinc-tion between the mechanism and the technic of nature' (59). It is owing to the nature of our understanding, which moves from the universal to the particular, that the problem of finality assumes the form it does for us. On the one hand the particular by its nature contains something contingent in respect of a universal. On the other hand, reason demands a unity in the synthesis of the particular laws of nature and hence conformity to law. It is this conformity to law on the part of the contingent that is termed finality. For Kant this necessarily means that the conception we come up with of a finality of nature in its products can only be a subjective principle of reason and only a necessary conception of the 'human power of judgement' (60). More specifically, what determines this kind of conception of a technic of nature is the fact that objects of experience have to assume for us the form of *possible*, and not actual, objects (the transcendental argument). It is quite conceivable, Kant concedes, to imagine an understanding that is quite different from the human. Such a non-human intuition, conceived, as an 'intuitive understanding' and as a *'complete spontaneity of intuition'*, would be one 'distinct from sensibility and wholly independent of it. Hence it would be an understanding in the widest sense of the term' (62). For an intuitive understanding all objects would be actual. The fact that such an intuition is denied us means that the harmonization of nature with our faculty of conceptions can only assume the form of a 'contingent accord'. Kant fully realizes that in moving from the analytic universal to the particular, that is, from conceptions to given empirical intuitions, nothing is determined or known with respect to the multiplicity of the particular. We thereby reach the crucial hesitation of the critique of teleological judgement: on the one hand, we have the dissatisfaction in natural science with an explanation of the products of nature in terms of a causality of ends (a dissatisfaction that arises from realizing that such an estimation is being made to adapt to our critical faculty of reflective judgement rather than to the things themselves), and, on the other hand, we have the recognition that while not every technic of nature can be subject to a teleological judgement (a formative capacity of nature that displays a finality of structure), it would be equally unscientific not to allow for a teleological principle in the investigation of nature. In short, it is necessary to estimate nature in accordance with two kinds of principles. It is clear, however, that Kant accords priority to the principles of mechanism and argues that a maxim of finality should only be deployed when the 'proper occasion' presents itself (section 70: 38; section 82: 91). Strangely though, it seems as if both determinations of nature, that of mechanism and that of teleology, reflect the subjective conditions of the human point of view. It is both that Bergson argues we must go beyond: 'We must get beyond both points of view, both mechanism and finalism being, at bottom, only standpoints to which the human mind has been led by considering the work of man' (Bergson 1983: 89).

Bergson's response

Kant, as we have seen, allows for the possibility of a non-human intuition but denies that we, given our transcendental constitution, can have access to it. Bergson responds by insisting upon the need to provide a genesis of the intellect. According to Bergson, the abstract intellect, which has evolved as an organ of utility and calculability, proceeds by beginning with the immobile and simply reconstructs movement with juxtaposed immobilities. By contrast, intuition, as he conceives it, starts from movement and sees in immobility only a snapshot taken by our mind (Bergson 1965: 34–5). He argues that in order to reach this intuition it is not necessary, as Kant supposed, to transport ourselves outside the domain of the senses:

> After having proved by decisive arguments that no dialectical effort will ever introduce us into the beyond and that an effective metaphysics would necessarily be an intuitive metaphysics, he added that we lack this intuition and that this metaphysics is impossible. It would in fact be so *if there were no other time or change* than those which Kant perceived . . .
>
> (Bergson 1965: 128; my emphasis)

So while Kant acknowledges the 'peculiar' character of '*our* (human) understanding relative to our power of judgement in reflecting on things in nature', and concedes that this peculiarity implies the idea 'of a possible understanding different from the human' (he mentions a similar implication in the first Critique regarding its allowing for 'another possible form of intuition', Kant 1952: section 77: 61), it is this route intimated at but blocked off by Kant that is pursued by Bergson. By recovering intuition Bergson hopes to save science from the charge of producing a relativity of knowledge (it is rather to be regarded as 'approximative') and metaphysics from the charge of indulging in empty and idle speculation.

Bergson conceives intuition as a form of mental attentiveness, it is a special kind of 'attention that the mind gives to itself, over and above, while it is fixed upon matter, its object' (Bergson 1965: 79). It is an attention that can be 'methodically cultivated and developed', forming the basis of a new science of the mind and a veritable metaphysics. Metaphysics will no longer be the activity of a pure intelligence, an intelligence that defined the mind by a set of negations. It is a gross error, Bergson argues, to confuse his method of intuition with instinct or feeling (1965: 88).[6] Furthermore, he insists on the ontologically neutral character of the new philosophical praxis he is advocating: the principles of its new understanding do not provide the basis for any maxims of conduct, and a metaphysics of continuity and hetero-geneity is not an ethics: 'One might just as well imagine that the bacteri-ologist recommends microbic diseases to us when he shows us microbes everywhere', he jests referring to his metaphysics of change and how people might read this as legitimizing all kinds of things on a social and cultural level.[7]

This metaphysics will operate via 'differentiations and qualitative intergra-tions', and in an effort to reverse the normal directions of the workings of thought it will have a rapport with modern mathematics, notably the infinitesimal calculus:

> Modern mathematics is precisely an effort to substitute for the *ready-made* what is in process of *becoming*, to follow the growth of magnitudes, to seize movement no longer from outside and in its manifest result, but from within and in its tendency towards change, in short, to adopt the mobile continuity of the pattern of things.[8]
>
> (1965: 190)

Metaphysics differs from modern mathematics (the science of magnitudes), however, in that it has no need to make the move from intuition to symbol. Its understanding of the real is potentially boundless because of this: 'Exempt from the obligation of arriving at results useful from a practical standpoint, it will indefinitely enlarge the domain of its investigations' (191). Metaphysics can adopt the 'generative idea' of mathematics and seek to extend it to all qualities, 'to reality in general' (ibid.). The aim is not to effect another Platonism of the real, as in Kant's system, he contends, but rather to enable thought to reestablish contact with continuity and mobility.[9] A form of knowledge can be said to be relative when, through an act of forgetting, it ignores the basis of symbolic knowledge in intuition, and is forced to rely on pre-existing concepts and to proceed from the fixed to the mobile. Absolute knowledge by contrast refuses to accept what is pre-formed and instead cultivates 'fluid concepts', seeking to place itself in a mobile reality from the start and so adopting 'the life itself of things' (1965: 192) and to follow 'the real in all its sinuosities' (1983: 363).[10] To achieve this requires relinquishing the method of construction that leads only to higher and higher generalities and thinking in terms of a concrete duration 'in which a radical recasting of the whole is always going on' (ibid.).

Bergson seeks to overcome Kant not by simply nullifying the effects of his critical philosophy but rather by retrieving its buried or concealed potentialities. Although Kant himself did not pursue thought in the direction he had opened for it – the direction of a 'revivified Cartesianism' Bergson calls it – it is the prospect of an 'extra-intellectual matter of knowledge by a higher effort of intuition' that Bergson seeks to cultivate from his engagement with Kant (1983: 358). Kant has reawakened, if only half-heartedly, a view that was the essential element of Descartes' thinking but which was abandoned by the Cartesians: knowledge is not completely resolvable into the terms of intelligence.

Bergson does not, let it be noted, establish a relation of opposition between sensuous (infra-intellectual) intuition and intellectual (what he calls an 'ultra-intellectual') intuition but seeks to show that there is a continuity and reciprocity between the two. Moreover, sensuous intuition can be promoted to a different set of operations, no longer simply being the phantom of an unattainable and unscrutable thing-in-itself:

> The barriers between the matter of sensible knowledge and its form are lowered, as also between the 'pure forms' of sensibility and the categories of the understanding. The matter and form of intellectual knowledge (restricted to its own object) are seen to be engendering each other by a reciprocal adaptation, intellect modeling itself on corporeity, and corporeity on intellect. But this duality of intuition Kant neither would nor could admit.[11]
>
> (1983: 361)

Bergson's main contention is that Kant could not admit this duality of intuition because for him to do so would have meant granting to duration an absolute reality and treating the geometry immanent in space as an ideal limit (the direction in which material things develop but never actually attain).

In his text *Bergsonism* Deleuze argued that intuition could be approached as a method of division that bore a resemblance to transcendental analysis. Conceived as a method intuition enables us to dissolve false problems and to go beyond badly stated questions. A false problem is one whose terms contain a confusion of the more and the less, as in the example of disorder treated in essay three of this volume, in which Bergson shows that there is more and not less in the idea of nonbeing than that of being, in disorder than in order, and in the possible than in the real. The notion of disorder, for example, contains the idea of order plus its negation. A false problem partakes of a fundamental illusion, a 'retrograde movement of the true', in which being and order are held to precede themselves and to come before the creative act that constitutes them. A badly stated question or problem involves cases of badly analysed composites which group together in an arbitrary fashion things that differ in kind (such as duration and extensity, or perception and recollection, or the quality of a sensation confused with the muscular space that is allied with it). The question 'by how much does a sensation grow?' can only take us back to a badly stated problem. There is an intimate link between the two cases in as much as the first rests on the second, that is, we are only able to think in terms of more or less because we have already disregarded the differences in kind between things. So, for example, the idea of disorder arises from a general idea of order as a badly analysed composite. Deleuze maintains in *Bergsonism* that this inability to perceive or intuit differences in kind is an error common to science and metaphysics (Deleuze 1991: 20). Moreover, the 'obsession with the *pure* in Bergson goes back to this restoration of differences in kind' (22). The way out of this neglect of such differences is to divide a composite in accordance with qualitative and qualified *tendencies*; for example, the way in which a composite combines duration and extensity defined as movements and directions of movements (the contractions of duration and the expansions of matter). Such tendencies can be said to exist *en droit* (by right or in principle); and while there is a resemblance to transcendental analysis in this approach, insofar as it enables us to go beyond experience towards its conditions, these are not the conditions of all *possible* experience but those of real experience (in both its virtual and actual aspects). This is to engage in a transcendental empiricism which approaches experience neither in terms of the general nor the abstract. It enables us to go beyond our experience as given, and what we take this experience to narrowly be, and opens thinking up to a pure perception on the one hand and a pure memory on the other. When Bergson compares the approach of philosophy to the procedure of infinitesimal calculus it is in the sense that it shows us a line of articulation that can be extended beyond experience in the same way that the mathematician reconstitutes with the infinitely small elements that s/he perceives of the real curve, 'the curve itself' as it stretches out into the darkness behind' him or her (27).

Bergson argues that science operates with an 'unconscious metaphysics', while Kantianism rests on an uncritical acceptance of the diagrams for modelling reality that are specific to the tasks of science. In short, neither are able to produce a genesis of the intellect that would account for the relativity of our knowledge. Bergson cognizes the specific achievement of Kant's transcendental aesthetic: extension cannot be regarded as a material attribute of the same kind as others simply because while we cannot determine the modalities of heat, colour and weight without recourse to actual experiences of these things, it is quite different with the notion of space. Even if it is given empirically by sight and touch, this does not rule out the ability of the mind to cut out in it *a priori* figures and whose properties we also determine *a priori*. It is this transcendental ideality of space that infuses the whole of Kant's enterprise, including the antinomies. But this means not simply that intelligence bathes in an atmosphere of spatiality but that this atmosphere closes down the possibilities of knowledge. If our perceptions are 'impregnated by our geometry' we should not be surprised when thinking finds in matter the mathematical properties which the faculty of perception has already deposed there. Matter yields itself to the docility of our reasonings. Because any other knowledge of matter and the real has been denied, such as that offered by the intuition of mobility, we should also not be surprised if the result is a set of antinomies in which one affirmation immediately gives rise to a contrary affirmation equally plausible and equally demonstrable.

Kant's peremptory refutation of empiricist theories of knowledge is, Bergson argues, definitive in what it denies. However, does it give us a solution to the problem in what it affirms (such as the transcendental ideality of space and time)? It is worth citing him at length in response to this question:

> With Kant, space is given as a ready-made form of our perceptive faculty – a veritable *deus ex machina*, of which we see neither how it arises, nor why it is what it is rather than anything else. 'Things-in-themselves' are also given of which he claims that we can know nothing: by what right, then, can he affirm their existence, even as 'problematic'? If the unknowable reality projects into our perceptive faculty a 'sensuous manifold' capable of fitting into it exactly, is it not, by that very fact, in part known? And when we examine this exact fitting, shall we not be led, in one point at least, to suppose a pre-established harmony between things and our mind – an idle hypothesis, which Kant was right in wishing to avoid? At bottom, it is for not having distinguished degrees in spatiality that he has had to take space ready-made as given – whence the question how the 'sensuous manifold' is adapted to it. It is for the same reason that he has supposed matter wholly developed into parts absolutely external to one another . . .
>
> (1983: 205)

Matter and the intellect can be understood in terms of a double genesis insofar as they have progressively adapted themselves to each other and assumed a common form. Both the practical intellect and science deal with inert matter and are unable to think duration, for even when they treat time they do so on the model of homogeneous space (a line, for example, made up of infinitely divisible points going in any direction; a closed system is any system in which duration has been artificially left out). If Kant is to be completed two things are necessary: one is to develop a genesis of the intellect (to show why we have the habits of mind we do and follow through the consequences of this for a philosophy of nature and a theory of matter), and the second is to resist the uncritical adoption of modern science into philosophy which then serves to unnecessarily limit our conception of metaphysics:

> The molds of the understanding had to be accepted as they are, already made. Between the matter presented to our intellect and this intellect itself there was no relationship. The agreement between the two was due to the fact that intellect imposed its form upon matter. So that not only was it necessary to posit the intellectual form of knowledge as a kind of absolute and give up the quest of its genesis, but the very matter of this knowledge seemed too ground down by the intellect for us to be able to hope to get it back in its original purity. If we now inquire why Kant did not believe that the matter of our knowledge extends beyond its form, this is what we find. The criticism of our knowledge of nature that was instituted by Kant consisted in ascertaining what our mind must be and what Nature must be *if* the claims of our science are justified; but of these claims themselves Kant has not made the criticism. I mean that he took for granted the idea of a science that is one, capable of binding with the same force all the parts of what is given, and of co-ordinating them into a system presenting on all sides an equal solidity. He did not consider . . . that science became less and less objective, more and more symbolical, to the extent that it went from the physical to the vital, from the vital to the psychical.
>
> (1983: 358–9)

Bergson's argument is that science has developed out of the habits of our intellect, and these are primarily habits of acting upon inert matter. They are not habits that have been designed for comprehending *life*. His contention is that Kant's system rests on an uncritical utilization of science and an unwillingness to produce a genesis of the intellect. To unfold life as duration (a becoming or a movement that cannot be thought in terms of divisible points or external parts) requires, for Bergson, a different method, namely, the method of intuition. Bergson acknowledges that some successors of Kant, such as Schelling and Schopenhauer for example, tried to escape relativism by appealing to intuition (1965: 30). He argues, however, that this was a *non-temporal* intuition that was being appealed to, and, as such, was largely a return to *Spinozism*, that is, a deduction of the form of life or duration from 'one complete Being'.[12] He writes:

> The post-Kantian philosophy, severe as it may have been on mechanistic theories, accepts from mechanism the idea of a science that is

one and the same for all kinds of reality. And it is nearer to mechanism than it imagines; for although, in the consideration of matter,
of life and of thought, it replaces the successive degrees of complexity, that mechanism supposed by degrees of the realization of an
Idea or by degrees of the objectification of the Will, it still speaks of
degrees, and these degrees are those of a scale which Being traverses
in a single direction. In short, it makes out the same articulations in
nature that mechanism does. Of mechanism it retains the whole
design; it merely gives it a different colouring. But it is the design
itself, or at least one half of the design, that needs to be re-made.

(1983: 362)

Both science and the intellect for Bergson concern themselves with the aspect
of repetition. The intellect selects in a given situation whatever is like
something it already knows so as to fit it into a pre-existing mould or
schema; in this way it applies 'its principle that "like produces like"' (1983:
29). It rebels against the idea of an originality and unforeseeability of forms.
Similarly, science focuses its attention on isolable or closed systems, simply
because anything 'that is irreducible and irreversible in the successive
moments of a history eludes' it (29–30). In cases of organic evolution
Bergson insists that foreseeing the form in advance is not possible. This is
not because there are no conditions or specific causes of evolution but rather
owing to the fact that they are built into, are part and parcel of, the
particular form of organic life and so 'are peculiar to that phase of its
history in which life finds itself at the moment of producing the form' (28).

The need for a philosophy of life arises for Bergson, therefore, out of the
deficiency of the intellect and the inability of science to adequately think a
creative evolution. It is this insight that informs the need to think beyond
mechanism and not to accept the restrictions Kant places on a different
thinking of nature.

The more duration marks the living being with its imprint, the more
the organism differs from a mere mechanism, over which duration
glides without penetrating. And the demonstration has most force
when it applies to the evolution of life as a whole . . . inasmuch as
this evolution constitutes, through the unity and continuity of the
animated matter which supports it, a single indivisible history.

(1983: 37)

Bergson and finality

Bergson does not accept the restrictions Kant places either on our knowledge of nature or on our conception of finality. We do not have to think
finality simply in accordance with our own patterns or habits of thought.

Although it is not possible to argue that evolution contains a plan or a programme, say one that inevitably leads to the point of man (there is contingency, there are many different lines of evolution, and the Aristotelian conception of evolution that posits successive degrees of the development of one and the same tendency is untenable), for Bergson it is possible to argue that evolution is not simply an entirely accidental and aimless process. In what way then can a notion of finality be upheld? In this section I propose to address this issue by examining how Bergson ends up espousing finality in a 'special sense'. This will return us to the problems Kant was grappling with in his critique of teleological judgement but in a transformed manner. While Bergson's treatment of evolution can be said to be successful in showing the need to think beyond both mechanism and anthropomorphic finality, it cannot be said to amount to a clear-cut transcendence of Kant's problematic. To negotiate this point it will be necessary to look at the way in which Bergson construes the vital impetus as an 'image', as an image thought gives itself in order to think life beyond the mechanistic and spatial habits of the intellect. This we will do in the final section of the essay; the focus for now is on how Bergson comes to uphold a notion of finality only in a special sense.

As we noted in the introduction of this essay, Kant was led to question the limits of the mathematical and mechanical method by the example of the biological sciences and the study of life. The concept of the purposive character of the organism is one forced upon mechanical science by the empirical observation of living things. Bergson, however, refuses to accept the terms in which Kant frames the problem of the organism: either as a pure mechanism of nature (which supposes the externality and discreteness of parts, and sees the construction of the organism as a strictly mechanical affair) or as a problem of finality (in which there is not external design but the intentionality of a whole that precedes the parts).[13] The problem of the organism is a problem of complexity, he argues, and it is this complexity that the intellect has difficulty in comprehending. However, this is not because complexity transcends the level of a discursive understanding and necessitates a new kind of judgement; complexity exists as a problem only for the understanding. This complexity presupposes a multitude of interwoven analyses and syntheses, and the idea that a simple play of physical and chemical forces could have produced such complexity on their own accord is one we find it difficult to accept. Instead our intellect prefers to operate with a hylomorphic schema that supposes the imposition of matterless form upon formless matter. The understanding can only perceive 'parts external to parts' and is thus allowed only two kinds of explanation: either to treat the infinitely complex organization as a fortuitous concatenation of atoms or to appeal to the idea of a potent external force that has grouped the elements together. Now, in this argument that we need to go beyond the level of the understanding which would posit statically ready-made material elements or particles juxtaposed to one another, and an equally static external cause, is

Bergson not simply refining Kant's insights into the need for teleological estimation?[14] I believe he is. However, some important differences between the two remain. We can identify these differences as follows:

1 Bergson cannot accept the priority of mechanism over teleology simply because he holds that mechanism is itself rooted in the habits of our intellect. It thus requires a special genesis and a determination of its own. The alternatives to mechanism cannot be accorded merely a secondary function in our investigations into nature and life.

2 Kant's problem with hylozoism is well known. After having argued that it is insufficient to construct the organizational capacities of nature in terms of an 'analogue of art' Kant proffers the suggestion, only to close it down, that we might do better if we were to come up with an 'analogue of life' (1952: section 65, 23). He cannot, however, allow himself this move as it entails a view of matter that he will not entertain, namely, endowing matter 'as mere matter with a property (hylozoism) that contradicts its essential nature' (ibid.). For Kant this essential property is inertness. Kant's rejection of hylozoism explains why he is led to the view that the organization of nature is not analogous to any causality that is known to us. Bergson, by contrast, does not hesitate to accord to matter itself capacities of self-organization (he states this, in fact, in terms of a critique of Darwinism and its passive conception of matter in which evolutionary change is attributed to the blind and mechanical process of selection). This does not, however, mean that Bergson's position commits him to hylozoism simply because he upholds a distinction between life and matter on the level of tendencies, with matter being conceived in terms of a tendency towards inertness.[15] Life and matter are co-implicated in contractions and expansions (tensions, de-tensions, and ex-tension). Matter admits of relaxation and 'shows a certain elasticity', with the result that its inertia, geometry and determinism cannot be said to be absolute (1920: 17–18). More than this, however, Bergson conceives organization not in terms of the organism and its finality but rather from the point of view of life itself as a creative process of actualization and materialization. This leads us to the most important difference separating Bergson from Kant.

3 Bergson insists that the limitations of mechanism with respect to the coordination of parts with the whole do not demand we make the move to finality (Bergson 1977: 114). Here he is supposing that the doctrine of finality is committed to the view that the whole presupposes an infinity of parts external to one another. Although for Kant it is the whole which precedes the parts and accounts for their organization and co-ordination his argument still relies, Bergson argues, on a principle of abstract divisibility. What now needs clarifying is how Bergson will re-situate the problem of finality. This takes place in terms of a move from

the whole of internal finality to the whole of an external finality. Finality is to be accounted for in terms of the 'intention' of life itself and in terms of its general directionality, without which evolution would be an entirely chance and accidental process.[16] As Deleuze notes: 'There is finality because life does not operate without directions; but there is no "goal", because these directions do not pre-exist ready-made, and are themselves created "along with" the act that runs through them' (1991: 106). Whether this conception of finality takes Bergson beyond the problematic of teleological judgement, especially with respect to the issue of regulative knowledge, we shall leave on hold for now and address in the final section of the essay.

For Bergson it is possible to think of a genuinely creative evolution in which the creation of actual living forms is unforeseeable and takes place in nonmechanistic terms. The problem with finalism as a doctrine, as Bergson sees it, is that as generally articulated it offers little more than an inverted mechanism, substituting the attraction of the future for the compulsion of the past. In both cases evolution is reduced to a programme of realization. Furthermore, while he has a similar conception of the organism, conceived as a product of nature capable of self-repair and self-maintenance and the task for Bergson of the sensori-nervous system, he does not accept the stress on internal finality. Bergson will argue that we need to expand or widen both our conception of the organism (it is neither a given whole nor, in more complex terms, an autopoietic whole that is organizationally closed) and of the whole of life of which it is a part.[17] We have examined the reasons informing Bergson's reduction of finalism to inverted mechanism in essay three. Let's now concentrate attention on his claim that finality has to be external.[18]

What can no longer be assumed for Bergson, within both philosophy and science, is an 'indifferent matter'. In the case of Darwinism the word 'adaptation' has simply not been properly worked out. We readily understand that the relation of the eye to light is obvious, but when this relation is called an adaptation we must know precisely what we mean. A purely mechanistic biology errs in making the passive adaptation of inert matter – a matter that simply submits to the influence of the environment – mean the same as the active adaptation of an organism. Doctrines of finality, on the other hand, err in construing active adaptation along merely anthropomorphic lines, in which the evolution of some elaborate organ is compared to a task of manufacturing. This is to reduce evolution to the realization of a pre-existent possible and is the point at which finalism becomes an inverted mechanism. When we speak of the gradual evolution of the eye, taking into account what is inseparably connected with it, we are no longer simply speaking of the direct action of light physically causing something like the formation of the various systems (nervous, muscular, osseous) that are continuous with the apparatus of vision in the case of verterbrate animals;

on the contrary, we are implicitly attributing 'to organized matter a certain capacity *sui generis* . . . the power of building up very complicated machines to utilize the simple excitation that it undergoes' (1983: 72).

In *CE* Bergson discusses the doctrine of teleology with reference not to Kant but to Leibniz and his view that beings simply realize a programme that has been previously arranged. But again this is to assume that time is without effect (the thesis that 'all is given' is once again advanced). Bergson goes on to argue that, unlike mechanism, finalism is not a doctrine with rigid outlines and so admits of different inflections. The theory of final causes, he aims to show, cannot be definitively refuted: 'If one form of it be put aside, it will take another' (40) (within the theory of natural selection, for example, finality is being attributed, implicitly or explicitly, to the natural). His own argument on creative evolution, he tells us, necessarily partakes of a certain finalism. We can speak of finalism in different ways; for example, the finalism of the whole of life (carrying out a definite plan, although such a hypothesis clearly admits of no empirical demonstration or confirmation); or the finalism of each part of life, each organism for example, taken separately. Here the stress is placed on internal finality, in which there is a 'marvellous solidarity among the parts of an organism' and a division of labour that is infinite in its complexity: 'each being is made for itself, all its parts conspire for the greatest good of the whole and are intelligently organized in view of that end' (41).

Bergson is not happy with these two doctrines of finality for a number of reasons. The first finalism, that of the whole, reduces finality to little more than the execution of a programme, while the doctrine of internal finality naïvely assumes that the organism exists as a self-subsisting single whole. He argues that the different elements that are said to work for the greater good of the whole may themselves be organisms in certain cases. If we follow through the logic of the internalist argument on finality we discover that it proves to be a 'self-destructive notion'. The elements of what is taken to be a unitary whole possess a true autonomy; for example, the various tissues of an organism all live for themselves, while there are phagocytes which are so independent that they attack the organism that nourishes them. In nature, therefore, we observe neither purely internal finality nor absolutely distinct individuality. Rather, each individual organism, including the most individuated such as the higher vertebrates, remains united with the totality of all living things by invisible bonds. Bergson reaches the not very helpful, but nonetheless consistent, conclusion that, 'If there is finality in the world of life, it includes the whole of life in a single indivisible embrace' (43). This life is not, however, a mathematical one, but admits of differing individuations.

Bergson replaces finality with virtuality then. This is contained in his argument that life is a continuation of one and the same impetus that has divided into divergent lines of evolution (different tendencies of instinct and intelligence, different contractions and excitations of matter found in plant and animal). But between the virtual and the divergent lines of actual evolution there is no putting into action a plan or a programme, and neither is there simply a mechanistic realization of the possible. If there is finality in evolution this is owing to a common impulsion, in which problems persist, and not a common aspiration:

> The more we reflect on it, the more we shall see that this production of the same effect by two different accumulations of an enormous number of small causes is contrary to the principles of mechanistic philosophy . . . Every moment, right before our eyes, nature arrives at identical results, in sometimes neighboring species, by entirely different embryogenic processes.
>
> (74–5)

Bergson is suggesting that only his version of finalism can actually account for a creative evolution. He focuses his attention on the divergency between the actual lines of evolution and the complexity of similar structures found within these lines. On the model of mechanism there is simply a mechanical accumulation of accidents that natural selection has preserved owing to the advantages they have bestowed on a form of life. This leads Bergson to ask: what is the likelihood that two entirely different evolutions will arrive at similar results by two entirely different series of accidents being added together? However, if something of the virtual whole persists across the divergent lines, abiding in the parts, then *'Pure mechanism would be refutable, and finality, in the special sense in which we understand it, would be demonstrable in a certain aspect . . .'* (54).[19]

Having now gained insight into how Bergson conceives finality in a special sense, what problems can be identified with it? Does it completely escape the predicaments of the teleological judgement as presented by Kant?

The image of the *élan vital*

Bergson acknowledges the hypothetical character of his explanation of the evolution of life in terms of an *élan vital*. Indeed, it has some highly speculative aspects, notably, and we commented upon this critically in the preceding essays, the claim that cases of convergent evolution (such as the evolution of the eye across different phylogenetic lineages) can be explained in terms of the persistence of the impetus in terms of it setting the same virtual problem across divergent lines. It was noted in essay three that other explanations of convergent evolution are equally, if not more, credible. It would seem, then, in this aspect that the hypothesis of the *élan vital* could serve only a regulative function with respect to the scientific investigation of nature. Moreover, this would be a judgement that the scientist of life would have to make, it could not be the judgement given to science by the metaphysician. Bergson himself, we can note, endorses this view in his essay on the experimental method of Claude Bernard which proceeds, he notes, without recourse to a vital principle (Bergson 1965: 203). And although he argues that Bernard's attack was directed only against a 'superficial vitalism', he does acknowledge the need for a difference between a science of life and a metaphysics of life. We would, then, seem to be still operating within the space of Kant's teleological judgement. I shall argue in a moment that, strictly speaking, this is not the case. For Bergson the important thing is that both science and metaphysics display a readiness to be taken by surprise in the study of nature and life and learn to appreciate that there might be a difference between human logic and the logic of nature (206). The scientist has to cultivate a feeling for the complexity of natural phenomena. In this respect we cannot approach nature with any *a priori* conceptions of parts and wholes or any *a priori* conception of what constitutes life, including how we delimit the boundaries of an organism and hence define it. We must resist the temptation to place or hold nature within our own ideas or shrink reality to the measure of them. Contra Kant, therefore, we should not allow our need for a unity of knowledge to impose itself upon the multiplicity of nature. To follow the sinuosities of the real means that we cannot slot the real into a concept of all concepts, be it Spirit, Substance, Ego, or Will (1965: 49). Bergson notes that all thought becomes lodged into concepts which congeal and harden, including duration itself, and we have to be aware of this and the dangers presented by it (ibid.: 35).

Bergson does believe that the hypothesis of the *élan vital* has an empirical application and validity. This is a view he states most clearly in the pages he devotes to the notion in his last work, *The Two Sources of Morality and Religion* (1977: 112–16). In *CE* itself Bergson will, in fact, champion the 'empirical study of evolution' while at the same time insisting that although science and philosophy have the same 'object' (life) they each approach this object in a radically different manner and expect different results from their encounter with it. The difference of method between science and metaphysics has to be upheld (Bergson 1965: 43). They present us with two halves of the absolute; it is certainly not the case that for Bergson metaphysics is the 'superior of positive science' which would come after it and obtain a higher knowledge of the same object (ibid.). If we conceive the relation between the two in this way we will wrong both and metaphysics will inevitably be construed as a vague and solely hypothetical type of knowledge. In the case of philosophy, 'intuition may bring the intellect to recognize that life does not quite go into the category of the many nor yet into that of the one; that neither mechanical causality nor finality can give a sufficient interpretation of the vital process' (1983: 177). It is clear that in Bergson's thinking a distinction is to be made between what philosophical notions can claim when they function in concert with science and what validity they have when they are being developed on their own plane. A philosophy of life provides a vision and an intuition of life that may well be considered speculatively

136

otiose by science. But the possibilities and actualities of thinking cannot be dictated to by the requirements of science simply because for Bergson its own praxis is an approximation of the real and not the whole explanation of it. In *CE*, for example, Bergson outlines a metaphysics of life in which the duty of philosophy is said to be one of examining the living without any interest in practical utility: 'Its own special object is to speculate, that is to say, to see . . .' (1983: 196). The relation of science and philosophy to life is different because the method each employs is different.

The difficult task he leaves his readers with is that of seeking to determine the scope of the different levels or planes of thinking and negotiating the rapport between them. In this respect Bergson remains Kantian. The difference, however, is that Bergson seeks to overturn the subjection of metaphysics to science that he believes Kant's Critique has effected and to liberate it on its own plane. In so doing the aim, one might suggest, is to give back to metaphysics a good conscience. Although it is clear for Bergson that science is not simply relative but bears on reality itself, it has to be educated into how to respect 'the limits of its own domain' (1983: 207). It is thus not only metaphysics that needs an education in limits.

There is a further problem to be identified with the *élan vital*, and this concerns its status as an 'image' of thought. In describing it in such terms Bergson is clearly showing that we can only think life *analogically*. There is no immediate intuition or direct comprehension of life, and even though Bergson brilliantly exposes the assumptions on which Kant builds the edifice of a critical philosophy his own thinking remains necessarily caught within the limits of the human mind. The question is whether this necessary reliance upon analogy proves fatal to the endeavour of his entire philosophy considered as a philosophy of intuition and of life.[20] To respond to this let us inquire further into the status of the *élan vital* as an image.

Life is being spoken of in terms of an impetus, says Bergson, simply because 'no image borrowed from the physical world can give more nearly the idea of it' (1983: 257). An image borrowed from psychology provides us with insight into life as the enfolding of a plurality of interpenetrating terms. Life can be characterized in terms of an enormous multiplicity of open-ended potentialities that have to be seen as interwoven. This interwovenness is owing to the nature of a tendency when conceived in virtual terms:

> The elements of a tendency are not like objects set beside each other in space and mutually exclusive, but rather like psychic states, each of which, although it is itself to begin with, yet partakes of others, and so virtually includes in itself the whole personality to which it belongs.
>
> (1983: 118)

Now, while this clarifies the philosophical thinking informing Bergson's qualified vitalism it does not help us to see how it can acquire any empirical or regulative application.

It is in letters Bergson wrote to two of his critical commentators that we can find some invaluable insight into how he conceived the *élan vital* working as a hypothesis with empirical purchase. In a letter to Höffding of 1915, who had recently sent Bergson a copy of his book on the history of philosophy which also contained his lectures on Bergson of 1913, he tries to make it clear that he wishes to produce an *empirical* refutation of mechanistic philosophy; he does not wish to espouse a vitalism that will only be able to express 'admiration and wonder' in the face of nature (*Mélanges* 1972: 1148). He stresses the point that life has a history (or rather, is its history) in which 'every moment is *unique* and carries with it the representation of the whole past' (ibid.). But the most important letter Bergson wrote on the topic was towards the end of his life, a letter to F. Delattre of December 1935.

It is in this letter that Bergson expands upon the status of the *élan vital* as an image and endeavours to illuminate the entire issue by dissociating it from what we might take to be allied notions. He points out that when he relates the phenomena of evolution to an *élan vital* it is not for reasons of stylistic flourish and neither is it to mask our ignorance of a deep cause with a mere image. This is precisely, he argues, what the customary invocation of a vital principle does, and he gives Samuel Butler's notion of a 'life-force' as an example (ibid.: 1526). The *élan vital* is not to be confused, he insists, with the 'sterile images' offered by either Schopenhauer's will to life or Butler's life-force.[21] He finds himself, he says, situated between mechanism and finalism, dissatisfied with both but seeking a concept of life that can play an intermediary role. By itself the concept is without value. It can only become valuable and instructive when it works within the context of the field of problems presented to thought by 'life'. It is the task and responsibility of philosophy to involve itself in special problems 'as is done in the positive sciences'. The true difficulty is to 'pose the problem' and this involves abstracting oneself from language which has been made for conversation, not for philosophy, and which satisfies the requirements of common sense and social action but not those of thinking. The genuine philosopher, as opposed to the amateur, Bergson argues, is one who does not accept the terms of a problem as a 'common problem' that has been definitively posed and which only then requires that he or she select from the available solutions to the problem, as if the solution pre-existed the choice to be made. This, he suggests, is the case with Butler's vitalism and its rejection of Darwin's solution in favour of Lamarck's. But if we are committed to the tasks of thinking then a real intellectual effort is required of us in which the positing of the problem is actually *created* and done so in '*creating* the solution' (ibid.: 1527).

Do we remain on Kant's terrain? I would like to suggest that we do not. The way in which Kant is forced to negotiate the issues in his critique of teleological judgement means that he ends up advocating extreme measures, such as seeking the answers to the questions of nature *outside* nature; while providing an instructive rationale for the deployment of the reflective judgement in terms of regulative knowledge, he nonetheless stresses the point that the extension of science by another principle (finality) does not interfere with the principle of the mechanism of physical causation (Kant 1952: section 67: 28). The aim of the science of teleology is a strictly negative one for Kant, which is why it assumes the form of critique and is not allowed to become a branch of doctrine. It is a critique of a cognitive faculty, that of judgement, concerned with laying down the principles for the *correct* judgement of nature according to the principle of final causes. Thus, the principle of finality tells us nothing about the things in terms of their own 'intrinsic nature'; rather, they 'only assert that by the constitution of our understanding and our reason we are unable to conceive the origin in the case of beings of this kind otherwise than in the light of final causes' (1952: section 82: 91). This judgement of finality is given once and for all and it is given, as this passage demonstrates, solely on account of our constitution. The idea of finality in nature is on the point of degenerating into mere whim and fancy. The problems we create with respect to nature are problems entirely peculiar to our own mind and its constitution. Ultimately, the solution to the problem of finality in nature lies for Kant in the intelligent will of a supernatural creator, a will that is not in nature but in a noumenal reality. The 'Being' of finality cannot be given to us in any experience (1952: section 74: 50).

Bergson, by contrast, wishes to remain firmly on empiricist ground. This is why he held to the view that 'true empiricism' is 'the real metaphysics' (1965: 175). The *élan vital* is offered as an image of thought but not one without reference to experience. This is experience enlarged and gone beyond and is valid for both science and metaphysics. If science and metaphysics are to 'meet in intuition', and the demarcation that Kant imposed is not to be accepted *as given*, then this requires putting more of science into metaphysics and more of metaphysics into science (1965: 192). Conceived as an image of thought, then, the *élan vital* is part of Bergson's effort to cultivate a 'superior' empiricism. It exists to remind us of our ignorance and to encourage us to go further with our inquiry into the real free of pre-formed ideas and immediate intuitions. In this respect it can serve to *regulate* knowledge but not because it has accepted mechanism as the unquestionable basis of our conception of life or nature. What is important is not the name we give it but that we have such an image of thought. In this respect it could legitimately be said that in key aspects and elements contemporary science is Bergsonian.

Finally, then, is it the case that Bergson's philosophy of life rests on the analogy of the vital impetus fatal to it? I think not. It is better, I think, to suggest that what it demonstrates is the degree of intellectual effort involved in thinking beyond the human condition. As we shall now see, such an effort is what characterizes the extraordinary movements of thought at work in Bergson's text *Matter and Memory*.

6

VIRTUAL IMAGE

Bergson on matter and perception

The *actuality* of our perception lies in its *activity.*
(Bergson, *Matter and Memory*)

To believe in realities, distinct from that which is perceived, is
above all to recognize that the order of our perceptions depends
on them, and not on us.
(Bergson, *Matter and Memory*)

Whether other perceptions than those belonging to our whole
possible experience, and therefore a quite different field of
matter, may exist, the understanding is not in a position to
decide. It can deal only with the synthesis of that which is
given.
(Kant, *Critique of Pure Reason*)

We operate only with things that do not exist . . . divisible time
spans, divisible spaces . . . In truth we are confronted by a
continuum out of which we isolate a couple of pieces, just as
we perceive motion only as isolated points and then infer it
without ever actually seeing it.
(Nietzsche 1974: section 112)

Introduction

Matter and Memory is a book that has perplexed and beguiled its readers
since it was first published in 1896. William James compared its effect to a
Copernican Revolution, making it a philosophical work to be ranked with
Berkeley's *Principles of Human Knowledge* and Kant's *Critique of Pure
Reason.* Unlike the revolutions of Berkeley and Kant, however, that effected
by Bergson in *MM* consists in neither reducing the world to our perception
or idea of it nor restricting knowledge of it to our *a priori* sensible and
cognitive forms. The opening part of the book, however, gives the impression
that Bergson is a kind of idealist or empiricist in the Berkeleyean sense. The
book cannot, then, be read without due regard for its complex movements of
thought. *MM* is a text that anticipates many of the recent moves made in the
philosophy of mind, such as the stress on approaching perception not in

140

representational terms but rather as bound up with the action and movement of a body and on consciousness as an emergent property of a network
or assemblage of components; it is only abstractly that we can separate
brain, body, and world (see Clark 1997). I shall not pursue the contempo-
raneity of the text with respect to these issues. My focus is on the virtual. In
particular, in this first of two essays devoted to *MM* I wish to examine how
the virtual works in Bergson's figuration of the image.

MM is composed of four chapters and a summary and conclusion.
Chapter 1 unfolds the argument that perception is not an interior subjective
vision, or some mysterious manifestation of matter. The perception of a
consciousness has its basis in an impersonal perception that is a feature of
matter in its most immanent mode. To demonstrate this Bergson uses the
notion of a 'pure perception', a perception without memory, and it is here
that we can locate the source of Deleuze's claim that in *MM* there is a
'Spinozist inspiration' at work, namely, the presentation of a plane which
'slices through the chaos' in terms of the infinite movement of a self-
propagating substance and the positing of a pure consciousness 'by right' (*en
droit*) (Deleuze and Guattari 1994: 49).[1] For Deleuze *Matter and Memory* is
one of those rare modern texts – Sartre's *Transcendence of the Ego* is another
– in which thinking undergoes the 'vertigo of immanence'. In this essay my
concern is to examine *MM* in terms of its uniquely Bergsonian inspiration.
Only in this way can we hope to gain an appreciation of the complexity of
the book.

In the opening chapter of the book Bergson approaches the question of
matter and its perception in terms of the notion of image. He uses this
notion extensively: chapter 1 of the book is devoted to the 'selection of
images',[2] chapter 2 to the 'recognition of images', chapter 3 to the 'survival
of images', and chapter 4 to the 'delimiting and fixing of images'. All
becomes image on his model, including the body, nerve centres, the brain,
etc. (in the essay on 'Brain and Thought' in *Mind-Energy* these get described as 'ideas'). The notion has more than one sense in Bergson and the
tensions within his usage reflect its complex application in the history of
philosophy. The notion plays an important role in Lucretius' naturalism
and an equally important, if different role, in Berkeley's immaterialism.
Lucretius, for example, uses various Latin words for image: *simulacra*,
imago and *effigiae*. Images enjoy a virtual, even spectral, existence for him
being

> a sort of outer skin [membrane or film] perpetually peeled off the
> surface of objects and flying about this way and that through the
> air. It is these whose impact scares our minds, whether waking or
> sleeping, on those occasions when we catch a glimpse of strange
> shapes and phantoms of the dead.
>
> (Lucretius 1994: 95–6)

Moreover,

> Just as a great many particles of light must be emitted in a brief space of time by the sun to keep the world continually filled with it, so objects in general must correspondingly send off a great many images in a great many ways from every surface and in all directions instantaneously.
>
> (ibid.: 99)

In contrast to this naturalism of the image, in which there is no separation between matter and image, Berkeley strictly reserves the notion for his immaterialist account of sensation and perception (all exists as 'idea' or image in the mind). In 1884 Bergson provided an extended commentary on Lucretius' text for a new edition; it is also interesting to note that in the part of the *Principles* where the claim that perception is primary is initially made, Berkeley refers to 'a *rerum natura*' and maintains that his theory continues to uphold the distinction between real and imaginary things (chimeras), the point being that both exist as realities in the mind (Berkeley 1962: 80–1).[3]

In the opening chapter of *MM* it is clear that in his depiction of matter as having no virtuality – precisely what this amounts to will shortly become clear – Bergson is relying upon an essentially Berkeleyean argument. It is in this opening chapter that Bergson introduces a notion of the virtual and establishes its conditions. In Bergson's thinking on perception the virtual is not deployed in abstract or mysterious terms. It is not all the stuff that is not actual and outside a field of perception. As Sartre noted in a critical appreciation of *MM*, the emergence of individuated consciousness is not to be explained in Bergson in terms of an unheralded light; such a consciousness, moreover, functions by extracting 'from the whole that is real a part that is virtual' (Sartre 1962: 248).

The difficulty in determining the precise character of Bergson's philosophical position in *MM* is compounded by the fact that he makes concessions to idealism – for example, in his very usage of the term image – and sees it as an inevitable component in our thinking about the world. But, as we shall see, he ultimately wants to move beyond idealism, whether in its Berkeleyean or Kantian presentation, and he aims to show how this is possible (Kant is depicted as both an idealist and a realist, though Bergson is careful not to equate his position with Berkeley's).[4] In chapters 2 and 3 of the book, which will be examined in the next essay, the focus shifts to memory, and the treatment here includes an elaboration of his well-known claim that memory-images are not stored in the brain and unfolds a distinction between psychological memory, the memory of habit-formation (a bodily memory), and an ontological memory (the memory of pure recollection). A concentration on Bergson's treatment of matter will show how he is constantly navigating a course between the poles of idealism and realism.

One of the novel aspects of the book is how it aims to show that realism also ends up in an idealist trap. Briefly: for the idealist the world is the product of our ideas and cannot exist independently of them. For the realist (sometimes called a materialist) – at least in the way Bergson presents this position – the mental is reduced to the cerebral and in this way the brain is made into the progenitor of our representations of the world. Bergson will take both to task for reducing the relation of the body to the world into one of speculative knowledge as opposed to vital activity. Realism becomes an idealism when it locates perception and consciousness in a centre or some detached isolated object that has been abstractly divorced from its conditions of action in the world.[5] Both err in making the presentation of the part – the mind or the brain – equivalent to the presentation of the whole (the real).

All is image

The very opening paragraph of chapter 1 contains some of the essential matters that demand a careful and precise reading:

> We will assume for the moment that we know nothing of theories of matter and theories of spirit, nothing of the discussions as to the reality or ideality of the external world. Here I am in the presence of images, in the vaguest sense of the word, images perceived when my senses are opened to them, unperceived when they are closed. All these images act and react upon one another in all their elementary parts according to constant laws which I call laws of nature, and, as a perfect knowledge of these laws would probably allow us to calculate and to foresee what will happen in each of these images, the future of the images must be contained in their present and will add to them nothing new.
>
> (1991: 17)

The opening paragraph is revealing in key respects: it is misleading if we suppose that Bergson is committed to a strong Berkeleyean position (images exist only when perceived) for he will go on to argue that images exist when unperceived. By describing the objects of matter and of the world as images Bergson is suggesting that they have the potential to be perceived.[6] Secondly, while Bergson will give an important place to the conception of a multiplicity of images acting and reacting upon one another in all their parts and facets, the view he adheres to most in the text is that which holds such action and reaction to be reducible to the mathematical treatment of mechanism, in which the future *is* contained in the past and calculable in advance. This is owing to him placing a distinction between matter and *esprit* – which is also, as we shall see, a distinction between actual and virtual – at the very centre of his inquiry. In *MM* the virtual is taken to be the sole preserve of *esprit*.

A key question guides Bergson's analysis in chapter 1. He poses it as follows: what is the relation between the image I term my body, which is an image that occupies a centre, and the image I call the universe? Moreover, how is it possible for the same images to belong at one and the same time to two different systems, to one in which each image varies for itself and another in which images change for a single image that occupies a privileged centre? To see why Bergson should raise this question about the existence of these two systems of images we have to jump ahead a little in the unfolding of the argument and appreciate that Bergson gives primacy to a continuity of material extensity. In its aspects this continuity changes from moment to moment and can be conceived in terms of a whole that changes like a kaleidoscope: there is no centre since everything is bound together in relations. Indeed, Bergson argues that empiricism has only a vague conception of the artificial character of the relations uniting the terms but it holds to these terms and neglects the relations (1991: 183). Once we have artificially broken up the moving continuity of the whole we seek to reestablish the unions and bonds that exist between things but we do so by replacing a 'living unity' with an empty diagram that is as 'lifeless as the parts which it holds together' in which relations are being conceived in logical and spatial terms.

We have already seen how Bergson repeatedly privileges this material continuity. However, in addition to the moving whole of this material extensity we also speak of bodies with clearly defined outlines – they have their own substance and individuality – and that move in terms of their relations with each other. The move must be made, ultimately, to construing things in terms of the continuity of a moving whole since this allows us to develop a plausible account of the formation of individuated bodies which emerge from it as 'zones of indetermination'. At the same time, however, he is concerned to expose the illusions that the intellect generates for itself in its neglect of the whole: generating, for example, the illusion of bodies changing in homogeneous space, a space which is then extended to time itself. As we shall see, Bergson believes that both philosophy and science are able to provide insight into the universal continuity and so recover the 'natural articulations' of a universe that has been carved artificially by the intellect (a faculty of abstraction). First, however, attention needs to be focused on Bergson's conception of a lived body.

My body is unique in that I do not simply know it 'from without' in terms of perception but also 'from within', as it were, in terms of 'affections', which interpose themselves between the excitations a body receives from the outside and the movements it executes in response. My body exists, then, amidst the aggregate of images that makes up the material world, and, as such, it can only be regarded as one image amongst many which, like other images, receives movement and gives it back. It is at this point that Bergson begins to describe everything as image: afferent and efferent nerves, the brain, my body, and so on. If the brain is an image existing in the material world amongst other images, then it cannot be reified into the condition upon which the *whole* image of the world depends (that is, its part cannot be made equivalent to the whole): 'Neither nerves nor nerve centers can, then, condition the image of the universe' (19). Moreover, in claiming that the brain is part of the material world, and resisting the view that the material world is somehow contained in the physical entity we call the bounded brain, Bergson is aiming to show that if the image that is the material world is eliminated then we at the same time destroy the brain and its cerebral disturbances: the brain cannot exist in the absence of the images of the material world that feed it. This leads him to exposing what he calls 'the fiction of an isolated material object' that results in an absurd position, namely, that such an object as the nervous system, in its physical properties, can exist independently of its relations with the rest of the universe, such as the organism which nourishes it, the body that houses it, and the atmosphere of the earth that envelopes the organism, and so on. If we keep hold of the relations then it makes no sense to reduce perceptions to the molecular movements of the cerebral mass, simply because these movements remain bound up with the rest of the material world. In addition, Bergson advances the argument that on the model he has constructed it can be seen that the body, as a living centre, is first and foremost a centre of action and not a house of representation. It is not abstracted from the world, simply contemplative in relation to it; rather it is intimately bound up with it and with its movements, with actions and reactions. Replacing the self-transparency of the Cartesian cogito with the isolated brain divorced from the images that inform it leads to the illusion that if we could penetrate into the inside of the brain it would be possible to understand the phenomenon of consciousness simply by observing the dance of the atoms of the cortex. This is to commit the error of positing a simple, linear or automatic account of the relation between the cerebral and the mental. Bergson does not deny that there is a relation, only that it is one of either parallelism or epiphenomenalism. Psychic life can be said to be highly varied, varying in accordance with the 'attention to life' and made up of diverse tones and rhythms.

The reader may already have a sense of the unorthodox character of Bergson's utilization of the notion of image. His usage does not conform to certain patterns that have established themselves within our thinking, such as the classic divisions of subject and object, mind and matter.[7] He neither construes the problem of perception or consciousness in representational terms nor does he hold that images are simply in our heads.[8] The person who might wish to claim that, although the world is not dependent on our consciousness – it would still exist should the consciousness that reflects on the being of its being disappear – the images our minds produce of it are dependent on our consciousness, is not even entitled to say this on Bergson's model. Precisely why Bergson is entitled to uphold this view I shall disclose shortly.

But why construe the brain as an image or idea? Is this not already to concede too much to idealism (all that I know of the brain is what I perceive of it or what is available to me as an idea)? Perhaps it is useful to bear in mind that in the opening chapter of the book Bergson is thinking in terms of common sense and has not yet, at this point in the book, developed an engagement with the realism of science. In the essay of 1904 on 'Brain and Thought' Bergson speaks of nerve centres as images in the sense of 'moving pictures' that contain 'movable parts', taking in movements from the outside and producing in response internal movements. On this level, therefore, all that the brain is doing is receiving the influences from the movements of other images and responding to them. It exists only as a part in relation to the whole, it is not identical with this whole (the moving images that compose the material universe). It is clear that Bergson has deployed an idealist category in an unconventional sense. However, this is only made clear in the 1910 Introduction he wrote to the book, and in it Bergson clarifies his relation to Berkeley.

A central thesis of the opening chapter of *MM* is that matter has no virtuality. What does this mean? When Bergson argues that matter enjoys no virtuality – the virtual is going to be situated strictly on the level of mind or spirit in this text – he means that it has no hidden powers or potentialities. Matter is as it appears to us, and although it may have unperceived physical properties this is all it has (physical properties without hidden potentialities). This view is somewhat modified in *CE*. In *MM* he gives the nervous system as an example of something that has only physical properties and no hidden potentialities. Indeed, in an awkward formulation he describes the nervous system as the 'material symbol' of an inner energy (1991: 71). In *CE* the nervous system is now spoken of as a 'reservoir of potentialities' (1983: 126) It is only in the essay of 1911 on 'Philosophical Intuition' that Bergson makes it explicit that the conception of matter as devoid of virtuality is part of Berkeleyean idealism. On Bergson's reading, Berkeley's immaterialism – matter is a cluster of ideas or images – does not consist simply in claiming that bodies are ideas. This rests on an inadequate appreciation of what Berkeley is doing simply because it is so uninformative: all we are doing is substituting one word for another (we would still be affirming of ideas what we had previously affirmed of bodies). Berkeley's idealism or immaterialism does not amount to the view that matter will cease to exist when we stop living but rather holds that it is co-extensive with our representation of it. In other words, matter has no underneath (no 'substratum' in Berkeley's words), so it is impossible for it to hide or contain anything. It is spread out as a mere surface, possessing no virtual power, and at any given moment it presents itself to us as it is – it is the plane of presentation (1965: 116). Indeed, this is the real challenge of Berkeley's idealism: it is not that matter is unreal but rather that the causes of ideas are to be located in an immaterial substance (Spirit). This is because of the way in which Berkeley has delimited the notion of matter. As Bergson notes, 'Berkeley perceives matter as a *thin transparent film situated between man and God*' (ibid.: 119). This film becomes opaque and forms a screen only when abstract concepts like 'force' and 'substance' are allowed to slip behind it and settle like a layer of dust. It is in the attempt to clear away this dust that Berkeley's *Principles of Human Knowledge* offers a kind of Copernican Revolution; and, in its attempt to delimit the field of metaphysics – the scope for endless speculation about things that transcend our capacities and result only in 'absurdities' and 'contradictions' – it clearly anticipates something of the sense of Kant's critique of pure reason (of course, it must always be noted that Kant is not Berkeley; his refutation of idealism attempts to make the differences between them clear, *CPR*: B 275–9).

The issue of matter not enjoying virtuality is also treated in the 1904 essay on the brain. In this essay Bergson treats idealism and realism as two notation systems and the purpose of the essay is to show how realism ends up reproducing the error of idealism by making the part equivalent to the whole. Idealism is associated with the conception that matter has no virtuality since whatever exists does so in actual terms. Interestingly, realism is said to consist in the opposite claim, namely, that matter exists independently of our idea (which is precisely the principal position advocated in chapter 4 of *MM*) and that behind an actual perception there are hidden powers and virtualities. This is because realism wishes to claim 'that the divisions and articulations visible in our perception are purely relative to our manner of perceiving' (1920: 235) (once again this neatly captures the position Bergson advocates in the final chapter of the book and in the context of a critique of the limitations of Kantian idealism). In this essay from *M-E* Bergson insists that it is contradictory to uphold both of these doctrines and yet this is precisely what we seem to find in *MM*. Or do we? The opening chapter makes central the claim that matter is as it appears and cannot be said to possess hidden potentialities. Matter is thus co-extensive with our representation of it. However, it is not until the final chapter that Bergson will complicate this conception of matter, conceiving it in terms of 'numberless vibrations'. Clearly, this does not necessarily mean that he is forced to relinquish the view upheld in the opening chapter that matter has no virtuality (a position which, I have argued, is complicated in *CE*); but it does mean that he holds that it is possible for philosophy and science to provide us with access to a different conception of matter. For now we simply note that the thesis that matter has no virtuality is the same as the thesis that matter is image (or an aggregate of movement images).

The 1910 Introduction to *MM* is helpful insofar as Bergson, while not addressing or clarifying these tensions and possible contradictions in his position, does make clear that his usage of the word image and that his adherence to the claim of idealism that matter has no virtuality does not commit him to a Berkeleyean position. Bergson begins by saying that both idealism and realism go too far when they reduce matter to the perception we have of it. This is confusing since, as we have seen, in chapter 1 of *MM* he argues in favour of the thesis that matter is coextensive with our perception of it, while elsewhere he will provide a different conception of realism (in the essay 'Brain and Thought' realism is discussed as the doctrine that holds that matter is not reducible to or equivalent with our perception of it). The claim makes sense only at the point at which realism reaches an idealist moment, namely when it posits a seat of consciousness and construes this seat as residing in some isolated material object (the brain). He then goes on to speak of his reliance on a notion of image, saying that what is meant by it is something more than what an idealist calls a representation and something less than what a realist calls a thing. Image is situated, then, midway between the two. Precisely what exact status this gives to image is unclear. Now, although Bergson will stick throughout the text to the position that matter exists just as we perceive it, he insists that this does not commit him to Berkeley's immaterialism. This is because on his deployment of matter as image it makes no sense to say that the objects that we see and touch exist only in the mind:

> Philosophy made a great step forward on the day when Berkeley proved, as against the 'mechanical philosophers', that the secondary qualities of matter have at least as much reality as the primary qualities. His mistake lay in believing that, for this, it was necessary to place matter within the mind and make it into a pure idea.
>
> (1991: 10–11)

(Descartes would be one such 'mechanical philosopher for Bergson). For Bergson if the world is approached as an aggregate of images then it makes little sense to ask whether the world is within or without us. This is because 'interiority and exteriority are only relations among images'. Thus, 'to ask whether the universe exists only in our thought, or outside of our thought, is to put the problem in terms that are insoluble, even if we suppose them to be intelligible' (ibid.: 25).

Bergson's attempt to clarify his position is not entirely successful. Just how he can hold to the position that he does – matter is image and has no virtuality but matter is not in the mind – will become more comprehensible once we have unfolded the remaining argument of chapter 1. Once this has been done, we shall turn our attention to chapter 4 and follow the major movements that have taken place in his thinking in *MM*. We shall also see how the notion of the virtual is brought into play as a component of Bergson's thinking on perception.

Between idealism and realism

Let's begin with this premise: matter is the aggregate of images and the perception of these same images refers to the possible action of a particular image, namely, an individuated body. For Bergson the difference between matter and its perception is only a difference in degree and not, like the difference between perception and memory, a difference in kind (if the latter difference is treated as one of degree then memory is being reduced to being little more than a weakened form of perception, a position that Bergson will vigorously contest in later chapters of the book). If matter is made into something completely different from perception it becomes difficult to see how we can have an image of matter or how perception could be explained as arising out of matter – as a specific organization of matter in an individuated form – except in miraculous terms. How can there be a relation between a 'formless matter' and a 'matterless thought'? The only solution is to conceive of matter as inseparable from its movement, which means to posit it in terms of an aggregate of images. Bergson acknowledges that 'images cannot create images'; rather what they do is to 'indicate at each moment, like a compass that is being moved about, the position of a certain image, my body, in relation to the surrounding images' (1991: 23). Within an acentred universe of images there emerges a centred perception, the individuated body with degrees of complexification, from the simple irritable and contractile protoplasm to the animal organism with a complex nervous system, or what Bergson calls a living centre of activity and 'zone of indetermination'. Bergson insists that the difference between the perceptive faculty of the brain and the reflex functions of the spinal cord is also one of degree and not kind. This is because both deal with movements (their co-ordination and inhibition), with the cord transforming external stimulations into movements and the brain prolonging them into reactions. The materialist, as Bergson now designates the realist, errs in making the modifications of the grey matter sufficient to themselves, leading to the illusion that perception is identical with the movements of cerebral activity. Bergson is not denying that there is a relation between the cerebral and the mental, only that it is one of identity.

It is in responding to this badly posed problem that Bergson advocates we approach the problem in terms of 'images, and of images alone' (1991: 26). This is because he holds that idealism and realism both draw on the notion and in recognizing the inadequacy of both we can find an alternative way of positing the relation between the two systems of images (the material universe and the body). In the case of realism we begin with the material universe and its mutual relations which are held to be governed by constant natural laws, and within which there is an 'absence of centre, all the images unfolding on one and the same plane . . .' The problem for the realist is how to account for the perceptions of the body in a way that does not reduce them to a mere phosphorescence of cerebral activity or that is forced to appeal to some *deus ex machina* to generate perception. Idealism begins the other way round, starting with the privileged image of the body, establishing perhaps the transcendental character of the mind in relation to matter, and either claiming matter to be unreal or being compelled to rely on some pre-established harmony between the mind and the things that make up the material world. Both views go wrong for Bergson in supposing that the interest of perception is speculative as opposed to vital. Rather, perception has to be seen as bound up with the vital adaptive needs and interests of a living body. It is for this reason that Bergson will restrict the brain to being essentially an instrument or organ of analysis with respect to received movement and of selection with respect to executed movement. The job of the nervous system is not to fabricate representations but simply to receive stimulations and to present an array of motor apparatuses to any given stimuli. If living matter is conceived in terms of centres of real action (real action that is also virtual action), then it becomes possible to envisage how conscious perception – a centre that subordinates images to it and that are variable with it – emerges. It is also possible to envisage a scale of perceptions from the simple (tactile perception or simple contact) to the complex (virtual action as opposed to necessary or automatic action).

The body is not just any image but exists as a privileged one. If matter is stripped of virtuality this also means that amongst the movement images of simple matter there is only natural necessity and mechanism (Bergson will not cast doubt on the legitimacy of this construal of matter until almost the very end of the book, and even then he will only raise the question whether a different approach to matter might be possible). My body, however, is capable of effecting a new action upon the objects that surround it. A body has the power to choose and decide a step of action among several that are materially possible. The objects surrounding a body, therefore, reflect its possible action upon them. It is for this reason that it is capable of *virtual* action. Bergson will define consciousness as the measure of virtual action. Before the character of this virtual can be defined in more precise terms (what is the nature of its difference?), we need to ask: how do we arrive at a notion of the body?

Bergson himself chooses to focus on two questions: why *conscious* perception? And how does it happen that we think such perception takes place as if it were the effect of the internal movements of a cerebral substance? Bergson approaches the issues by simplifying the conditions under which conscious perception actually takes place. This is his hypothesis of an ideal or pure perception, which is a perception without memory (the impregnation of the present by the past), a perception confined to the present and fully absorbed in the task of moulding itself upon some external object. For Bergson this is not an idle hypothesis, even though he concedes its ideal status. This is because it is designed to show that the individuality of a conscious perception – a perception bound up with memory – is one 'grafted onto this impersonal perception' and that lies at the very root of our knowledge of things. This construction of types of perception aims to combat the reduction of perception to a kind of interior, subjective vision, which is then held to differ from memory only in terms of its degree of intensity (memory being construed as a merely weakened form of perception, rather than as something that is different in kind from it). However short or brief perception is taken to be it has to occupy a certain duration, which, in turn, presupposes the effort of memory that prolongs into one another a plurality of moments (it binds and synthesizes them). Even the so-called secondary qualities require this 'contraction of the real' that is effected by memory. Memory serves to cover a set of immediate perceptions with a cloak of recollections – past recollections are brought to bear on problems encountered in the present – and also to contract into a single experience a number of external moments. It is these habits of contraction through memory that serve to further individuate conscious perception.

On the basis of this presentation of perception there is no need, Bergson believes, to offer a deduction of consciousness. This is because he holds that the emergence of a conscious perception is explicable solely in terms of this positing of matter as an aggregate of images. It is in his treatment of this issue that we perhaps find the clearest account of why Bergson is relying so heavily on the notion of images. And what we might take to be a phenomenology of images – in the sense that they refer to an intentional consciousness – turns out to be a strict *empiricism* of images.

Bergson advances the argument that no theory of matter can escape the necessity of conceiving matter in terms of images. For example, if we take matter to be atoms in motion such atoms, though denuded of physical qualities, can only be determined in relation to an 'eventual vision' and an 'eventual contact' (it should be noted that for Bergson all perceptions, whether tactile or visual are extensive; he takes Berkeley to task for regarding extensity as a property of tactile perceptions, seeing nothing in sensible qualities but sensations, and in the sensations themselves nothing but mental states, 1991: 212–17). Bergson insists that even when atoms are converted into centres of force which are then dissolved into vortices that revolve in a continuous fluid, such centres can only be determined in relation to touch (albeit an impotent one) and light (albeit colourless). In short, matter, however it is depicted, remains as image in the sense that for it to become real for us it has to become translated into images. Bergson concedes that images may exist without being perceived, but that simply means something is present without being represented or imagined (1991: 35). It should perhaps be stressed that at this stage in his argument Bergson is not offering an account of the praxis of science in his theory of images but focusing his attention on the issue of perception and accounting for its emergence and possibility.

Indeed, it is in the context of this insistence upon matter as image that Bergson begins to develop his claim that perception operates in a subtractive fashion. Although such a conception of perception is often held to be one of the distinctive features of Bergson's thought, it can already be found articulated in strikingly similar terms in earlier thinkers, such as Schopenhauer and Nietzsche, for example.[9] Bergson invites us to think about the difference between 'presence' and 'representation', a difference that seems to explain the 'interval' between matter and its conscious perception. He argues that if we were to move from the one to the other in terms of adding something – the representation of matter being greater than its simple presence – then the passage from matter to perception becomes mysterious. If we make the less obvious move and construe perception as involving a narrowing or subtracting of the real then the passage to perception can be rendered intelligible. It is in his treatment of the subtractive perception that we get the first proper sense of the role the notion of the virtual is playing within Bergson's thinking on perception and consciousness:

> ... here is the image which I call a material object; I have the representation of it. How then does it not appear to be in itself that which it is for me? It is because, being bound up with all other images, it is continued in those which follow it, just as it prolonged those which preceded it. To transform its existence into representation, it would be enough to suppress what follows it, what precedes it, and also all that fills it, and to retain only its external crust, its superficial skin. That which distinguishes it as a *present* image, as an objective reality, from a *represented* image is the necessity which obliges it to act through every one of its points upon all the other points of all other images, to transmit the whole of what it receives, to oppose to every action an equal and contrary reaction, to be, in short, merely a road by which pass, in every direction, the modifications propagated throughout the immensity of the universe.
>
> (1991: 36)

Deleuze will make significant use of such a passage in his Bergsonism of the 1980s. If there is no moving body that is distinct from an executed movement, and nothing moved without received movement, meaning that any and every image is indistinguishable from its actions and reactions, then we can construct a world of 'universal variation' out of the movement image, conceive the plane of immanence as a 'plane of matter' and bring about a novel rapport between Bergsonism and Relativity: 'a set of movement-images, a collection of lines or figures of light; a series of blocs of space-time' (Deleuze 1986: 60). If the identity of the image and movement is conceived as an identity of matter and light – the plane of immanence itself is said to be made up entirely of light – then this means, for Deleuze, that 'things are luminous by themselves without anything illuminating them' (ibid.). Deleuze argues that phenomenology and Bergsonism are two responses to the 'historical crisis' of psychology and maintains that the opposition between them on the issue of consciousness – How do we posit it by right? Is it immanent to matter-energy? – is a radical one.

In contrast to the proposition of (Husserlian) phenomenology that all consciousness is *of* something we have the proposition that all consciousness *is* something (see Husserl 1931: 141–2, 241–4). The eye is in things and not simply in a centred subject of perception or a consciousness capable of *Sinngebung*.[10] This inversion of transcendental idealism and phenomenology (Kant and Husserl) by a spiritualized realism or materialism reminds one of Goethe's riposte to Schopenhauer's insistence on the primacy of idealism:

> That man Goethe . . . was so completely a *realist* that he absolutely could not get it into his head that the *objects* as such exist only to the extent that they are *projected* by the perceiving subject. What, he once said to me, looking at me with his Jovian eyes, you suggest that the light exists only in so far as you can see it? No, *you* would not exist if the light did not see *you*.
>
> (Schopenhauer quoted in Safranski 1991: 183)

Deleuze writes: 'The more the privileged centre is itself put into movement, the more it will tend towards an acentred system where the images vary in relation to one another and tend to become like the reciprocal actions and vibrations of a pure matter' (1986: 76).[11] This is the moment of Deleuze's realism.

Let us now return to Bergson's treatment of the two systems in *MM* and note that while a deduction of consciousness would constitute a 'bold undertaking' (Bergson) it is rendered superfluous once we posit a material world made up of an aggregate of mobile images and within which interiority and exteriority are only relations among these images (an insight that we find taken up in the later Merleau-Ponty).[12] No other assumption works, says Bergson (1991: 35). The passage cited above from *Matter and Memory* continues:

> I should convert it into a representation if I could isolate it, especially if I could isolate its shell. Representation is there, but always virtual – being neutralized, at the very moment when it might become actual, by the obligation to continue itself and to lose itself in something else. To obtain this conversion [from the virtual to the actual], it would be necessary, not to throw more light on the object, but, on the contrary, to obscure some of its aspects, to diminish it by the greater part of itself, so that the remainder, instead of being encased in its surroundings as a *thing*, should detach itself from them as a *picture*. Now, if living beings are, within

153

the universe, just 'centers of indetermination', and if the degree of this indetermination is measured by the number and rank of their functions, we can conceive that their mere presence is equivalent to the suppression of all those parts of objects in which their functions find no interest.

(1991: 36)

Bergson approaches the matter of perception, then, in terms of a relation between a part and the whole. Perception is an activity that subtracts from a mobile whole in accordance with its interests and functions. But what of the virtual? This is bound up with the conditions of actual perception and the living centre of action. Outside of this all is actual or potentially actual. In the passage just cited the conversion from the virtual to the actual does not refer to a process of translation from one mode of being to another; rather, it indicates the conditions under which an actual representation or perception comes into being, namely through a process of selection of images. The spontaneity of reaction that characterizes the activity of a living centre interrupts the radical mechanism which binds together all images, mutually acting and reacting in all their elements, and in which 'none of them perceives or is perceived consciously'. The representation effects a diminution of the action of surrounding images. It is within the context of establishing the conditions of the emergence of perception and representation that Bergson invokes the idea of a virtual image:

When a ray of light passes from one medium into another, it usually traverses it with a change of direction. But the respective densities of the two media may be such that, for a given angle of incidence, refraction is no longer possible. Then we have total reflection. The luminous point gives rise to a *virtual image* which symbolizes so to speak, the fact that the luminous rays cannot pursue their way. Perception is just a phenomenon of the same kind.

(1991: 37)

The spontaneous activity of a living zone or centre means that the rays of light that reach and interest it do not just pass through it but appear reflected and thus indicate 'the outlines of the object which emits them'. Now, Bergson insists that, conceived in these terms, perception does not add anything new to images; there is, in fact, no addition at all. Rather, what happens is that objects abandon aspects of their 'real action in order to manifest the virtual action of the living being upon them' (ibid., translation modified). This explains why he compares the phenomenon of perception to the effect of a mirage. The difference between 'being' and 'being consciously perceived' can only be one of degree in Bergson's schema of images. There is then no fundamental difference for Bergson between the existence of the

154

material world and the 'virtual perception of all things' (ibid.: 39). Bergson argues that this is not a hypothesis but an essential part of the data which no adequate theory of perception can dispense with. If we imagine that perception is a kind of photographic image of things that is taken from a fixed point of view – and in which the photograph is developed in the brain conceived as the supposed central organ of perception – then no metaphysics or physics can escape the conclusion, Bergson argues, that the photograph, supposing there be one, is 'developed in the very heart of things and at all the points of space . . .'. He writes:

> Build up the universe with atoms: each of them is subject to the action, variable in quantity and quality according to the distance, exerted on it by all material atoms. Bring in Faraday's centers of force: the lines of force emitted in every direction from every center bring to bear upon each the influences of the whole material world. Call up the Leibnizian monads: each is the mirror of the universe. All philosophers, then, agree on this point.
>
> (38)

This argument helps us to clarify the role the notion of the virtual is playing in Bergson's account of perception. On one level there is at any given place in the universe the action of all matter passing through it without resistance or loss and in which the photograph of the whole is translucent. On another level, however, behind the photographic plate we can posit a black screen on which an image is shown. It is the 'zones of indetermination' that play the role of this screen and whose role is not to add to what is there but rather to effect the situation in which while real action passes through, the virtual action remains.

Beyond the identity thinking of materialism

Sartre astutely notes that Bergson's laying out of the universe as a world of images ends up embracing an empiricism and a realism that he had apparently set out to criticize. The difference from someone like Hume, notes Sartre, is whereas in Hume the term image is reserved for things only insofar as they are actually perceived, in Bergson the term is applied to every kind of reality, that is, not just objects of actual knowledge but every possible object of a representation (images can be without being perceived, and when they are perceived it is in terms of subtraction and selection). This means, Sartre further notes, that Bergson has no need, as in Descartes, to distinguish between the thing and its image (the thing is its images) or to resolve the problem of how to establish a relation between two modes of being (in Bergson's model there are *not* two modes). Neither does the sceptical issue of a reality existing in and for itself that haunts Hume's enterprise ever surface in Bergson's text. When Bergson insists that the difference between being and being consciously perceived is only a difference of degree, this, says Sartre, amounts to the claim that everything is first given as 'participating in consciousness, or rather *as consciousness*' (Sartre 1962: 39). If this was not the case then for Bergson the fact that reality does become consciousness – in the form of individuated and complexified organizations of matter and energy – could never be accounted for except in mysterious or miraculous terms. Sartre then goes on to note the extent to which this configuration of consciousness differs from Husserl's phenomenological reduction. The terms in which he presents this difference anticipate the way in which Deleuze construes the significance of Bergson's *Matter and Memory* in *Cinema 1* on the movement-image:

> Bergson was not of the opinion that consciousness must have a correlate, or, to speak like Husserl, that a consciousness is always consciousness *of* something. Consciousness, for Bergson, seems to be a kind of quality . . . very nearly, a sort of substantial form of reality. It cannot arise where it is not, it cannot begin or cease to be. What is more, it can be in a purely virtual state, unaccompanied by an act or by any manifestation whatsoever of its presence. The 'unconscious', Bergson was to dub this reality endowed with a secret quality. Yet this unconscious is of exactly the same nature as consciousness. There was no nonconscious for Bergson, only a consciousness unaware of itself. There is no illuminated object blocking and receiving light. There is a pure light, a phosphorescence, and no illuminated matter. But this pure light diffused on all sides becomes actual only by reflecting off certain surfaces which serve simultaneously as the screen for other luminous zones. We have here a sort of reversal of the classic analogy: instead of consciousness being a light going from the subject to the thing, it is a luminosity which goes from the thing to the subject.
>
> (Sartre 1962: 39–40)

We may note that whereas Sartre is unhappy about the nonphenomenological character of Bergson's laying-out of consciousness, Deleuze holds to the importance of beginning precisely with this aspect. Indeed, he will credit Sartre's own essay of 1936–7 (drafted in Berlin in 1934–5) on the 'transcendence of the ego' with effecting a decisive move for a thinking of immanence by opening up an *impersonal* transcendental field, although Sartre did not, Deleuze argues, remain faithful to his original insight (Deleuze 1990: 97–8: 102).[13]

Bergson's own attention is focused throughout the text on the two systems. The difference between pure perception and the perception *of* memory amounts to a difference between a difference in degree and a difference in kind. The question of *esprit* is posed in specific terms in the text. First, we have the reality of matter which is made up of the totality of its elements and of their actions and reactions. Second, we have a representation of matter as the measure of the possible action one individuated body has upon another, and this emerges through a process of selection, in which these bodies discard that which has no interest for their needs and functions. For Bergson it is possible, *in one sense*, to say that the perception of some 'unconscious material point' is 'in its instantaneousness . . . infinitely greater and more complete than ours'. This is because it 'gathers and transmits the influence of all the points of the material universe, whereas our consciousness only attains to certain parts and to certain aspects of those parts'. But within the poverty of conscious perception we can locate something positive, namely, 'discernment', and it is here that we can 'foretell spirit'. Now, the reason why Bergson will maintain that it is mistaken to make the intra-cerebral process equivalent to the whole of perception is because he holds that (a) although it is quite true to claim that the details of any perception are moulded upon sensory nerves, the two cannot be rendered identical because there is a 'tendency of the body to movement' and (b) this movement is not the movement studied by abstract mechanics; rather, such movement possesess a unity, an indivisibility, and a qualitative heterogeneity of memory (sensible qualities are contracted with the aid of memory). There is then for Bergson a difference to be upheld between 'exigencies of scientific method', which rightly insists upon subjecting nervous elements which receive and transmit impressions to experiment and calculation, and an account of the real process in terms of a qualitative movement. When there takes place a lesion of the nerves we should not be surprised that perception is diminished:

> That matter should be perceived without the help of a nervous system and without organs of sense, is not theoretically inconceivable; but it is practically impossible because such perception would be of no use. It would suit a phantom, not a living, and, therefore, acting, being.
>
> (1991: 44)

But it is mistaken to infer from this that motor activity functions autonomously and can assume the role of some miraculous generator of our perception of the world. The character of movement differs in accordance with the differences between visual, auditory and tactile impressions. Perceptions do not spring from automatic sensory vibrations but rather from the kind of questions posed to motor activity.

A great deal of neuroscience, and what passes for the philosophy of mind (identity theory, for example), inadvertently produces an idealism of the cerebral substance by severing motor activity from the processes of perception, localizing perception in the sensory nervous elements.[14] But this is an error in thinking: '. . . the truth is that perception is no more in the sensory centers than in the motor centers; it measures the complexity of their relations, and is, in fact, where it appears to be' (ibid.: 46). The view that Bergson wishes to combat most is that which would, in treating sensations merely as signals, in which the office of each sense is to translate homogeneous and mechanical movements into its language, posit on the one hand homogeneous movements in space and, on the other, extended sensations in consciousness (a quantitative outside and a qualitative inside). In contrast with this view Bergson wishes to argue that the identity resides not between the cerebral and the mental or spiritual, but rather between the real action of sensory elements and the *virtual* action of perception (including the motor diagrams).[15] Thus, perception is a part of things (it is not an interior, subjective vision), just as an affective sensation (such as the capacity to experience pain or pleasure) does not spring from the depths of inner consciousness by extending itself into an outer realm (affection is not a simple movement from an inner intensive state to an outer extensity), simply because it is intimately bound up with the modifications that inform the movement of one body with other bodies. The virtual character of the movement of bodies becomes radically complexified when this is thought in terms of duration and in terms of the addition of memory. This virtual being of a body in its becoming certainly has its material conditions in a nervous system – 'The greater the power of action of a body, symbolized by a higher degree of complexity in the nervous system, the wider is the field that perception embraces' (1991: 56) – but this virtuality cannot be rendered reducible to its physical embodiment or incarnated existence by locating it in some specific organ.

Here we anticipate Bergson's unique and challenging account of memory, in particular his claim that because we are so preoccupied by images drawn from space we think that there has to be a place where memories are stored up. If physico-chemical phenomena take place in the brain, if the brain is in the body, and the body is in the air which surrounds it, etc., then surely it follows that the achieved or actualized past must also be 'in' something? It seems obvious that the place this past is 'in' is the cerebral substance conceived as a kind of given receptacle and which only has to be opened in order to allow the latent images to flow into a present consciousness. Bergson argues against this model of the brain as a warehouse that stores accumulated images for two main reasons: first, he holds that the brain, conceived as an image extended in space, is essentially an organ of utility which never occupies more than the present moment and so constitutes along with the rest of the material universe 'an ever-renewed section of universal becoming' (149); second, that there is a survival of the past in itself: the past is that which has ceased to be useful but it does not follow from this that it has, therefore, ceased to be. As difficult as we might find such a proposition, it is an essential claim of Bergsonism and its attempted philosophical demonstration that the preservation of the past takes place not in space but in duration, and so it is 'in' time that we will find the survival of the past. Now, we encounter, in a most challenging manner, the limits of perception: for while any perception, no matter how instantaneous, consists in an incalculable multiplicity of remembered elements, that is, every perception is already memory, we perceive *practically* only that which interests us at any given moment. Thus, the reluctance to admit the integral survival of the past has its source in the 'very bent of our psychical life'. Although the 'pure present' is nothing other than the 'invisible progress of the past gnawing in to the future' (150), the virtual reality of a time-becoming is not perceived by us. Time is invisible and is rendered visible only when the interests of effective action are suspended or relaxed, for example, in unique circumstances such as states of dreams or through special non-utilitarian praxes (forms of art such as painting and cinema, for example). Bergson draws the truly radical conclusion that it is an error to wish to localize present and past perceptions in the brain since these perceptions (and memories) are not in the brain but rather the brain is *in them*. This is a conclusion that we can never expect science to adhere to or acknowledge but which is strictly a matter for philosophical thinking.

Bergson draws to a close the opening chapter of *MM*, in which he has sought to demonstrate the *external* character of perception with the aid of a theory of pure or impersonal perception, by insisting that whereas the difference between matter and its perception is one of degree, the difference between perception and memory is a difference in kind. Demonstrating this difference is the task that occupies him in chapters 2 and 3 of the book. I propose to postpone Bergson's treatment of memory until the next essay, when I shall examine his argument with the aid of Deleuze's writing on the subject. In contrast to other commentators, who expressed deep reservations concerning the issue, Deleuze always championed the significance of Bergson's laying-out of a virtual memory conceived as a pure past, in which psychology has to take the 'leap' into ontology, into the being of time that is peculiar to the being of memory, in order to find its adequate conditions. In the final section of this essay I want now to turn attention to the final chapter of the book and examine the conception of matter Bergson is outlining there.

Beyond idealism

Bergson's achievements in *MM* are manifold. One of them consists in having shown that matter does not need to be placed in the mind (in which it becomes pure ideas) and neither does it need to be equated with simple geometrical extensity. The innovations he has made in the text with respect to *this* issue open the way for a new alliance between science and metaphysics. It is in the final chapter of the book that we gain insight into the nature of this new alliance.

Let's begin thinking about this alliance by returning to the issue of idealism versus realism. Throughout the book Bergson will contest the idea that our representation of the world is something merely relative and subjective. But the precise sense of his contesting of this view needs to be made clear and rendered coherent. It is not that Bergson holds our representation of the world to be an absolute representation, in the sense that it is a faithful reflection of the world as it really is in terms of some identity between thought and being. Representation is essentially subtractive and selective. The relationship between mind and world, however, is not a question of a relation between appearance and reality, or phenomenon and noumenon, but rather of a relation between part and whole. Bergson is, in fact, contesting the relativity of knowledge on two fronts. First, while it is true that our representation of the world is partial and selective we err if we think that this must mean we are trapped within a world of our own making; or, as Bergson puts it, 'that it has, so to speak, emerged from us, rather than that we have emerged from it' (1991: 54). It is in this sense that he is unhappy with the designation of representation as merely relative and subjective (which it is, but only in the specific sense of being a part connected to and bound up with the whole, a whole that is not ever static and simply given). Second, and more ambitiously perhaps, Bergson will contest – and this is the significance of the final chapter of the book – the view that philosophy is restricted to representation and to a relative appreciation of both matter and duration.

Bergson ends up developing his own unique form of realism in the final part of *MM*. On one definition he gives realism is identified with the view that behind ideas is a cause which is not itself an idea. Now, we have seen that Bergson does not, in fact, reduce matter as image to idea. His dissatisfaction with realism arises because of what he regards as its essential mistake, that of reducing the complexity of perception – complex because it involves movement, relations between different components – to the actual physical and mechanical movement of atoms in the brain. If perception and memory are not in the head but distributed across an assemblage of body and movement images unfolded in time, then it makes no sense to ask after the 'where' of perception and memory ('where is the seat of consciousness'?, 'where are memories stored'?). There is no actual physical place of perception and memory since they are not spatialized entities or things. If the realism of science could move in the direction of treating the universe in terms of an acentred system of moving images, in which what would be key to inquire into would be the interactions and transversal communications between components (whether we conventionally designate them as 'atoms', 'material points', or 'centres of force'), then there would be the beginning of a new rapport between the realism of science and metaphysics. The error in treating the brain in reified terms as the material centre of consciousness is that it withdraws the objects which encase it, so also withdrawing in the process the very thing we designate as a cerebral state, simply because it is dependent on the objects for its properties and its actual reality (Bergson 1920: 245). It is in making this move, of privileging the brain as a material centre and treating its operations in terms of a series of discrete states, that realism surreptitiously passes over into idealism where it posits as isolable by right what is isolated only in idea.

In the essay on 'Brain and Thought' in *Mind-Energy* Bergson argues that 'we are always more or less in idealism ... when we have to do with knowledge or science' (1920: 248). This would seem to present a challenge to my argument on a novel alliance being constructed between science and metaphysics. Indeed, one might argue that Bergson is placing an *a priori* limitation on the development of knowledge within science. In other pieces of writing, however, he seems to be arguing against imposing any such *a priori* limitation. This is even hinted at in the final chapter of *MM*. Before exploring this, it might be useful to ask and consider: why does idealism constitute a limit to thinking?

The answer can actually be found in the essay on 'Brain and Thought', in which Bergson suggests that we always encounter idealism in our quest for knowledge of the real. Idealism, according to Bergson, is a limited form of understanding that stops at what is presented 'spread out in space and at spatial divisions' (1920: 247). In contrast, realism regards this display as superficial and treats the divisions the intellect has carved in order to make reality something intelligible for itself as largely artificial. But then how can Bergson so brazenly declare that we are always idealists 'more or less', which means binding thought *to space*, when his entire metaphysics is a metaphysics (and an empiricism) of *duration*? In fact, it would appear that Bergson is drawing attention to the necessity of our idealism in order to spur science on to ever greater and greater realism, resulting in a thinking beyond the human condition, that is, beyond the utilitarian and spatial habits of the intellect. The following passage should bring this out:

> The hypothesis of the realist is therefore only an ideal, whose purpose is to remind him that he has never gone deep enough down in his explanation of reality, and that he must discover more and more fundamental relations between the parts of the real which to our eyes are juxtaposed in space. But the realist cannot help hypostatizing this ideal. He hypostatizes it in the ideas or pictures, set side by side, which for the idealist are reality itself. These ideas become therefore for the realist so many *things* – that is to say, reservoirs of hidden potentialities – and he can now think of the intra-cerebral movement (no longer simple ideas, but things) as enclosing potentially the whole complete world as idea.
>
> (1920: 248)

161

In short, where the scientist goes wrong is not in his or her reliance upon ideas or images of the real but in their reification of them in which the virtuality of a movement, a becoming, or a process, is reduced to an *actuality* and a *materiality*. The virtual is not in space – in matter, for example, including the brain-matter which would then serve as the source or origin of some hidden potentiality – but in time. And time is not a hidden potentiality, it is not hidden from us on account of its possession of secret powers; it is rather that we necessarily hide time from ourselves. For us time is space and even when we desire to have an experience of time our preference is for the remembrance of things past rather than the search for lost time. Precisely what an adequately conceived search for time entails will be addressed and opened up in the next essay.

The contradictions and problems – indeed, the antinomies of modern thinking – stem in large measure from our imposition of symbolic diagrams upon the movement of the real, which serve to make it something uniform, regular and calculable for us, but which also cover it up and comes to constitute our only experience of the real. To break free of these mental habits would make it possible to transcend space without stepping outside extensity. In short, there is no fixed logic or established law that compels us to equate a continuous and diversified extensity with the amorphous and inert space that subtends it, and within which movement can only be constructed in terms of a multiplicity of instantaneous positions. Bergson wants to demonstrate that movement is something absolute, not merely relative. It is important we understand him correctly on this issue. In declaring movement to be absolute and place to be relative (Bergson argues contra Newton explicitly on this point) he is claiming it to be something real and not merely an effect of measurement (the mathematical symbols of the geometrician are unable to demonstrate that it is a moving body that is in motion and not the axes and points to which it is referred). But if motion is merely 'relative' then change must be an illusion (1991: 194–5). The change Bergson holds to be real concerns not merely changes of position among parts of matter. We have, then, a conception of motion studied by mechanics, on the one hand, in which it serves as a mere symbol (a common measure and denominator) and that allows for a comparison of different movements, and, on the other hand, we have the reality of the movements themselves conceived as indivisibles that occupy duration, that is, that link together successive moments of time by a thread of variable quality and which cannot be entirely dissimilar from the continuous heterogeneity that characterizes the syntheses of our consciousness and the contractions of our memory (this is the single time of a virtual multiplicity that is valid for the entire universe).

The fundamental habit of thought that needs to be overcome is the one which would attribute qualities (in the form of sensations) to consciousness and conceive movements (always divisible) in terms of calculable differences of direction and velocity. This gives us two entirely different worlds that are unable to communicate except in miraculous terms. Bergson now argues that while the difference between quality and quantity is irreducible it cannot be located in terms of an opposition between extensive movement and intensive consciousness (sensation): 'do real movements present merely differences of quantity, or are they not quality itself, vibrating, so to speak, internally, and beating time for its own existence through an often incalculable number of moments?' (202). How, for example, do we adequately account for the irreducible nature of two perceived colours except in terms of the narrow duration into which the billions of vibrations that they execute in one of our moments get contracted? If this duration could be lived at a slower rhythm then would we not see these colours pale and lengthen into successive impressions as the rhythm slowed down, almost to the point where they would coincide with pure vibrations? Our habit of construing motion in terms of little more than an accident involving a series of positions and a change of relations among diminutive bodies (atoms or corpuscles) of matter, not only provides us with an inadequate conception of matter and motion, but equally conceals from us the process by which in perception there is always a state of our consciousness and a reality that is independent of us. Bergson reaches the conclusion that just as motion is not without quality, so sensation is not without movement. In order to become quality sensation must go beyond itself, that is, become implicated in movements: 'Motionless on the surface, in its very depth it lives and vibrates' (204).

It is at this point in his presentation that Bergson opens up the possibility of a new dialogue between science and metaphysics, with science rediscovering the 'natural articulations of a universe we have carved artificially', and metaphysics cultivating not an immediate intuition but a *philosophical* one that is able to demonstrate the possibility of thinking beyond our spatial habits of representation (ibid.: 197). Science is able to provide an 'evermore complete demonstration of the reciprocal action of all material points upon each other', so producing an insight into the universal moving continuity between things. We might suppose that all we need to do is to replace the notion of matter with that of force, but this is still insufficient for what is decisive are 'movements and lines of force whose reciprocal solidarity brings back to us universal continuity'. It should, therefore, be the task of a theory of matter to find the reality hidden beneath our customary images of it and that are relative to our needs of adaptation (ibid.: 200). This attempt to think and go beyond our customary images of matter explains why Bergson claims that 'every philosophy of nature' ends by finding the discontinuity that our senses perceive incompatible with the general properties of matter' (201).

In terms of a thinking of duration, however, a gulf remains between the philosopher and the physicist. This is because whereas the philosopher holds that a lived time has its uniquely determined rhythms, the physicist approaches time as a homogeneous medium which in any given interval can store up as great a number of phenomena as is sought. Bergson does not deny that durational time exists in terms of different tensions and rhythms; on the contrary, he goes on to insist upon this very point: 'In reality, there is no one rhythm of duration . . .' (207). It is our obsession with an 'homogeneous and independent Time' which prevents us from being able to conceive of durations of different tensions and relaxations. Bergson's argument, then, is not simply against division; rather, his argument revolves around whether the division is carried out in terms of an actual multiplicity or a virtual one. And this makes all the difference between science and philosophy. It is, in fact, in this part of the argument of chapter 4 of *MM* that we can locate the true character of Bergson's quarrel with Relativity. For example, our lived consciousness experiences a light in terms of a contraction of billions of successive vibrations (in the case of red light, the light with the longest wavelength, this involves 400 billion successive vibrations). Let us now imagine a consciousness which could observe the actual and instantaneous succession of each vibration with each one separated from the next by the 0.002 of a second necessary to distinguish them. This refers in Bergson to the smallest interval of empty time which we can detect and he points out that a simple calculation shows that, in the case of red light, more than 25,000 years would elapse before the operation would be concluded. Now, if we suppose this time to be infinitely divisible the crucial issue to think about concerns whether the division takes place purely in terms of a homogeneous time or in terms of the division of a virtual multiplicity of duration. This gives us the difference between the two multiplicities as one in which the division is either actually infinite because it is taking place in space and which can be carried as far as one pleases, or potentially unlimited because it involves the multiplicity of different tensions and rhythms of lived durations. The difference Bergson draws and insists upon between space and time, between the two multiplicities, between the actual and the virtual, does not expose a naïveté about the 'lived' on his part and it has *nothing* 'phenomenological' about it; the issue is rather bound up with his whole thinking of matter and perception. It is not that Bergson cannot entertain the possibility of there being durations other than the ones we 'actually' live or perceive (this is precisely what he wishes to think and is a concern that lies at the very heart of the philosophical project as he conceives it). His argument is directed against the reduction of these different durations to a homogeneous time that would be the same for everything and everyone. This time is a fiction and an 'idol of language' whose origins lie within our evolved condition as creatures of social action and adaptation. The time of the physicist is, then, a time devoid of qualitative contractions. It is not the time of life but the time of space and infinite and actual divisibility. It is the time of the human condition, a condition it does not know how to think beyond.

Bergson now seeks to make clear the conception of the universe he has arrived at with respect to his thinking on the relationship between matter and perception. There is a difference between the material universe and the different perceptions of it, a difference that lies in the qualitative differentiations of different durations. This difference, however, is not a radical one but one of degree. Only the correct conception of perception, however, is able to demonstrate the difference in these terms. If our consciousness were eliminated the material universe would continue to subsist as it was and matter would resolve itself into numberless vibrations linked together in an uninterrupted continuity 'and traveling in every direction like shivers through an immense body' (208). Now, although such a vision of matter may prove fatiguing for our imagination, since it has been freed from what the exigencies of life compel us to add to it in external perception, it also serves to show us the role played by *conscious* perception (a perception of memory and not simply a pure perception at the heart of things). Perception is one with the universe but also, and at the same time, fundamentally different from it. So even with this new vision of matter, in which the spatial divisibility and homogeneity of matter is shown to be relative to our modes of acting and thinking, Bergson will still maintain the difference between matter and spirit. This is because in his view the whole of extended matter is 'like a consciousness where everything balances and compensates and neutralizes everything else' (219; matter is 'a slumber of the mind', 1965: 238). In other words, all is mechanically actual, a succession of infinitely rapid movements that can be deduced from one another and that are also equivalent to one another. As a neutralized form of consciousness nothing within matter can stand out and escape the law of necessity. Matter is repetition without the difference of an evolution (221). In order for this standing-out to take place there needs to emerge individuated centres of perception.

It is only in the very final pages of the text that Bergson poses the question whether the duration of the material universe can be adequately approached in terms of absolute necessity: 'Can each moment be mathematically deduced from the preceding moment?' (248). In other words, is there a perfect equivalence within the successive moments of duration that characterizes the universe? Although he advances novel movements of thought which demonstrate the need to think beyond both idealism and materialism – contra the first Bergson shows that matter exceeds our representation of it (our understanding does not design the 'plan of nature'), contra the latter he shows that perception overflows the cerebral state (the isolable brain cannot beget representations) – he feels compelled to withhold a concrete and qualitative duration from the universe. What is necessitated and called for, as Bergson soon came to appreciate, is the possibility of thinking a durational life which is immanent to the universe. It is not that a philosophy of life annuls the need to account for the emergence of individuated forms of matter (such as organisms) and the progress of living matter in the direction of increasing complexification; what is needed is an account of the *creative* evolution of life and the universe.

MM is a complicated philosophical text that seeks to both effect a reconciliation between matter and its perception and to demonstrate the difference between them. In this essay I have sought to show the intricate manner in which the text draws upon a notion of the image and also provide insight into how Bergson utilizes the notion of the virtual and conceives it as bound up with *esprit*. Bergson will go on in later works, notably *CE*, to develop further reconciliations (between inorganic and organic life, for example), but also to mark anew the differences. But what is the significance, if any, of the 'and' in the title of Bergson's remarkable book, *Matter and Memory*? The separation of the two phenomena, of matter and memory, is not simply or impatiently to be overturned and quashed. On the contrary, there are reasons, to do with the operations and movements of memory, for upholding the difference. Memory can be granted an *autonomous* vital and virtual life, even though matter and duration are two extreme levels of relaxation and contraction (with memory displaying both features). It is to the strange, creative life of memory I now turn in the final essay of the volume. For Deleuze what is important about *Matter and Memory* is its 'marriage' of radical materialism and pure spiritualism (Deleuze 1995: 48). Indeed, one fruitful way of reading the relation between Deleuze's two books on cinema – the movement image and the time image – is in terms of such a marriage. There is movement in Deleuze's reading of *MM*. He does not simply remain with the movement image of pure perception but makes the move to time on the level of subjectivity. Does this mean that Deleuze becomes, in the end, a phenomenologist?

In essay four the nature of Deleuze's commitment to an ontology of the virtual was shown. Now, we are going to encounter this ontology on a different level, namely, in terms of a Being of memory in which the ontology can be located on the plane of psychology itself but which also entails making a move through and beyond psychology. In following and pursuing this complex move we will also encounter and negotiate some quite extraordinary paradoxes and complications of time.

7

THE BEING OF MEMORY AND THE TIME OF THE SELF

From psychology to an ontology of the virtual

Memory is the real name of the relation to oneself, or the affect on self by self ... Not that brief memory that comes afterwards and is the opposite of forgetting, but the 'absolute memory' which doubles the present and the outside and is one with forgetting, since it is itself endlessly forgotten and reconstituted.

(Deleuze 1988: 107)

Is not Proust's *mémoire involontaire* much closer to forgetting than what is usually called memory? ... Proust's method is actualization, not reflection. He is filled with the insight that none of us have time to live the true dramas of the life that we are destined for. This is what ages us – this and nothing else. The wrinkles and creases are the registration of the great passions, vices, insights that are called on us; but we, the masters, were not home.

(Benjamin 1973: 204, 213–14)

Proust's psychological work attacks psychology itself.

(Adorno 1991: 177)

Bergsonism makes possible a whole *pathology* of duration.

(Deleuze 1991: 118; my emphasis)

Is seeing itself not – seeing abysses?

(Nietzsche, 'Of the Vision and the Riddle', section 1, *Thus Spoke Zarathustra*)

... if it belongs to the essence of the finite subject to be able to be activated as a self, then time as pure self-affection forms the essential structure of subjectivity.

(Heidegger 1997b: 132)

167

Introduction

In this final essay of the volume I want to provide some insight into the innovative nature of Bergson's thinking of memory and into how Deleuze's creative utilization of it produces a Bergsonism that complicates the time of *durée*. I am not able to address all the myriad questions and issues Bergson's treatment of memory throws up. My aim is simply to open things up a little and demonstrate the tremendous significance of Bergson's thinking of memory and the pure past for Deleuze's encounter with time, with the being of time and the time of the self.

At the centre of Bergson's thinking of memory is the notion of the pure past. This is not an easy notion to render either sensible or intelligible. For Deleuze, however, it is Bergson's discovery of the pure past which makes *Matter and Memory* a 'great book', and it requires the resources of a transcendental empiricism to open it up. The pure past concerns a time that has never been lived and so is beyond psychological recollection (the recollection of some former present). It is the pure past which enables us to speak of a *being* of memory and provides us with an ontology of the virtual: the time of the self and its becoming can be shown to be virtual. Deleuze utilizes Bergson's discovery of this past to address a number of quite specific problems, such as: how does time actually pass? How can time be regained and redeemed? How is time put out of joint and how does duration become pathological? These are questions Deleuze addresses in a number of texts ranging across the entire span of his *oeuvre*: in *Bergsonism* the focus is on the paradoxes of time; in *Difference and Repetition* the focus is on the three syntheses of time (the pure past is designated as the second synthesis); and in *Cinema 2* Deleuze draws on Bergson's insights into time-memory to come up with a new image of time, what he calls the 'crystal-image' of time.

Deleuze is committed to *saving* time and to saving it 'for us'. His position, however, is deeply paradoxical since he also holds that subjectivity is never ours but always virtual. The time that is saved (redeemed or regained) is one in which the self necessarily encounters the other (*Autre*). Time can be laid out as a form of interiority, but this interiority requires a complication if we are to adequately present it in its condition of virtuality: for even on the level of interiority it is not simply that time is *in us* but rather that we are, and we become, *in it* (there is a being *of* time). It is also possible to speak of a memory that is not the opposite of forgetting but which is one with it. This is the memory that is endlessly forgotten and reconstituted. All is not lost for time is regained and gained again precisely because it has been lost. Deleuze finds resources within Bergson for complicating time and subjectivity in this way but he also finds it necessary to mine other sources, such as Proust, Nietzsche and Kant. He will bring these figures to bear on Bergsonism but also bring Bergsonism to bear on them, so producing a novel and fertile encounter between Bergson and Kant for example. Deleuze is making a number of highly intricate and complicated moves with respect to his usage of the texts of these thinkers as they bear on the question of time. It is important to try and get right the nature of the inversion he is carrying out: when he approaches time on the level of subjectivity, and says that time is the interiority in which we move and change, he is not grounding time *in* subjectivity or in an intentional consciousness. The *depths* of time that are involved in the exploration of the pure past, and in the 'volcanic spatium' of Nietzsche's eternal return, are beyond the ambit of a simple or straight-forward phenomenology of time (we would do better to speak of a geology of time).

Indeed, phenomenology never really understood the challenge Bergson was laying down to philosophy and psychology in his thinking on time and memory. Phenomenologists like Sartre and Merleau-Ponty identified a set of problems with Bergsonism. For Sartre the problem centred precisely on what he took to be the *lack* of a 'positive description' of the *intentional* character of thought within Bergson's account of the subject. 'Bergsonian dynamism', Sartre writes, 'amounts to 'melodic syntheses without a synthetic act; organizations without an organizing power' (1995: 67; compare Merleau-Ponty 1989: 420–1, 427–8).[1] Sartre speaks of the 'magic' performed by Bergson's *durée* conceived as a 'multiplicity of interpenetration' because, in his terms, it is devoid of the structure of the 'For-itself' (Sartre 1989: 166–7). Moreover, he refuses to accept the reality of the being of the past and breaks with Bergson (and Husserl) on this very issue. For Sartre there is no in-itself of the past, rather we can only make sense of a 'present which *is* its past' (1989: 113). For Sartre, we might say, subjectivity is always ours. In his 1953 study Lyotard notes that phenomenology separates itself from Bergsonism precisely on the question of time, replacing a flowing time in consciousness with a consciousness that constitutes time, which requires, Lyotard notes, conceiving both the past as both 'no longer' and 'now' and the future as a 'not yet' and a 'now' (1991: 113). Phenomenology's break with Bergsonism is clearly, and as Deleuze's careful and inventive reading shows, founded on an inadequate reading of Bergson. Time does not flow for Bergson in any simple sense; there is a contracting time of life, including the time of subjectivity although this is not to be conceived along the lines of a self-constituting subject. Subjectivity is virtual, and this is the challenge Deleuze presents to phenomenology in both the treatment of the syntheses of time in *Difference and Repetition* and in his presentation of a non-organic image of time in *Cinema 2*.[2] Time is never ours, it is always our other, even though it provides the ground of subjectivity and is the only form that does. It is the ground of an *abyss* and the form of the *formless*.

Bergson's conception of memory affords valuable insight into the figuration of the virtual in his work and enables us to see how it is possible to speak of a *Being* of memory. The distinction Deleuze draws between empirical and transcendental memory is designed to open up this ontology of memory.

In *Difference and Repetition* Deleuze suggests that every image of thought presupposes a certain distribution of the empirical (lived, intuited, or sensed experience) and the transcendental (the formal conditions of experience, experience gone beyond). Deleuze seeks a transcendental empiricism that will break with key assumptions of the Kantian project, such as a harmonious accord between the faculties, and a break with common sense and good sense as the natural determinations of thought. Only in this way can philosophy find the means to break with *doxa*. If Kant is the discoverer of the 'prodigious domain of the transcendental' (Deleuze 1994: 135), he does not execute a genuinely transcendental project so as to enlarge and go beyond experience since the transcendental structures or forms are traced from the empirical acts of a psychological consciousness. Kant's thinking remains a psychologism (Husserl had argued this forcefully several decades earlier in his *Formal and Transcendental Logic* but in the context of a set of different concerns).[3] The transcendental must be made 'answerable to a superior empiricism' so that its domain and regions may be explored more freely (1994: 143). For example, we can develop the idea of a transcendental memory in contrast to a purely empirical memory. The transcendental memory serves to show that there is a being of the past presupposed in any adequate conception of the syntheses of time. Whereas empirical memory concerns those things which are quite readily grasped since what is recalled needs to have been seen, heard, imagined, or thought, a transcendental memory seeks to grasp that which from the outset can only be recalled, even the first time of something. It deals not with a contingent past but the being of the past, the past of every time. Memory cannot be addressed without addressing the forgetting concealed within its operations: 'Forgetting is no longer a contingent incapacity separating us from a memory which is itself contingent: it exists within essential memory as though it were the "nth" power of memory with regard to its own limit or to that which can only be recalled' (ibid.: 140). One might suggest that even empirical memory operates on the level of the 'first time'. Deleuze's point, however, is that the empirical or actual workings of memory cannot be adequately explained without recourse to a transcendental memory in which neither recollection nor forgetting are simply contingent capacities. That which moves the soul and perplexes it through being sensed (the being of the sensible) forces the soul to pose a problem and it is the very object of encounter, the sign, which is the bearer of the problem (signs are constituted by contractions, habitudes, and passive syntheses, see Deleuze 1994: 77 for further insight). We don't have to think and we don't think naturally, rather we are forced to think by certain encounters: the problem of memory is one such sign and encounter. Common sense forbids such encounters and resists such a conception of the transcendental. Instead it presents us with an image of thought that does not allow thought to encounter itself and to face the strange, it is a dogmatic (and moral) image (131). Transcendental memory provides us with a case of experience enlarged and gone beyond.

Is Deleuze not renowned for saying that he detests memory? Deleuze's opposition to memory is an opposition to its treatment as merely a former present (recollection), not memory as an event (the memory which Deleuze continued to configure in so many of his texts).[4] To conceive memory in this way requires a new image of time. If time-relations are not visible in ordinary perception – for the psychological reasons Bergson lays out, as we shall see – then a creative time-image is one which makes the time-relations that are irreducible to the present sensible and visible: 'The image itself is a collection (*ensemble*) of time relations from which the present merely flows, whether as the common multiple, as the lowest divisor' (Deleuze 1998c: 53). This means that perception is itself enlarged as we encounter times irreducible to the present, such as the pure past and the alterior future (Deleuze 1998d: 71–2). 'To enlarge perception', Deleuze wrote in an essay on the composer Pierre Boulez and Proust, 'means to render sensible, sonorous (or visible), those forces that are ordinarily imperceptible' (Deleuze 1998d: 72). But how can time be something invisible or imperceptible? Although invisible forces – molecular affections and perceptions – are not time they are intertwined with its passages, intervals, echoes, and tunnels. Deleuze argues that while we readily, and sometimes painfully, perceive what is in time, what we do not perceive is 'time as *force*', or a 'little time in the pure state' (see also Deleuze and Guattari 1994: 189).

What is time in its 'pure state'? And what is the time that is being regained and redeemed? We will now begin our adventure into the virtual nature of the time of our lives and explore the depths of these questions.

From psychology to ontology: Bergson on pure memory

Bergson lays great stress on the importance of approaching existence in terms of a plurality of planes (a plane of action, a plane of recollection, a plane of dreams, etc.).[5] His thinking on memory can only be adequately understood when it is viewed in terms of the presentation of these different planes. What is the 'present'? And what is the 'past'? Neither can be adequately defined in abstraction from the planes of existence and the time of memory and its operations.

Bergson's distinction between two types of memory, habit-memory and recollection-memory, is well-known and even a hostile critic such as Russell could bring himself to credit Bergson with making a major innovation here (Russell 1912: 328).[6] The past is preserved under two distinct forms, namely, motor mechanisms and independent recollections (today the difference is drawn in terms of a distinction between declarative memory, which includes semantic and episodic memory – the knowledge of facts and the recollection of events – and non-declarative memory covering motor skills).[7] This means that the usefulness of memory can manifest itself in different ways, sometimes through action, which will involve an automatic setting in motion of an adaptive mechanism, and sometimes through an intellectual effort when we place ourselves directly in the past and contract elements of it to suit a present requirement. A lived body is one embedded in a flux of time, but one in which it is the praxial requirements of the present that inform its constant movement within the dimension of the past and horizon of the future. If the link with the 'real' is severed, in this case the field of action in which a lived body is immersed, then it is not so much the past images that are destroyed but the possibility of their actualization, since they can no longer act on the real: 'It is in this sense, and in this sense only, that an injury to the brain can abolish any part of memory' (1991: 79; see also McNamara 1999: 42).

In a chapter on Bergson in his recent study of mental Darwinism, Patrick McNamara presents a succint and instructive account of how the contraction of the past takes place as a way of addressing the present. When a level of the past gets contracted the contraction is experienced by present consciousness as an expansion, simply because its repertoire of images and moments of duration are increased and intensified (1999: 37).[8] Memory enables us to contract in a single intuition multiple moments of time. In this way it 'frees' us from the movement of the flow of things and from the rhythm of mechanical necessity. Memory can be triggered by an external cue, but it also has its own rhythms and laws – its own spontaneous 'agenda' (ibid.: 36). The activation of memory involves a series of phases. Firstly, there is a relaxation of the inhibitory powers of the brain; this is followed by a proliferation of memory-images that can flood the cognitive system; and then, finally, there takes place a selection phase in which the inhibitory processes are once again called upon. The proliferation of images opens up a plurality of possible states of affairs and possible worlds; the process of actualization, however, requires contraction take place in order to contextualize a cue and provide an adequate response to the problem in the environment that has been encountered (ibid.: 37). The needs of the present demand that they are addressed and the movement and actualization of the past is rendered subservient to this praxial end. What is selected *may not* be the 'best match or the most optimal solution to a current perception' (38).

Bergson's theory of memory rests on an understanding of these contractions and expansions in relation to the syntheses of past and present. However, our grasp of this theory remains inadequate so long as we do not appreciate its addition of a third term, that of pure memory. As Mullarkey notes, Bergson's 'is a tripartite theory with a concept of "pure memory" alongside those of habit- and representational-memory' (1999: 51). How do we arrive at this third term of memory?

When we learn something a kind of natural division takes place between the contractions of habit and the independent recollection of events that

172

involve dating. If I wish to learn a poem by heart I have to repeat again and again through an effort of learning, in which I decompose and recompose a whole. In the case of specific bodily actions and movements habitual learning is stored in a mechanism that is set in motion by some initial impulse and that involves releasing automatic movements within a closed system of succession and duration. The operations of independent recollection, however, are altogether different. In the formation of memory-images the events of our daily life are recorded as they take place in a unique time and providing each gesture with a place and a date. This past is retained regardless of its utility and practical application. As beings of action and creatures of habit we are always remounting the slope of our past. The past is preserved in itself and, at the same time, contracted in various states of virtuality by the needs of action that are always seated in an actual present. This repetition of memory-images through action merits the ascription of the word memory not because it is involved in the conservation of past images but rather because it prolongs their utility into a present moment. The task of this kind of memory is to ensure that the accumulation of memory-images is rendered subservient to praxis, making sure that only those past images come into operation that can be co-ordinated with a present perception and so enabling a useful combination to emerge between past and present images: 'Thus is ensured the appropriate reaction, the correspondence to environment – adaptation, in a word – which is the general aim of life' (Bergson 1991: 84). An *actual* consciousness is one which simply reflects the adaptation of the nervous system to the present situation. Without this co-ordination of memory-images by the adaptive consciousness the practical character of life would be distorted and the plane of dreams would mingle with the plane of action (in fact, as Bergson fully concedes, the planes do communicate and cannot be treated as isolable dimensions of consciousness and unconsciousness; the issue is rather to be approached in terms of different tensions, different stresses and strains of time).

There is nothing that is mechanical or simply automatic about the interplay between the different planes. The pure past – by which is simply meant the preservation of the past in and for itself, that is, independent of its actualization in a present – is inhibited from freely expressing itself by the practical bent of our bodily comportment, 'by the sensori-motor equilibrium of a nervous system connecting perception with action' (95). Not only is there more than one kind of memory, but memory-images enjoy more than the one kind of existence, being actualized in multiple ways in accordance with their virtual plane of existence: 'Memory thus creates anew the present perception, or rather it doubles this perception by reflecting upon it either its own image or some other memory-image of the same kind' (101). Our life moves – contracts, expands and relaxes – in terms of circuits and it is the whole of memory that passes over into each of these circuits but always in a specific form or state of contraction and in terms of certain variable dominant recollections: 'The whole of our past psychical life conditions our present state, without being its necessary determinant' (148).[9]

What Bergson has uncovered is an autonomous life of memory. Memory is related to bodily habits and to present needs, but it also enjoys a life of its own. This is owing to the fact that the image does not simply represent the *object* of representation or perception (memory does not simply preserve *traces* of things).[10] The essential difference between an object image and a memory-image is as follows: whereas the former is firmly situated in a sequential time, the latter is not; a memory-image is an image that has been removed from the aggregate of images and is now part of a subjective duration. The crucial points to be derived from this insight have been ably articulated by McNamara:

> Memories are not weakened versions of percepts. The contents of memory do not reflect or correspond in any simple way to the things we have perceived throughout our lifetimes. . . . Thus memory cannot reflect the environment, and empiricist approaches to memory must fail.
>
> (41)

In chapter 3 of *MM* Bergson penetrates further into the internal mechanism of psychical and psycho-physical actions in order to show how the past actualizes itself and thus 'reconquers the influence it had lost' (Bergson 1991: 131). He has posited a unity made up of three processes: pure memory, memory-images and perception. The latter is never simply a contact of the mind with a present object but is impregnated with memory-images; in turn these images partake of a pure memory that they materialize or actualize and are bound up with the perception that provide it with an actual embodiment. Pure memory is, like pure perception, a theoretical hypothesis designed to enable a 'superior' empiricism to pursue various lines of inquiry and to overcome the limits of associationism. Pure memory shows us that there is a movement at work in the actualization of memory-images, we do not just pass from one isolated perception or memory to another.[11] Bergson is thus proposing a truly innovative theory of the mind in which there are different planes and in which its operations and movements are approached in terms of virtual-actual circuits. In this respect the movement of the mind is akin to the movement of life itself, involving a passage from the less realized to the more realized, from the intensive to the extensive, and from a reciprocal implication of parts and elements to their juxtaposition (Bergson 1920: 230; see also 203).

In order to develop this conception of the movement of mind and memory it is necessary to dispel a number of illusions, a key one being that memory only comes into being once an actual perception has taken place. This illusion is generated by the requirements of perception itself, which is always focused on the needs of a present. While the mind or consciousness is attending to things themselves it has no need of pure memory which it holds to be useless. Moreover, although each new perception requires the powers afforded by memory, a reanimated memory appears to us as the effect of perception. This leads us to suppose that the difference between perception and memory is simply one of intensity or degree, in which the remembrance of a perception is held to be nothing other than the same perception in a weakened state, resulting in the illegitimate inference that the remembrance of a perception cannot be created while the perception itself is being created or be developed at the same time (1920: 160–1).

It is by recognizing the virtual character of pure memory and its images that we can begin to appreciate that the difference between perception and memory is one of kind and not merely degree; in short, memory has to be credited with its own specific and peculiar modality of being. Memory is made up of memory-images but the recollection of an image is not itself an image (it is closer to a concentrated act of intellectual effort). Bergson insists that 'To *picture* is not to *remember*' (*Imaginer n'est pas se souvenir*) (Bergson 1991: 135).[12] As a recollection becomes actual it comes to live in an image, 'but the converse is not true, and the image, pure and simple, will not be referred to the past unless, indeed, it was in the past that I sought it . . .' (ibid.). The progress of memory consists in a process of materialization.

The relation between memory and perception can be compared to that between an image reflected in a mirror and the actual object in front of the mirror. Such an object can be touched and it allows itself to be acted upon and it acts upon us. In this regard it can be said to be 'pregnant with possible actions'. But although it is pregnant with possibility such an object is always *actual*. The image, by contrast, is necessarily *virtual*, in that while it obviously resembles the object it is also fundamentally different from it since it is not capable of doing what the object does. Far from being chimerical or hallucinatory the virtual image is fully real, though clearly it can be assigned a specific mode of the real. This division between the actual object and the virtual image is what leads Bergson to claim that at every moment of our lives we are presented with two aspects, even though the virtual aspect may be imperceptible owing to the very nature of the operations of perception:

> Our actual existence, then, whilst it is unrolled in time, duplicates itself all along with a virtual existence, a mirror-image. Every moment of our life presents two aspects, it is actual and virtual, perception on the one side and memory on the other. Each moment is split up as and when it is posited. Or rather, it consists in this very splitting, for the present moment, always going forward, fleeting limit between the immediate past which is now no more and the immediate future which is not yet, would be a mere abstraction were

it not the moving mirror which continually reflects perception as a memory.[13]

(1920: 165)

It is because the past does not simply follow the present but coexists with it that we can develop an explanation of paramnesia or the illusion of *déjà-vu*. As Deleuze notes, 'there is a recollection of the present, contemporaneous with the present itself, as closely coupled as a role to an actor' (1989: 79). The illusion is generated from thinking that we are actually undergoing an experience we have already lived through when in fact what is taking place is the perception of the duplication we do not normally perceive, namely, of time into the two aspects of actual and virtual. It is from this idea of a splitting of time, one that requires a complex articulation, that we get the paradoxes of time. To comprehend these paradoxes we need to acquire a better grasp of the notion of a pure past. This is the past in general which every present contracts into particular states of tension and extension but which exists – or rather, insists – as a being of the past.

Bergson insists that what is being duplicated at each moment in our lives into perception and memory is not simply the actual past of particular dates, times and places, but rather a totality. This is a totality, however, which on the plane of actual existence only ever exists in states of contraction and expansion. There is always a virtual whole that is being actualized and such a whole exists in a confused intensive form. In life we never simply re-live the past, that is, it is not a question of rendering actual what is simply virtual and making the two identical. Being is always of the order of difference, which explains why Bergson insists that our memory is always, in the element or dimension of its virtuality, and on the plane of action, a memory of the present and a function of the future.[14] Memory, *qua* the virtual, is a movement of differences and time, by its very nature, is the impossibility of equivalence.

It is in working through the paradoxes of time that Deleuze unravels the nature of the move from a psychology of the present to an ontology of memory. He seeks to show that the reason why we have such difficulty in understanding a survival of the past in itself is because we hold the past to no longer be. The past is precisely that which is without Being. But this is to confuse Being with Being-present. Could we not say that it is, in fact, the present which 'is' *not*? The present can be so characterized because it is always outside itself. Its correct domain is not that of Being but rather that of action and utility. The past, in comparison, is that which no longer acts and in its pure aspects it is also no longer useful. Hence Deleuze writes of it: 'Useless and inactive, impassive, it IS in the full sense of the word' (Deleuze 1991: 55). Moreover, we can go so far as to reverse the ordinary determination of time by saying of the present at every instant that 'it was' and of the past, in its pure dimension, that 'it is' and is 'eternally, for all time' (ibid.; it is with this conception of the pure past that Deleuze will provide a unique rendition of Plato's figuration of time as a moving image of eternity: eternity refers to nothing other than the complicated state of time itself).

It is a truism that 'time goes by', and that this going by is of the essence of time and that the time that has gone by is now in the past. Bergson insists, however, that 'there can be no question here of a mathematical instant' (Bergson, 1991: 137). While we can posit an ideal present as some indivisible limit separating past from future, in the case of the concrete living present this necessarily occupies the duration of a virtual multiplicity. But this is the virtual of the 'present' and not the virtual of a more profound time. It is the depths of time that Deleuze is in search of and seeking to explore with the aid of Proust, of Nietzsche, and of cinema. It is important to get this right if we are to avoid some real confusions. Bergson correctly implicates the time of the present in a virtual multiplicity of duration; Deleuze, however, insists on drawing the distinction between virtual and actual by placing both memory and the pure past in the virtual and perception and the present in the actual.[15] The sense of this move, however, can only be grasped if we adequately understand what is meant by the present here: it refers not to an abstract mathematical point but to the present of our sensori-motor being in which there is always only a past of the present (a former present) and a future of the present. But this gives us only a limited conception of the virtual, we have not as yet accessed its true depths.

Let me continue for now with Deleuze's elaboration of the paradoxes of time found in his treatment of Bergson on the time of memory in the 1966 text. Four essential paradoxes can be articulated:

1   The paradox of the leap in which we place ourselves directly in the onto-logical dimension of the past.
2   The paradox of Being which is found in the difference between past and present as a difference in kind.
3   The paradox of coexistence in which the past coexists with the present in a virtual state.
4   The paradox of psychic repetition in which what coexists with each present is the whole of the past on a plurality of levels of contraction and relaxation.

Not only are these paradoxes interconnected, they also form a critique of another set of propositions which misconceive the nature of time and present us with a badly analysed composite which leads us to believe:

1   that the past can be reconstituted simply with the present;
2   that we pass gradually from one to the other in terms of discrete steps;
3   that the passing of time takes place in terms of a chronological 'before' and 'after';

4   that the activity of the mind takes place in terms of a mere addition of elements, as opposed to changes in level, leaps and the reworking of closed and open systems.

The fundamental illusion that has to be overcome, as one that lies at the heart of all physiological and psychological accounts of memory, is that which holds the past to *be* only once it has been constituted after the present it is the double of (here the mirror image would be nothing more than the simple copy of an original model, an image without real difference). This confusion is unavoidable so long as we do not recognize that the difference between past and present, like that between perception and memory, is a difference in kind.[16] This difference can be explained in the following terms: our present is the 'very materiality of our existence' in the specific sense that it is 'a system of sensations and movements and nothing else' (Bergson 1991: 139). This system is unique for each moment of duration 'just because sensations and movements occupy space, and because there cannot be in the same place several things at the same time' (ibid.). One's present at any moment of time is sensori-motor, again in the specific sense that the present comes from the consciousness of my body: actual sensations occupy definite portions of the surface of my body. The concern of my body, manifest in the consciousness I have of it, is with an immediate future and impending actions. The contrast with pure memory can now be brought into view: one's past is 'essentially powerless' in the specific sense that it interests no part of my body conceived as a centre of action or praxis. No doubt, Bergson notes, it begets sensations as it materializes, but when it does so it ceases to be a memory and becomes something actually lived by passing into the condition of a present thing (139). In order for such a memory to become materialized and rendered an actual present I have to carry myself back into the process by which I called it up, 'at it was virtual, from the depths of my past'. Bergson insists that this pure memory is neither merely a weakened perception nor simply an assembly of nascent sensations. When conceived in terms of the latter, memory becomes little more than the form of an image contained in already embodied nascent sensations. Let us once again clarify the difference between the present and the past: it is because they are two opposed *degrees* that it is possible to distinguish them in *nature* or kind. Deleuze insists: 'To say that the present is the most contracted degree of the past is also to say that it is opposed by nature to the past' (1999: 60). This is because as duration splits it moves in two directions.

With this demonstration of the 'fundamental position of time' we also reach the profound paradox of memory: 'The past is "contemporaneous" with the present that it *has been*' (Deleuze 1991: 58). Deleuze goes on to explain this difficult point:

> If the past had to wait in order to be no longer, if it was not immediately and now that it had passed, 'past in general', it could

never become what it is, it would never be *that* past. ... The past
would never be constituted if it did not coexist with the present
whose past it is. The past and the present do not denote two
successive moments, but two elements which coexist: One is the
present, which does not cease to pass, and the other is the past,
which does not cease to be but through which all presents pass.

(ibid.: 58–9)

If the past is preserved not only in motor mechanisms but also as a pure
past then this means that it is the whole of one's past which coexists with
each present. However, the crucial point concerns how we configure this
whole. Deleuze insists, correctly, in my view, that it can only be conceived in
a way that is faithful to the ontological move Bergson has made (with the
claim that the being of memory is virtual) if it is thought in terms of levels
and sections, each one of which is itself virtual. The universe of memory is a
pluralistic one. The formula that Deleuze comes up with of 'monism=
pluralism' may be a magical one, but it also emerges out of a series of
specific demonstrations concerning the reality of the virtual. In the case of
ontological memory the whole of the past is inseparable from a plurality of
virtual wholes, in which the particular elements of the past in general are to
be thought always in terms of a totality of the past at a specific contracted
or expanded level. On the plane of action recollection-memory is inseparable
from a contraction-memory. Deleuze insists:

> It is not a case of one region containing particular elements of the
> past, particular recollections, in opposition to another region which
> contains other recollections. It is a case of there being distinct levels,
> each one of which contains the whole of our past, but in a more or
> less contracted state.

(1991: 61)

Once we grasp the character of its peculiar and specific reality it becomes
legitimate to grant to the being of the past an extra-psychological range. As
Bergson notes, if consciousness is the characteristic 'note of the present',
then that which is not *actually* lived and no longer active may cease to
belong to consciousness without thereby ceasing to exist. In the domain of
psychology existence cannot be rendered reducible to consciousness. If we
delimit the term in this way then we shall not find it so difficult to envisage
unconscious psychical states whose unconsciousness arises from their
ineffectiveness (Bergson 1991: 141).[17] Just as we may legitimately suppose
that material objects do not cease to exist when we stop to perceive them, so
we can suppose that the past is not simply effaced once it becomes perceived.
This move is crucial to Deleuze's own configuration of the significance of
Bergson's original conception of a pure past as the *being* of time. Deleuze

179

writes, for example: 'What Bergson calls "pure recollection" has no psychological existence. This is why it is called *virtual*, inactive, and unconscious'
(1991: 55). Contra what he takes to be the Freudian conception Deleuze
locates in Bergson's thinking a nonpsychological reality of the unconscious,
that is, the unconscious is not simply another psychological reality, one
situated outside of consciousness.[18] As Bergson himself asks: how is it that
an existence outside of consciousness appears clear to us in the case of
objects but less clear when we speak of the subject? (Bergson, 1991: 142). In
conceiving of a past that preserves itself we have to envisage a past that
while ceasing to be useful has not thereby ceased to be. To properly think
this requires that we make a profound ontological shift: 'Only the present is
"psychological"; but the past is pure ontology; pure recollection has only
ontological significance' (Deleuze 1991: 56).

Virtual memory and a crystal-image of time

Although independent recollection involves a psychological act or intellectual effort, it does so Deleuze claims, only because it has made a genuine
leap in which it places itself at once and directly in the past (the past in
general). It is this ontological past that is the condition of the passage of
every particular present and that makes possible all pasts. It is only once the
leap has been made into the Being of the past that recollections are able to
gradually assume a psychological existence. The past can never be recom-
posed with presents since this would be to negate its specific mode of being.
To elaborate an adequate thinking of time, including the time of the present,
requires that we make the move to an ontology of the pure past. Psychological consciousness is born and emerges into being only when it has found
its proper ontological conditions. Regarding the movement of a virtual
memory Bergson himself provides the necessary insight:

> Whenever we are trying to recover a recollection, to call up some
> period of our history, we become conscious of an act *sui generis* by
> which we detach ourselves from the present in order to replace
> ourselves, first, in the past in general, then, in a certain region of the
> past – a work of adjustment like the focusing of a camera. But our
> recollection still remains virtual . . .
>
> (1991: 133–4)

In short, we cannot reconstitute the past from the present but must make the
move into the past itself as a specific region of being. The past will never be
comprehended or experienced as something past unless we follow and adopt
the movement by which it expands into a present image, and this movement
by definition is something *virtual*: 'In vain do we seek its trace in anything
actual and already realized; we might as well look for darkness beneath the

light' (135). Bergson contends that this is, in fact, one of the chief errors of associationism:

> placed in the actual, it exhausts itself in vain attempts to discover in a realized and present state the mark of its past origin, to distinguish memory from perception, and to erect into a difference in kind that which it condemned in advance to be but a difference of magnitude.[19]
>
> (ibid.)

Because it has substituted a continuity of becoming with a discontinuous and discrete multiplicity of inert and juxtaposed elements, associationism is forced to sacrifice the movement of a becoming and to shut its eyes to pure memory. Its psychology of the mind is an impoverished one as a result.

As McNamara points out, the associationist stance for Bergson is either uninformative or trivial: to say that every idea has some kind of associate tells us nothing about the mechanisms of association:

> Association by resemblance and contiguity surely occurs, but that fact does not explain how recollection is possible. Why, during any given act of recognition or of remembering, does a single memory emerge into consciousness?
>
> (McNamara 1999: 43)

It is only in answering this kind of question that we are offered insight into the actual mechanisms of association and selection.[20] What is in need of explanation is not so much the cohesion of internal mental states but rather 'the double movement of contraction and expansion by which consciousness narrows or enlarges the development of its content' (Bergson 1991: 166). Associationism conceives the mechanism of linkage in terms of a perception remaining identical with itself, it is a 'psychical atom which gathers to itself others just as these happen to be passing by' (165). On Bergson's model of recollection, however, the linkages and connections forged by the mind are not simply the result of a discrete series of mechanical operations. This is because within any actual perception it is the totality of recollections that are present in an undivided, intensive state. If in turn this perception evokes different memories:

> it is not by a mechanical adjunction of more and more numerous elements which, while remaining unmoved, it attracts round it, but rather by an expansion of the entire consciousness which, spreading out over a larger area, discovers the fuller details of its wealth. So a nebulous mass, seen through more and more powerful telescopes, resolves itself into an ever greater number of stars.
>
> (1991: 165–6)

The first hypothesis, which rests on a physical atomism, has the virtue of simplicity. However, the simplicity is only apparent and it soon locks us into an untenable account of perception and memory in terms of fixed and independent states; in short, it cannot allow for movement within perception and memory except in abstract and artificially mechanical terms, with memory-traces jostling each other at random and exerting mysterious forces to produce the desired contiguity and resemblance. Bergson's theory of memory in terms of pure memory, memory-images, and actual perception, is designed to provide a more coherent account of how associations actually take place and form in the mind.[21]

As we have already noted, Bergson is keen to revise our prevailing idea about how recollections are formed and how memory operates. In short, his innovation is to suggest that a recollection is created alongside an actual perception and is contemporaraneous with it: 'Either the present leaves no trace in memory, or it is twofold at every moment, its very up-rush (*jaillissement*) being in two jets exactly symmetrical, one of which falls back towards the past whilst the other springs forward towards the future' (1920: 160). The illusion that memory comes after perception arises from the nature of practical consciousness, namely, the fact that it is only the forward-springing jet that interests it. Memory becomes superfluous and without actual interest. But it is precisely because of this lack of interest and suspension of need that it can reveal itself as a disruptive and creative power, and in spite of its demotion by consciousness to a more feeble form of perception. In insisting that memory is not a simple duplication of an unrolling actual existence, in which it would be possible to live twice through one and the same moment of a history, Bergson is granting the virtual an autonomous power. There is no bare or brute material repetition of the past. The disruptive and creative power of memory works contra the law of consciousness, suggesting that for Bergson there is something illegal or unlawful about its virtuality: 'In a general way, or *by right*, the past only reappears to consciousness in the measure in which it can aid us to understand the present and to foresee the future. It is the forerunner of action' (175). Because consciousness is bound up with an attentiveness to the life of praxis it 'only admits, legally' those recollections which provide assistance to the present action (177). This explains Bergson's interest in the anomalies of the life of *esprit*, one that informs and inspires Deleuze's analyses in the two *Cinema* books, such as deliriums, dreams, hallucinations, etc., which, Bergson insists, are 'positive facts' that consist in the presence, and not in the absence, of something: 'They seem to introduce into the mind certain new ways of feeling and thinking' (151).[22] Contrary to a recent argument Bergson does not have a wholly normative conception of personality; rather, he is actually attempting to give an account of the 'abnormal' workings of the mind.[23]

Deleuze transforms the image of time from an organic one to a crystal one. This image is modelled on Bergson's notion of jets of time, now rendered dissymmetrical, and serves to capture the 'bursting forth of life' in which time splits and divides into two flows, the presents that pass and the pasts that are preserved. Deleuze selects as an image of the thought of time the 'crystal-image' as it provides time with a *ratio cognoscendi*, a non-organic image of the totality of time as one of virtuality:

> What constitutes the crystal-image is the most fundamental operation of time: since the past is constituted not after the present that it was but at the same time, time has to split itself in two at each moment as present and past, which differ from each other in nature, or what amounts to the same thing, it has to split the present in two heterogeneous directions, one of which is launched towards the future while the other falls into the past. Time has to split at the same time as it sets itself out or unrolls itself: it splits in two dissymmetrical jets, one of which makes all the present pass on, while the other preserves all the past . . . We see in the crystal the perpetual foundation of time, non-chronological time, Cronos and not Chronos. This is the powerful, non-organic Life which grips the world.
>
> (ibid.: 81)

The crystal image gives us the following diagram:

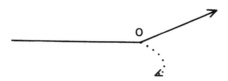

The crystal-image removes time from the realm of presence by complexifying it into regions, sheets and strata of time past and time to come. Between the primordial virtuality of the past and the present as an infinitely contracted past we can locate 'circles of the past' in which each region has its own tones, stresses, singularities, shining points, and dominant problems or themes (ibid.: 99). We see in the crystal the 'transcendental form of time' in this specific sense: such an image provides us with access to time in its constitutive division into a present that is passing and a past which is preserved, and this gives us a transcendental which opens up experience so that it can be enlarged and gone beyond. The depths of time open up a 'continuity of duration' that proves 'irreducible to the dimensions of space' (108).[24] Each region of the past opens up a continuum made up of unique accents, potentials, and critical moments.

The Being of memory provides the ground on which subjectivity is constituted in terms of an auto-affection: 'It is memory that grounds time' (Deleuze

1994: 79). In short, there is for Deleuze a being of time, and it is we who exist and become in time, not time that exists in us, even though time is subjectivity. Hence Deleuze's claim, initially strange when one first encounters it, that 'Subjectivity is never ours, it is time, that is, the soul, or the spirit, the virtual' (82–3). This is a dramatic transformation of the prevailing conception of what the transcendental determination of time carried out by Kant amounts to. Schopenhauer is not an untypical Kantian when he summarizes what is commonly taken to be Kant's Copernican Revolution with respect to time: 'time is nothing but the ground of being in it' (Schopenhauer 1969: vol. 1, p. 34); 'before Kant we were *in* time; now time is in us' (ibid.: 424). Clearly, this is not wrong. It is not a mistaken reading of Kant. Deleuze, however, in bringing a Bergsonism to bear on Kant's thinking of time radically reconfigures its sense:

> Bergsonism has often been reduced to the following idea: duration is subjective, and constitutes our internal life. And it is true that Bergson had to express himself in this way, at least at the outset. But, increasingly, he came to say something quite different: the only subjectivity is time, non-chronological time, grasped in its foundation, and it is we who are internal to time, not the other way round. That we are in time looks like a commonplace, yet it is the highest paradox. Time is not the interior in us, but just the opposite, the interiority in which we are, in which we move, live, and change . . . Subjectivity is never ours, it is time, that is the soul or the spirit, the virtual. The actual is always objective, but the virtual is subjective . . .
>
> (1989: 82–3)

Time is never a simple possession or property of the subject simply because it is in time that the self becomes other to itself, becomes double; both loses itself and creates itself.

In his reading of Kant Heidegger raises the important question: when we say that time is 'in' the subject what is exactly meant? The constant reference to the subjectivity of time yields little, he notes, if it is supposed that time is in the subject as cells are in the brain, which is to posit something being or existing as simply at hand (Heidegger 1997b: 131).[25] He then asks, 'is not the elucidating of the temporal character of the subject first permitted on the basis of the correctly understood subjective character of time?' (ibid.: 132). His response is to develop Kant's thinking on time in the direction of a thinking of auto-affection in which a 'finite subject' is 'able to be activated as a self'. As pure self-affection time forms the 'essential structure of subjectivity'. In other words, the self is not given (not even to itself), it is not something at hand; rather it becomes what it is only through time as the form of self-affection. Heidegger goes on to speak of a finite creature that 'takes things in stride' and which by coming to stand against things and be in 'opposition' to them – positionings of the self which are derived from thinking through the nature of pure affecting – provides us with something like self-consciousness conceived as a consciousness that is able to affect itself and to do so precisely because experience is *absent*, it has to be constituted and can only be so through the form of time (133). The time of the self is primordial, not simply chronological:

> if time as pure self-affection allows the pure succession of the sequence of nows to spring forth for the first time, then this, which springs forth from it and which, so to speak, comes to be discerned for itself alone in the customary 'chronology', essentially cannot be sufficient to determine the full essence of time.
>
> (ibid.: 135)

The self is not 'in' time, it 'is' time as auto-affection. Heidegger suggests that by interpreting time as self-affection Kant achieved a truly radical understanding of time, 'one that was not achieved either before or after' him (1997a: 104). But has Heidegger sufficiently clarified the time of the self as an affective time?

Deleuze's Bergsonism enriches this presentation of the complicated becoming of the self: the self becomes in time and cannot be conceived outside the terms of this becoming. Deleuze is able to effect this transformation of Kant – although time is an interiority this does not mean that time is simply 'in' us – owing to the way in which the virtual allows for a becoming of the self as a becoming 'in' time. The self is time, but equally its subjectivity is never simply its. Time is never simply at hand, never something physical or empirically extant, as Heidegger claims. But the affect on self by self bears on the very character of the passing of time and the *virtual* life of time. A self is never completely actual but always implicated in a virtual life.[26]

The synthesis of the pure past in *Difference and Repetition*

Time can be presented as a series of syntheses and among the most formative syntheses are the passive ones.[27] The synthesis of a living present is constitutive but not active: the synthesis 'is not carried out by the mind, but occurs *in* the mind which contemplates, prior to all memory and all reflection' (ibid.). If we string together a succession of instants we will not arrive at time, whether its creation or destruction, but only its constantly aborted moment of birth. A living present can only be constituted through an 'originary synthesis' that contracts the successive and independent instants into one another. The past and the future belong to this present, not as instants, but rather as dimensions of a *contracted* present. This is how an organism goes from the particular to the universal, from a contracted habit to a field of expectation, and ultimately to a reflexive past of reproduced particularity and a future of reflexive prediction. Deleuze wants to go beyond the level of sensible and perceptual syntheses and penetrate the nature of what he calls 'organic syntheses': 'The passive self is not defined simply by receptivity – that is, by means of the capacity to experience sensations – but by virtue of the contractile contemplation which constitutes the organism itself before it constitutes the sensations' (78). The presentation of time he is developing is by no means restricted to human time – the contraction of habits through an originary contemplation is a feature of organic life in general: 'Underneath the self which acts are little selves which contemplate and which render possible both the action and the active subject' (75).[28] There is a 'primary sensibility' consisting of contractions of the elements (water, air, light, etc.) which is prior to them being sensed. Every organism can be said to be a sum of contractions, of retentions and anticipations. The living present – the present that is the result of contracted habits – is one that passes and has a certain duration that will vary according to different species and organisms. It is possible to conceive of a perpetual present, which would be coextensive with time and amount to an infinite succession of instants. But this, Deleuze argues, is not a *physical* possibility for organisms since their contraction 'always qualifies an order of repetition according to the elements or cases involved' (76–7). It is the thousands of habits which compose us, and which assume the form of contractions, contemplations, anticipations, satisfactions, fatigues, and so on, that constitute the basic domain of passive syntheses. It is the 'illusions of psychology' which prevent our developing adequate insight into this domain of syntheses because it insists upon making a 'fetish of activity' (73).

Deleuze goes on in this part of *DR* to explore the nature of two further syntheses of time, the time of the pure past and its transcendental synthesis, the 'profound passive synthesis' of memory as the ground of habit, and the time of the future as the time of the caesura. I shall come back to this third synthesis later in the essay.

Although the first synthesis of time can be said to be 'originary' it is nonetheless intra-temporal. If we say that such a synthesis constitutes time as a contracted present, as a present which *passes*, then we reach the paradox of the present which can only be resolved by positing a second synthesis of time in which the first takes place. The paradox can be put as follows: if time is to be constituted in the way the first synthesis has opened up then this constitution of time must pass in the time which is constituted. How does the present pass? What prevents the time of a contracted present from being coextensive with time itself? Initially, it seems as if the past was simply the time that is trapped between two presents, the one that it has been and the one in relation to which it can now held to be past. The past itself is the domain not of a particular 'has been' but of a general 'was' (following

Husserl's terminology it is necessary to distinguish, Deleuze says, between 'retention' and 'reproduction' (80)). At this point, however, Deleuze insists on drawing a distinction between *active* and *passive* syntheses of memory. What is the nature of this distinction?

So far in his presentation of the syntheses of time Deleuze has opened up the possibility of there being a being of the past, that is, the past in general. From the perspective of the reproduction involved in memory it is this region of the general past which makes possible any particular present by solving the paradox of the passing of time (there has to be a time for time to pass into). It is this which allows for the representation of time to take place: if the past in general is the element in which each former present preserves itself, then any former present can find itself represented in the present present (for example through relations of resemblance and contiguity established by laws of association). This time of representation is the time in which memory is always 'of' the present: 'It is of the essence of representation not only to represent something but to represent its own representativity' (ibid.). Such a memory of the present operates on the level of an *active synthesis* providing both a reproduction of the former present and reflection of the present present. This active synthesis is founded on the passive one of habit which constitutes the general possibility of any present, but, more profoundly, it is founded on the *passive synthesis* which is peculiar to memory itself. This further aspect of the second synthesis of time can only be adequately comprehended in the transcendental terms of a pure past.

With regard to the passive synthesis of memory it is not enough to say of the past that it is simply a present that once was: 'we are unable to believe that the past is constituted after it has been present, or because a new present appears. If a new present were required for the past to be constituted as past, then the former present would never pass and the new one would never arrive' (81). It is the discovery of a pure past as a transcendental synthesis – that is, as a necessary condition of time conceived as synthesis – and of its constituent paradoxes that makes *MM* such a great book, says Deleuze. If the positing of such a pure past is transcendentally legitimate, then we can say that the past is not simply a dimension of time but the synthesis of all time, since it is the synthesis which allows for the (virtual-) actual passage of time: 'Habit is the originary synthesis of time, which constitutes the life of the passing present; memory is the fundamental synthesis of time which constitutes the being of the past' (80). No doubt, we live in the present, but this is a contracted present. There could not be a present without the passive syntheses of habit and memory and which entail different distributions of repetition and contraction.

In the case of the two passive syntheses of habit and memory we find a different contraction of the present. In the case of habit the present 'is the most contracted state of successive elements or instants which are in themselves independent of one another' (Deleuze 1994: 82). In the case of memory, however, the present designates something quite different, namely, the most contracted degree of the whole of the past. This means that the present is the 'maximal contraction of all this past which coexists with *it*' (ibid.). If this is the case, then it must follow that the whole past coexists with itself in varying formations of contraction and relaxation. As Deleuze argues, the present can only become the most contracted degree of the past which coexists with it if we suppose this to be the case: the past coexisting with itself in a variety of forms of contraction and relaxation and at an infinity of levels (this, he says, is the meaning of Bergson's metaphor of the cone presented in figure 5 in *MM*, 1991: 162; see also 194 below). Deleuze asks us to consider the repetition that characterizes a life. Here we find presents succeeding one another and encroaching on one another. However, although the potential opposition and conflicts between these presents have to be taken to be in a real sense very strong, there is also the impression that each of them is also playing out '"the same life" at different levels' (ibid.: 83). For Deleuze this provides us with a notion of 'destiny', which is not to be understood simply in terms of step-by-step deterministic relations between succeeding presents that inform our order of represented time; rather, it implies a more complicated conception of time, an enfolding time involving 'actions at a distance, systems of replay, resonance and echoes, objective chances, signs, signals, and roles which transcend spatial location and temporal successions' (ibid.). Our lives play out the same story but never at the same level (there is difference within repetition), and freedom consists precisely in 'choosing the levels':

> The succession of present presents is only the manifestation of something more profound – namely, the manner in which each continues the whole life, but at a different level or degree to the preceding, since all levels and degrees coexist and present themselves for our choice on the basis of a past that was never present.
>
> (ibid.)

Deleuze goes on to forge a distinction between the empirical self and the noumenal self to account for this freedom: 'what we live empirically as a succession of different presents from the point of view of active synthesis is also *the ever-increasing co-existence of levels of the past within passive synthesis*'. The difference can also be presented in terms of the difference between two repetitions and two modes of life, the material and the spiritual. However, although there is an important link with Kant, these differences cannot be construed in straightforwardly Kantian terms since it is clear that for Deleuze the empirical self and the virtual self are both real and both exist in contracted time. It is not that one is a mere phenomenal appearance in time and the other is the thing-in-itself existing outside time. The difference between them is that one is everyday, the other is rare; one is ordinary, the other is extra-ordinary.[29]

If Bergson has provided the theoretical resources which enable us to comprehend the pure past, and to articulate an adequate conception of the passage of time, then it is Proust (and Nietzsche, as we shall see) who shows us how it is possible to save time 'for us'. The eternity of time that Deleuze invokes and appeals to is that of time's *virtual* being, which is brought to life in the work of art and its search for lost time and the regaining of time (Deleuze 2000: 62–3: 87).[30] In both Bergson and Proust we are presented with a being of the past as a being of the virtual; in the case of Proust we get the formula, 'Real without being actual, ideal without being abstract' (Proust 1983: vol. 3, p. 906; cited in Deleuze 2000: 58; 1991: 96; 1994: 208). For Deleuze, however, the difference between them is that while it is enough for Bergson to comprehend this pure past, for Proust as an artist it is also necessary to explore how such a past can be 'saved for us' (2000: 59; see also 1991: note 16: 126 and 1994: 84–5 and the 'Note on the Proustian experiences' in the same text, 122). Deleuze makes it clear that the task is not one of penetrating the in-itself of the past in order to reduce it to the former present it once was or to the current present in relation to which it is now past. Rather, the artist presents us with the past, *qua* virtual being, as an *event*. In the case of Proust this concerns a Combray reappearing in the form of a past that was never present: 'Combray as cathedral or monument' (Deleuze and Guattari 1994: 168; see also Deleuze 1994: 85). Combray 'rises up in a pure past . . . out of reach of the present voluntary memory and of the past of conscious perception' (2000: 61). It is, Deleuze insists, '*within* Forgetting' that Combray returns in the form of a past that was never present, 'the in-itself of Combray' (1994: 85). Or, as the novelist writes: 'A moment of the past, did I say? Was it not perhaps very much more: something that, common both to the past and to the present, is much more essential than either of them? . . . a fragment of time in the pure state' (Proust 1983: 905; see also 1087 on the 'different planes' of duration).[31]

How does this actually work? To adequately comprehend this we have to reflect on the complex mechanism of reminiscences which initially strikes us as being an associative one. On an associative model we would say that there is a resemblance between a present and a past sensation, as well as a contiguity of the past sensation with an experienced whole which gets revived as a result of the effect of a present sensation. This would lead us to say that the flavour of the madeleine is 'like' the one which was tasted at Combray, the place which is now revived as the place where it was tasted for the first time. However, Deleuze insists that the task is not as simple as either noting an associationist psychology at work in Proust or discarding such a psychology. Rather, we need to ask from what perspective the instances of reminiscence transcend associative mechanisms and from what perspective they do in fact draw on such mechanisms. In this way we will be able to appreciate the profound discovery of the pure past, or the disclosure of a fragment of time in its pure state: 'Combray rises up, not as it was experienced in contiguity with the past sensation, but in a splendor, with a "truth" that never had an equivalent in reality' (2000: 56). The associative mechanism provides only the occasion for something much more profound than the linkage of past and present sensations, namely, the 'joy of time regained' which overflows all associative mechanisms.

The pure past is unlocatable and invisible so long as we remain on the level of either conscious perception or voluntary memory. On the level of perception the madeleine has only an external relation of contiguity with Combray, while on the level of voluntary memory Combray can only be external to the madeleine 'as the separable context of the past sensation' (Deleuze 2000: 60). It is the characteristic of involuntary memory to inter-nalize the context, that is, to make the past context inseparable from the present sensation: '*The essential thing in involuntary memory is not resem-blance, nor even identity, which are merely conditions, but the internalized difference, which becomes immanent*' (ibid.; compare Deleuze 1994: 122). The art of the novelist presents us with a Combray as it could never be experienced: an involution in which two different objects, the flavour of the madeleine and Combray with its qualities of colour and temperature, are enveloped within one another and their relation made internal and resonant. Of course, this presents us with a new and strange paradox: the being of the pure past (time as eternity) is wholly implicated in the very passage of time. The time that passes constitutes the 'ground' on which the truths of time are to be constructed and created. This is why the search for lost time, understood first and foremost as a search for truth, must always remain a search for and of time: 'truth has an essential relation to time' (2000: 15). Nevertheless, it is vital that the past which is sought is the *being* of the pure past. This explains why the search for lost time cannot be carried out by voluntary memory simply because this memory fails to recognize the past's being as past: its past is always relative to the present which it has been and to the present with respect to which it is now past. It thus recomposes the past only with different presents. [32]

Our sense of time has been dramatically transformed: it is not in us but we are in it. Time is subjectivity but this subjectivity is never simply ours (it is virtual). This amounts to a transformation of Kant through a funda-mental aspect of Bergsonism. Indeed, in effecting this transformation Deleuze draws a parallel between Bergson and Kant that opens up the possibility of establishing a novel rapport between them. How is this possible? This will be explored in the final section of the essay.

The depths of time

> . . . duration is no longer actual but past and constantly sinks deeper into the past.
>
> (Husserl 1964: 50)

Let us consider the main criticism levelled at Bergsonism: how can the present ever actually be if it is simply the expression or realization of what has already been? We can only endeavour to point out the limited conception of the movement of time implied in this critique. The most common criticism made of Bergson is that he has failed to distinguish between 'the being of nature' of the past from the 'intentional being' of the same past. Such a criticism clearly misses everything that it at stake in the innovations Bergson effects with respect to accounting for the passing of time in terms of the virtual and the actual, the ontological and psychological, the past and the present: these differentiations are designed precisely to enable us to comprehend the distinction he is alleged to have overlooked *and* to comprehend the very notion of an intentional being of the past in the act of complicating it ('subjectivity is never ours').

John Mullarkey is one eminent commentator who expresses an unease over Bergson's theory of memory and he adds a criticism of his own. Bergson's realism about the pure past – a realism that is required, he correctly notes, in order to mark an ontological difference between perception and memory – leads one to wonder, he argues, how the present, 'being in part the actualized image of the past, can be anything more than the realisation of some stored-away memory' (Mullarkey 1999: 53). However, the argument that Bergson has, in effect, negated or obliterated the present by folding it back within a virtual memory, in which it then becomes indistinguishable from a rearrangement of something *pre-existent*, is in danger of neglecting everything he says about the movement of time-memory (involving contractions, expansions, and relaxations), a movement that determines that the junction of 'past' and 'present' happens in terms of an intersection of planes (planes of contemplation, of action, of dream-images, states of reverie, etc.). It is not, however, simply that Mullarkey is guilty of reifying the pure past by treating it as if it could exist independent of the contractions and expansions that actualize its virtuality, simply because Bergson's thinking stresses the need to allow for such a pure past.

For Mullarkey the notion of a pure past represents something mysterious and ethereal. He wishes to demote memory and accord primacy to perception in which our varying 'attention to life' is to be conceived not in terms of different types of memory but rather in terms of different types of perception. If, he argues, we posit a multiplicity of presents each with a correlatively different past and future, then the need to appeal to a pure past, a virtual memory, or 'any other ethereal entity' disappears. However, the effect of this privileging of perception and the present in terms of an actual multiplicity – albeit a complicated one – is to render Bergson's contribution to our thinking of time nugatory. It deprives the pure past of any ontological reality. A multiplicity of actual presents has the effect of situating the self purely on the level of psychology. Although we find it very difficult to think an immanence of the past there is nothing intrinsically 'mysterious' about it, as is claimed (Mullarkey 1999: 53). It is, in fact, only by adopting the psychological plane as the sole and privileged plane of existence that such a judgement of the past (of time itself) can be made. It is from the perspective of psychology and the actual that the ontological past and the virtual are deemed to be impotent or, in this case, non-existent. We must seek to demystify the notion of a pure past without forsaking anything of its strange and truly uncanny being. It is admittedly an extremely difficult notion to think; reasons can be given, however, to explain why it is so difficult for us to acknowledge the reality of a pure past and to make the ontological leap.

Let's remind ourselves of Bergson's response to the question concerning time, in which an adequate response requires that one places oneself in time's abyss: In order to pass on, the present must be both past and present at the same time. This means that the past does not simply follow the present that it is no longer, rather it coexists with the present it was. Deleuze puts it like this: 'The present is an actual image, and *its* contemporaneous past is the virtual image, the image in a mirror' (1989: 79). Time is not simply a succession of passing presents, and time does not only become past time when a new present arrives. To demonstrate this requires that we adequately determine the *transcendental* form of time. The empirical form of time – which Deleuze analyses in the 'cinema' books in terms of the movement-image – refers to a successive present existing in an extrinsic relation of before and after, in which the past is only ever a former present and the future only ever a present to come. To determine adequately the transcendental form of time requires that we go beyond time as an empirical progression and conceive time out of joint and in its pure state (1989: 271). This is what the crystal-image enables us to see, namely, the *seeds* of time, that is, not a succession of presents, and not simply intervals or wholes of time, but rather time's 'direct presentation' in the form of a constitutive division into two, a present which is passing and a past that is preserved. Deleuze has utilized Bergson's discovery of the pure past to arrive at a time-image which interrupts the flowing continuity of duration and introduces dis-locations into it (duration becomes pathological). Relations between past and present are no longer linear or chronological. It is on the basis of this clarification of empirical and transcendental forms of time that Deleuze's distribution of past and present in accordance with actual and virtual planes should be understood. The present is sensori-motor (psychology), the past can be said to be 'pure' in that it emerges out of the passing of time and enters into its own specific region of Being (ontology). The crystal-image of time is designed to demonstrate this. Such an image is not time; rather, the crystal enables us to gain an image of it (the foundation of time as both Cronos and non-Chronos). The crystal renders visible the invisible reality of time, that is, 'its differentiation into two flows, that of presents which pass and that of pasts which are preserved' (Deleuze 1989: 98). On the level of Cronos the difference between past and present is simply a difference in degree (the present being the most contracted level of the past). However, situated on the level of non-Chronos we see that the difference between the two is a difference in kind, like that between perception and memory, actual and virtual. For now we are dealing with a time (pure past, open future) which is no longer subordinated to an empirical succession of passing presents. This transfiguration of planes provides us with a more adequate conception of becoming:

> The before and the after are then no longer successive determinations of the course of time, but the two sides of the power, or the passage of the power to a higher power. The direct time-image does not appear in an order of coexistences or simultaneities, but in a becoming as potentialization, as series of powers.
>
> (1989: 275)

Becoming is that which transforms an empirical sequence into a series, or rather a 'burst of series'.

The ontological move which Deleuze proposes to make on the basis of this insight into time is a truly novel one. This comes out in his conception of the pure virtual image. Conceived as a small or relative circuit, the actual and its virtual (since the virtual is always both of the actual and of itself) expands into ever deeper circuits of virtuality. The virtual image that is peculiar to memory has to be distinguished from its allied images. Although things like recollection-images and dreams are variants of virtual images they exist as actualized images in psychological states of consciousness. Furthermore, while 'they are necessarily actualized in relation to a new present, in relation to a different present from the one that they have been', and proceed in terms of a chronological succession, the virtual image in its pure state cannot be defined simply in accordance with a new present in relation to which it would be past (Deleuze 1989: 79–80). The virtual images that are specific to the sphere of the mental (dreams, recollection-images) exist, therefore, only in an actualized state and in relation to some kind of present. By contrast, the virtual image that is pure recollection is the pure virtuality which does not need to be actualized in order to be. This is because 'it is strictly correlative with the actual image with which it forms the smallest circuit which serves as base or point for all the others. . . . It is an actual-virtual circuit on the spot, and not an actualization of the virtual in accordance with a shifting actual' (ibid.). The pure virtual image has to be defined not in accordance with a new present in relation to which it would be relatively past, but rather 'in accordance with the actual present *of which* it is the past, absolutely and simultaneously', and although it is specific it is also part of the past in general and receives its being there. Time-memory exists as *both* a memory of the present and as a pure past. Deleuze notes: 'What causes our mistake is that recollection-images, and even dream-images or dreaming, haunt a consciousness which necessarily accords them a capricious or intermittent allure, since they are actualized according to the momentary needs of this consciousness' (80). We are thus able to explain the confusions that take place in our heads between the real and the imaginary, the present and the past, the virtual and the actual: '. . . the confusion of the real and the imaginary is a simple error of fact, and does not affect their discernibility: the confusion is produced solely in "someone's head"' (69). But there is also an indiscernibility of past and present, actual and virtual, imaginary and real, which is *not* produced in the head but which is an objective characteristic of images which are by nature double: 'there is no virtual which does not become actual in relation to the actual, the latter becoming virtual through the same relation . . .' (ibid.). The actual and the virtual are, therefore, in continual exchange, and in this exchange we see the double existence of the crystal as something both solid and opaque: 'When the virtual becomes actual, it is then visible and limpid, as in the mirror or the solidity of the finished crystal. But the actual image becomes virtual in its turn, referred elsewhere, invisible, opaque and shadowy, like a crystal barely dislodged from the earth' (70). The crystal is both mirror and seed.[33]

Deleuze's conception of the virtual and actual involves a quite specific and precise interpretation of Bergson's cone of memory:

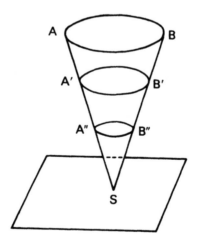

While point S denotes the actual present, we cannot treat it strictly as a point simply because it includes the past of this present, a virtual image that doubles the actual image. Moreover, the various sections of the cone, such as AB, A'B', etc., are not for Deleuze psychological circuits to which recollection-images would correspond, but rather purely *virtual* circuits with each one containing the whole of the past as it is preserved in itself (pure recollection). Psychological circuits can only come into operation by being actualized, and this involves leaping from S to a section of the cone; in short, it involves, an actualization of something that is purely virtual. It is the relative circuits between present and past that refer back, on the one hand, to a small internal circuit between a present and its own past (an actual image and its virtual image), and, on the other, to ever deeper and deeper virtual circuits which put into movement the whole of the past. So Deleuze writes:

> The crystal-image has these two aspects: internal limit of the all the relative circuits, but also outer-most, variable and reshapable envelope, at the edges of the world, beyond even moments of the world. The little crystalline seed and the vast crystallizable universe: everything is included in the capacity for expansion of the collection constituted by the seed and the universe. Memories, dreams, even worlds are only apparent relative circuits which depend on the variations of this Whole.
>
> (1989: 80–1)

One might suggest that Deleuze is seeking to give us a quite different lesson on the past and memory-recollection from the one that we encounter in Wittgenstein at the end of his *Philosophical Investigations*: 'Man learns the concept of the past by remembering.' Along with almost all other authors on the subject Wittgenstein can give us only the plane of psychology, memory and the past as recollection (in spite of his clearly stated and well-known anxieties about 'psychology'). It is necessary to render Wittgenstein's insight uncanny, so that the self which learns is doubled and de-psychologized: 'To learn is to remember; but to remember is nothing more than to learn . . .' (Deleuze 2000: 65). What we learn are the profound and uncanny 'truths' of time, and such truths can only be had by taking the leap into ontology. We will not learn of the past by simply engaging in acts of recollection or reminiscence.

The virtual image of time (pure recollection) does not denote a psychological state or a consciousness; rather, 'it exists outside of consciousness, in time, and we should have no more difficulty in admitting the virtual insistence of pure recollection in time than we do for the actual existence of non-perceived objects in space' (80). We need to learn to look for the past where it is, in time. The creative invention of a pure past requires the unique powers of the artist – including the artist in us; in ordinary, actual existence we necessarily live the past in disfigured form. We bear the scars of the past more than we eat its fruit in any pure form. But even here, and especially here, the reconstitution and working-through of the past calls upon an art of existing, a task of *germinal* life, in which these scars bear their own fruit. Scars and wounds are the signs and events of the fact that we have become in time. For beings like ourselves who are creatures of the present and of adaptation it is extremely difficult to inhabit the virtual plane of existence except now and again in rare or quite specific instances. Necessarily we appraise the being of the past from the perspective of a psychological present. Bergson's thinking on time explains why this is the case. But when we do this, reducing the past to recollection, we debase it (see Deleuze 1989: 124). The fact that we find it hard to make the leap into the past, since it is only the ever-onward jet of time which interests us – an interest also explained by Bergson's conception of time and how it passes – leads us to suppose that the past is impotent, nothing more than a dead time. But what if this dead time is full of *life*? (pure reserve or the life of the event).

'We are born in a crystal, but the crystal retains only death, and life must come out of it. . . .' (Deleuze 1989: 86). In truth, death and the dead never go away, it is simply that we forget them and for perfectly understandable reasons. Why this act of bringing back the dead and buried and the regaining of time? But then, where does life begin and death end? And what of the future – is a leap not also involved here? We have to leave the crystal at the same as we plummet into the depths of time, and in order to open up time as an event of individual and collective freedom it is sometimes necessary to mine and undermine the depths of the past. The pure past is, in fact, *contemporary* with the future:

> The child in us, says Fellini, is contemporary with the adult, the old man and the adolescent. Thus it is that the past which is preserved takes on all the virtues of beginning and beginning again: it is what holds in its depths or in its sides the surge (*l'élan*) of the new reality, the bursting forth of life (*le jaillissement de la vie*) . . . the present that passes and goes to death, the past which is preserved and retains the seed of life, repeatedly interfere and cut into each other.
>
> (92)

The struggle against entropy is not a struggle against the mere passing of time, a mad desire to mummify the living against the forces of decay and decomposition, a clinging on to life out of a fear of death and obliteration, but a struggle for the future. This is a struggle or battle that is necessarily born out of our becoming in time.

Deleuze's profound interest in cinema and its powers of creative fabulation arises out of his attachment to the extra-ordinary discoveries of Bergson's *Matter and Memory*. Modern cinema adopts as its basis the collapse and break-up of the sensori-motor schema, such as pure optical and sound sequences and situations in which expected actions and reactions are suspended or complexified. It is the motor habits of the brain that compel us to respond to crises and shocks in terms of cliché. Deleuze defines a cliché in accordance with Bergson's insights into the character of perception:

We have schemata for turning away when it is too unpleasant, for prompting resignation when it is terrible and for assimilating when it is too beautiful. . . . Now this is what a cliché is. A cliché is a sensory-motor image of the thing. As Bergson says, we do not perceive the thing or the image in its entirety, we always perceive less of it, we perceive only what we are interested in perceiving, or rather what it is in our interest to perceive, by virtue of our economic interests, ideological beliefs and psychological demands. We therefore normally perceive only clichés.

(1989: 20)

He then goes on to speak of a 'civilization' of the image and of the cliché. Only when the sensory-motor schemata is jammed or broken can a different type of image appear. In key aspects modern cinema is fundamentally Bergsonian since it does not present us simply with a psychological memory made up of recollections but with time-images that cut across chronological time, opening up 'a beyond of psychological memory' (1989: 109). With Bergsonism we are already on the level of the third synthesis of time: time unhinged and put out of joint. Speaking of the Bergsonian-inspired films of Alain Resnais, Deleuze writes:

In Resnais too it is time that we plunge into, not at the mercy of a psychological memory that would give us only an indirect representation, nor at the mercy of a recollection-image that would refer us back to a former present, but following a deeper memory, a memory of the world directly exploring time, reaching in the past that which conceals itself from memory. How feeble the flashback seems beside explorations of time as powerful as this . . .[34]

(Deleuze 1989: 38–9)

The straight line of time: Nietzsche and Kant

'Stop, dwarf!' I said. 'I! Or you! But I am the stronger of us two – you do not know my abysmal thought! That thought – you could not endure!' . . .
　'Everything straight lies', murmured the dwarf disdainfully. 'All truth is crooked, time itself is a circle'.
　'Spirit of Gravity!' I said angrily, 'do not treat this too lightly! Or I shall leave you squatting where you are, Lamefoot – and I have carried you *high*!'
　(Nietzsche, 'Of the Vision and the Riddle', 1969: section 2)

Deleuze refers to the third synthesis of time as the pure and empty form of time, associating it with the elusive time of Aion, with Nietzsche's eternal

197

return, and with Kant's straight line of time.[35] The use to which Deleuze puts Nietzsche's thought-experiment of eternal return in *Difference and Repetition* is quite extraordinary: it constitutes the highest possible thought of difference and repetition, a thought beyond the moral law and beyond the laws of nature which govern only the surface of the world. Here there is only space to take a cursory look at the way in which Deleuze constructs it as a third synthesis of time and to disclose something of the secret of its intimate rapport with the second synthesis.

There is desire or Eros in our exploration of the pure past. The present exists, the past insists, and the vertigo we undergo with time presents us with a persistent question concerning the nature of this desire, a 'rigorous imperative to search, to respond, to resolve' (Deleuze 1994: 85). If Eros allows us to 'penetrate the pure past in itself', the 'virginal repetition which is Mnemosyne', from where does it gain its power (a power of the 'three metamorphoses')? [36] The power of memory's fiancé comes from the third synthesis of time conceived as a belief in the future: all time is saved for its sake.[37] It is the time of the future that undoes time's circle, shatters the crystal, and takes the self beyond any coherence since the self must become equal to the unequal itself.[38] It is the future which is addressed and appealed to in the erotic effect of memory. There is, then, a secret intimacy between the pure past and the future. Only the 'to-come' comes back or returns again and again (at the gateway of the 'moment' [*Augenblick*] which offers us time as eternity and an eternity *of* folded time). If we can posit an irreducible past, a past that is neither a former present nor a present present, then the alterity of the future speaks of a future that is not a simply a future of the present. Upon the straight line time can be seen to run in two opposite directions (Zarathustra's 'lanes'), backwards and forwards, with both presenting themselves as eternities. Deleuze refuses to accept the opposition between (ancient) cyclical and linear time as a pertinent one simply because the modern time of the straight line is not linear or chronological in any simple sense; it is *both* Cronos and non-Chronos. At any 'moment' the time of the self can be unhinged and time put out of joint. It is for this reason that Deleuze approaches eternal return as the time of the caesura in which the past and the future do not denote empirical determinations of time, but are rather formal aspects of time conceived as the most 'radical form of change' (the form of change which does not itself change, Deleuze 1994: 89).

To regain time is to redeem time: this is a teaching that has been taken away from Nietzsche and denied him. When Deleuze first begins to develop a reading of Nietzsche's doctrine of eternal return in terms of a doctrine of time – time as becoming – in *Nietzsche and Philosophy* (1962), he does not credit eternal return with its own unique synthesis. It is read on the level of the second synthesis, that is, in terms of the problem of time's passage (how does time pass?). It is in terms of this synthesis that one can productively read the parable on 'Redemption' in *Thus Spoke Zarathustra* where the task is to show how the will can be emancipated from its revenge against time: *es war* or 'it was', time as the great devourer (time as blind justice). Deleuze writes:

> That the present moment is not a moment of being or of present 'in the strict sense', that it is the passing moment, *forces* us to think of becoming, but to think of it precisely as what could not have started, and cannot finish, becoming.
>
> (1983: 48)

The 'foundation' of eternal return is to be found in the thought of pure becoming. What is the being of becoming? Deleuze answers that 'returning is the being of that which becomes', and cites the well-known section 617 of *The Will to Power*: 'That everything recurs is the closest approximation of a world of becoming to a world of being – high point of the meditation.'

The problem of the meditation needs to be formulated in a specific way. How can the past be constituted in time? How can the present pass? 'The passing moment could never pass if it were not already past and yet to come – at the same time as being present.' In order for it to pass the moment must be simultaneously present and past, present and yet to come; a present can't wait for a new present in order to become past, there would be no past and time would never pass. The eternal return is thus a response to the problem of passage: 'The synthetic relation of the moment to itself as present, past and future grounds its relation to other moments' (ibid.). What returns is not the 'same' but the form of time, and it is the very passing of time which is being affirmed in the thought-experiment of eternal return. The eternal return of becoming speaks only of the becoming of difference: '. . . identity in the eternal return does not describe the nature of that which returns, but, on the contrary, the fact of returning for that which differs' (ibid.). For Deleuze this explains why eternal return has to be conceived in terms of a *synthesis*: it is a synthesis of time and its dimensions, of diversity and its reproduction, and of becoming.

Let us now apply these insights to a reading of the discourse in *Thus Spoke Zarathustra* called 'Of Redemption'. This is the discourse in the text in which the 'ground' is prepared and worked over for the subsequent presentation of the doctrine of return in the discourses 'Of the Vision and the Riddle' and 'The Convalescent' (in both cases the doctrine is articulated not by Zarathustra himself but either by his arch-enemy, the spirit of gravity, or by his animals). As Nietzsche informs us in *Ecce Homo*, in a disclosure we have to know how to hear and receive, there is only one occasion in the text when Zarathustra defines and openly declares his task (Nietzsche tells us it is his task too): 'the *meaning (Sinn)* of which cannot be misunderstood: he is *affirmative* to the point of justifying, of redeeming the entire past' (*alles Vergangenen*) (Nietzsche 1979: 110). The decisive question is: how is the redemption of time to be understood? And why the *whole* of the past? Might we suggest that Nietzsche is Bergsonian on this crucial point? It is in Bergson that we have seen how we might conceive of the 'whole' of the past in the dimension of its virtuality: the past never ceases to be or to insist, it gets lost but it also continues to be reconstituted. It is the dead time of the event (pure potentiality).

Clearly, it is not accidental that Nietzsche should focus on the problem of the past in this encounter with the being of time. The being of the past, its sheer brute facticity if one likes, is what alienates the will and makes it feel impotent. But this construction of the brute time of the past is one without a virtual becoming, it is a material and not a spiritual repetition. The will feels impotent in the face of time and time's passing – all becomes past and nothing endures, there is only the fleeting and the transitory, therefore everything is in vain – because it has alienated itself from its own conditions of action and becoming. Zarathustra walks among human beings as among fragments and limbs of humans. His task is to teach them the riddle of redemption, he is to become the redeemer of chance, by teaching them that the liberation of time's desire – a desire that is met by a spirit of revenge on our part – consists in learning that it is possible to transform every 'it was' into 'thus I willed it'. The will remains an angry spectator of time past to the extent that is fails to realize the virtual character of time's becoming and of its own becoming in time (the will remains fixed solely on the empirical level and cannot see into time's abyss). When Zarathustra declares that the creative will must will something higher than reconciliation this 'higher' points us in the direction of a higher form of time, namely, the empty form of time (Heidegger's claim that Nietzsche's thinking of eternal return fails to escape the spirit of revenge is an inadequate and impoverished one; such a reading has not adequately comprehended what it means to transcend the spirit of revenge through the redemption of time, this redemption it does not understand).[39] The task is not simply one of reconciling ourselves to the empirical character of time (this would mean reconciling oneself to the actual as that to which one is already firmly attached). What makes Zarathustra's teaching one of redemption is that it enlarges the perception of time by opening up time's *abyss* as a new vision and riddle. Subjectivity is virtual, never ours, and we are given the chance of a becoming (chance itself is redeemed and given a chance, but the chance might not be taken). This is not a doctrine of revenge against time but of time's emancipation.

Deleuze's reading of Nietzsche goes further than any other reading in insisting that the eternal return does not speak of a return of the same but only of difference. While there is an absence of depth in the sphere of the immutable, the eternal return opens up the intensive space of positive differences: 'The eternal return is neither qualitative nor extensive but intensive, purely intensive . . . it is said of difference' (1994: 243). The 'same' that is invoked and appealed to in Nietzsche's articulation of the doctrine and thought-experiment speaks only of the repetition of difference and the difference of repetition. There is only ever differences of intensity – 'a flashing world of metamorphoses' and 'communicating intensities, differences of differences' – although we do not readily perceive these intensities and differences. The eternal return gives us 'the most beautiful qualities', 'the most brilliant colours', and the 'most vibrant extensions' (ibid.: 244). Deleuze describes it as the 'superior form' of everything that is, of being. Conceived as becoming it speaks of the virtual and not the actual.

In *Nietzsche and Philosophy* Deleuze is reading eternal return through a Bergsonian lens in as much as the focus is on the problem of time's passage. A distinctly Nietzschean problematic is added, however, and this revolves around the determination of a becoming-active of forces. As the superior form of everything that is, eternal return guarantees that only active forces return. This does not suppose that reactive forces are simply eliminated but rather that *their* returning involves a becoming-active. A becoming of forces necessarily involves transmutation and eternal return provides a test of the creative will's affirmation of them in as much as, for example, a laziness, a stupidity or baseness that willed its own eternal return would no longer be the same laziness, stupidity or baseness. The eternal return of reactive forces involves a contradiction: reactive forces cannot return, where returning names the being of becoming, simply because they have not even begun to leave themselves, they want to remain what they are. This conception of a becoming-active of forces takes its inspiration from a Bergsonian ontology: the one (being) is always said of a multiplicity and a multiplicity can only become what it is (a becoming) (ibid.: 24). The only way that reactive forces can become active is by overcoming and conquering themselves. Hence Deleuze writes: 'It is no longer a question of the simple thought of eternal return eliminating from willing everything that falls outside this thought, but rather, of the eternal return making something come into being which cannot do so without changing nature' (71). On the basis of this differentiation of becoming-active and being reactive Deleuze marks a distinction between two memories, a memory fuelled by *ressentiment* that 'only invests traces' and an active memory 'that no longer rests on traces' (115).

In both Nietzsche *and* Kant it is the pure and empty form of time that 'abjures all empirical content' which is at stake for Deleuze. It is the pure order of time that creates the possibility of a temporal series since the series is not given (Deleuze 1994: 88). Deleuze argues that Kant is not effecting a straightforward spatialization of time, as Bergson held, but rather providing a specifically modern topology of time: 'time ceases to be a number or measure and becomes parameter'. This allows for a topology of the self which complicates the matter of its becoming. Although Bergson could find nothing new in Kant's presentation of time this did not prevent Deleuze from trying to forge a novel alliance between Kant and Bergson on time. 'Bergson is much closer to Kant than he himself thinks', Deleuze writes

(1989: 82). By this Deleuze means that both thinkers seek to show that time is not simply the 'interior in us' but rather that it is 'the interiority in which we move, live, and change'. We have seen how this works in the case of the pure past and how it allows for a becoming of the self in time (time as its other). Let us now see how Deleuze configures a similar becoming in Kant's straight line of time by putting a dramatic spin on it.

Deleuze suggests that Kant's presentation of an 'autonomous form' points to a profound mystery and requires a new definition of time (1998: 29; compare 1994: 87–9). How does this work?

Kant brings about a significant reversal: time is no longer subordinated to movement, rather movement is rendered subordinate to the time that conditions it (see also 1989: 271ff.). The notion of ancient philosophy that time is the measure of movement, as its interval or number, is overturned. There is no longer a hierarchization of movements to be appraised in terms of their proximity to the eternal, 'according to their necessity, their perfection, their uniformity, their rotation, their composite spirals, their particular axes and doors, and the numbers of Time that correspond to them' (1998a: 27). Bergson defines space as an empty homogeneous medium since it is space that enables us to distinguish from one another a number of identical and simultaneous sensations. Although it is a principle of differentiation it is a reality without quality or intensive differences. This conception of an empty homogeneous medium is a 'reaction against the heterogeneity which is the very ground of our experience' (Bergson 1960: 97). Deleuze is suggesting, however, that Kant cannot be readily credited with this reaction; on the contrary, his presentation provides a topological structure which enfolds the intensive character of our becoming in time.

In Kant's 'rectification of time' time 'ceases to be cardinal and becomes ordinal, the order of an empty time' (1998a: 28).[40] If there is nothing originary that depends on movement then time becomes emancipated from what is original or primary and within the line of time we can locate the most extraordinary labyrinth: 'The labyrinth takes on a new look – neither a circle nor a spiral, but a thread, a pure straight line, all the more mysterious in that it is simple, inexorable, terrible . . .'[41] There is something decidedly modern and secular in this reversal of the image of time, and Deleuze seeks to disclose the nature of the shift that has taken place through the figure of Hamlet:

> It is Hamlet . . . who completes the emancipation of time. He truly brings about the reversal because his own movement results from nothing other than the succession of the determination. Hamlet is the first hero who truly needed time in order to act, whereas earlier heroes were subject to time as the consequence of an original movement . . .
> (ibid.; see also Deleuze on Oedipus and Hamlet in 1994: 89 and Deleuze's second lesson on Kant, 21 March 1978; on Hamlet compare Nietzsche 1979: 59 and Levinas 1987: 78)

This pure empty form of time is perhaps concealed in Kant's presentation and Deleuze endeavours to bring it to light. Time cannot be defined by its modes, whether permanence, succession, or simultaneity (what Deleuze names duration, series and set). Succession cannot be used to define time, for example, because if time was succession then we would need to posit another time to succeed it and so on *ad infinitum*. Things can only succeed each other in diverse times, they can be simultaneous in the same time, and they subsist in an indeterminate time. If everything moves and changes this is not because time changes or moves. Time does not change and move and neither is it eternal. It is an autonomous form. It is not that we simply order our material sensations in accordance with a homogeneous medium, we also complicate the sense of our lives in accordance with this strange and terrible straight line. With Kant time is no longer a mode but a *being*; no longer marked by a modal character, as in antiquity, it has become 'tonal'.

Deleuze locates a second emancipation of time in Kant. Descartes brings about a secularization of monastic time with the cogito in which the 'I think' takes place in an act of instantaneous determination, implying an undetermined existence ('I am'), and determining it as the existence of a thinking substance, but he is unable to specify the *form* under which the determination can be applied to the undetermined. In Descartes time is expelled: the cogito is reduced to an empty series of instants and the time of a continuous creation is entrusted to a transcendent God. Kant's completion of Descartes's laicization of time consists in showing that 'our undetermined existence is determinable only in time, under the form of time' (29; and see Kant *CPR*: B 158, B 278). The self is passive and receptive in respect of its becoming what it is: 'the I (*Je*) and the Self (*Moi*) are thus separated by the line of time, which relates them to each other only under the condition of a fundamental difference' (ibid.). There is thus a paradox of the inner sense in which the self that represents to itself the 'I' as the spontaneity of the determination is an 'other' that affects it. This is the fate of the modern self – to experience its 'I' as other (Hamlet, Nietzsche, the characters of Beckett, etc.). Like Hamlet, we are not beings of skepticism or doubt but of critique:

> I am separated from myself by the form of time and yet I am one, because the I necessarily affects this form by bringing about its synthesis – not only of successive parts to each other, but at every moment – and because the Self is necessarily affected by the I as the content of this form. The form of the determinable makes the determined Self represent the determination to itself as an Other (*Autre*). In short, the madness of the subject corresponds to the time out of joint. There is, as it were, a double derivation of the I and the Self in time, and it is this derivation that links or stitches them together. Such is the thread of time.
>
> (30)

203

The self is not an object but a subject of auto-affection, constituting a modulation and not a mould, and 'to which all objects are related as to the continuous variation of its own successive states, and to the infinite modulation of its degrees at each instant' (ibid.). It is in this way that time assumes the status of an immutable form and appears as the 'form of interiority'. Thus, we cannot simply declare time to be interior to us since it is we who are always interior to time. For us time is constituted as a kind of vertigo, it subsists without end and its interiority constantly doubles and hollows us out.

Conclusion

Of course, it is necessary to grant a time to the present; but then the question is: what is the time which is peculiar to the present? Deleuze outlines a novel way of approaching an actual multiplicity of points of present in his idea of there being peaks of a *de-actualized* present that coexist with sheets of virtual past. This would give us a present of the future, a present of the present, and a present of the past, 'all implicated in the event, rolled up in the event . . .' (Deleuze 1989: 100). This determination of the time of the present as being implicated in the event becomes possible once we free the event from both the space that marks its place and the actual present which passes. This means that the *time* of the event comes to an end before the event does, so the event will start again at another time; this empty time of the event, as one where nothing happens but everything becomes, gives us a multiplicity of presents implicated in a virtual time of becoming. The actual has been broken up. The time of the event is, then, equally the event of time, and it speaks of time's redemption.

The virtual is the time of life. It is also the time of one's life, providing it with an enigmatic power and an abyssal freedom. Redeemed time is 'beyond good and evil'. It is not a fable of moral redemption we are being offered or taught in these lessons on, and explorations of, time. As Nietzsche says, going into the depths does not make us better human beings, only more profound ones.

Nietzsche defines spirit as 'the life that itself cuts into life . . .' (*Geist ist das Leben, das selber in's Leben schneidet . . .*) ('Of the Famous Philosophers', 1969, translation modified). The time of life cuts into our being, constituting a time of becoming, giving us the chance to become. But if time is something monstrous and a riddle, the one who has tamed monsters and solved riddles 'should also redeem his monsters and riddles' and 'transform them into beautiful (*himmlischen*) children' ('Of the Sublime Men'). It is often said that life is hard to bear, so making of us 'fine asses and assesses of burden' (ibid., 'Of Reading and Writing'). (One is also reminded of Hamlet's question concerning the bearing of the 'whips and scorns of time'.) Nietzsche invites us to reflect on what we have in common with the rosebud which trembles because a drop of dew is lying upon it. Are we this 'rosebud'? And what is it that lies upon us and our actions as our greatest weight or heaviest burden, giving us our pride in the morning and our resignation in the evening? If life, on account of time, proves to be a terrible burden, this should not be allowed to serve as an objection but viewed as a weight that needs to be endured and lightened. While the spirit of gravity exists to remind us of our abysses what it cannot comprehend is our most abysmal thought and the fact that with it we are able to take flight:

> I have learned to walk: since then I have run. I have learned to fly: since then I do not have to be pushed in order to move.
>
> Now I am nimble, now I fly, now I see myself under myself, now a god dances within me.
>
> (ibid.)

NOTES

INTRODUCTION

1 As early as his 1956 essay on Bergson and difference Deleuze is thinking the concept as an event and not in terms of the scientific function (the virtual is not a function of the lived but the event of life). On the distinction between concept and function see Deleuze and Guattari 1994, chapters 5 and 6, for example, p. 144. On the function in science, and in relation to the question of time *qua* duration, see Weyl 1987: 45–6, 93–4.

1 INTRODUCING TIME AS A VIRTUAL MULTIPLICITY

1 There is a Plotinian ring to this description of other durations in terms of 'inferior' and 'superior'; but, of course, the other realities are not to be conceived in terms of an inferior material or bodily life and a superior intellectual life. On Plotinus see Hadot 1993: 26–7. On the role of Plotinus in Bergson and Deleuze see essay four.

2 Both Levinas and Deleuze note some profound affinities between Bergsonism and phenomenology (Levinas 1987: 131; Deleuze 1991: 117–18). Coterminously Bergson and Husserl develop the idea of the two multiplicities (Bergson in *Time and Free Will* of 1889, Husserl in *Philosophy of Arithmetic* in 1891); Husserl conceives duration as a continuous multiplicity (Husserl 1964: 24); he appreciates the need to posit the distinction between perception and memory as one of kind and not simply degree (if the difference is one of degree then memory gets construed as little more than a weakened form of perception); he also recognizes the need for philosophy to go beyond the human condition, insisting upon the need to leave behind the natural attitude through undertaking the epoché and its reductions, which supposes a suspension of the habits of the human and an appeal to intuition (on the epoché see Husserl 1931: 110–12); finally, Husserl also appreciates that there is no contradiction between having a commitment to a transcendental project and being committed to a radical empiricism as well. In his pursuit of a pure phenomenology of pure consciousness Husserl came to insist upon a strict separation of the transcendental from the psychological. The overcoming of the empirical ego by the transcendental ego amounts to a thinking beyond the human condition in order to discover a pure consciousness of intentionalities, of meaning and sense-bestowing: the being of meaning uncovers special kinds of entities Husserl calls *noemata*. The categorial intuition of essence amounts to an immediate intuition irreducible to sensible intuition although it has to be related to it to acquire validity (there is not an intellectual intuition).

This is a radical empiricism because it claims that we have access to universals and concepts (states of affairs, ideal meanings) as genuine features of experience. Bergsonism, however, refuses to make this move to intentionality and meaning (*Sinn*). It is not only a text like *Creative Evolution* which is not a work in phenomenology, neither is *Matter and Memory*, which one might think has a relation to phenomenology but which in fact lays out consciousness and memory on a very different plane, providing a pure consciousness by right (pure perception) and a past which is *beyond intentionality* (pure memory). Subjectivity or intentionality is never self-constituting but always constituted. The relation between Bergsonism and Husserlian phenomenology, as well that between Deleuze and phenomenology (Husserl and Sartre), is a topic that merits an extensive investigation.

3 For further insight into the importance of Riemann for Bergson's distinction see Deleuze and Guattari 1988: 482–3; and Durie 2000: 154–5. Durie's essay contains an excellent rebuttal of Heidegger's peremptory critique of Bergson and his alleged failure to think the temporality of time outside the confines of an Aristotelian legacy. For insight into how Deleuze comes to figure multi-dimensional multiplicities in topological terms in his work on rhizomatics see my *Germinal Life*, 1999: 155–9. See also Husserl on Riemann and multiplicity, 1969: 193–4.

4 The challenge Bergson was presenting to mathematics and physics on the question of the continuum was clearly recognized and picked up on by the mathematician Hermann Weyl. In his essay on 'The Concept of Number and the Continuum' (first published 1918) Weyl notes, with reference to the opening pages of *Creative Evolution*: 'It is to the credit of Bergson's philosophy to have pointed out forcefully this deep division between the world of mathematical concepts and the immediately experienced continuity of phenomenal time ("*la durée*")' (1987: 90). Even more pertinently, Weyl notes: 'The view of a flow consisting of points and, therefore, also dissolving into points turns out to be false. Precisely what eludes us is the nature of the continuity, the flowing from point to point; in other words, the secret of how the continually enduring present can continually slip away into the receding past' (91–2). Weyl's presentation of the conflict between number and *durée*, or the two multiplicities, rests on a synthesis of insights and ideas taken from Bergson and Husserl.

5 See especially Hegel on magnitude in 1999 (1812): 190ff. This is not, of course, to deny that important differences will remain between Bergsonism and Hegelianism. Deleuze insists upon these differences in his text of 1966, noting the concrete, empirical richness of Bergson's method of intuition over the abstract movements of pure thought in the Hegelian dialectic (and, we may note, contesting the caricature of Bergson as a philosopher of the pre-discursive presented by one of his former teachers, see Hyppolite 1997: 48–9). For further insight into the fundamental differences between the two modes of thought see Baugh 1993: 15–31. For a thought-provoking recent treatment of Hegel on multiplicity see Haas 2000. The key issue concerns whether Hegel can only conceive of nature as pure externality (space), which would mean that something like a virtual multiplicity would be a feature only of mind or spirit.

6 See R. Durie, Introduction to *Duration and Simultaneity*, 1999: xix.

7 Russell is famous for his view that Bergson does not know what number is or have any clear idea of it (Russell 1912: 334). See also the exchange between Russell and Wildon Carr in Russell 1992: 344–6 and 456–60. Russell's harsh

judgement can be contrasted with the appreciation of Bergson's pertinence for mathematics to be found in Weyl. For a reply to Russell on Bergson see Capek 1970: 147–50 and especially his appendix on 'Russell's Hidden Bergsonism': 335–45, and, more recently, Dale Adamson 2000: 53–86, 60–70. See also Deleuze and Guattari's distinction between the 'numbering number' and the 'numbered number', which seeks to open up a 'minor' geometry of nonmetric multiplicities: 'The number distributes itself in smooth space; it does not divide without changing nature each time, without changing units, each of which represents a distance and not a magnitude', 1988 pp. 484–5. Whereas multiplicities of distance cannot be rendered separable from a process of continuous variation, those of magnitude must always distribute constants and variables (ibid.: 483).

8 As Moore points out Bergson is not approaching the issue of sensations and their recognition from the point of view of a 'private language argument': 'Bergson is as strong an opponent of the old empiricist view of sensations as Wittgenstein – not because of their supposed *privacy*, but because of their supposed *distinctness* . . .' (1996: 44–5).

9 On plurality and numerical difference as given by space compare Kant, *CPR* 'Identity and Difference': A 264/B 320.

10 Compare Kant 1978: 183–4 (*Critique of Pure Reason* A 143/B 182): '. . . the pure *schema* of magnitude (*quantitatis*), as a concept of the understanding, is *number*, a representation which comprises the successive addition of homogeneous units. Number is therefore simply the unity of the synthesis of the manifold of a homogeneous intuition in general, a unity due to my generating time itself in the apprehension of the intuition.' Kant is drawing our attention not to the act of counting and what it implies but rather what is implied in things being numerable. Over and above the successive marking of units we have a mental synthesis of the whole simultaneously apprehended. We count successively but intuit simultaneously, which we can only do by referring a multiplicity to space. A sum implies the simultaneous existence of the parts and unless we apprehend the whole of the sum in a single act no counting of successive units can produce a sum (we need to know when to stop counting). This means that number is the act of a synthetic unity. But in addition to an intuition of space it also rests on an intuition of time. The concept of a magnitude is explained 'by saying that it is that determination of a thing whereby we are enabled to think *how many times* a unit is posited in it' (*CPR*: A 241/B 300, my emphasis). This 'how-many-times' is, says Kant, based on successive repetition, that is, on time as a synthesis of the homogeneous in time. Bergson's contention is that Kant has illegitimately extended his treatment of space as a homogeneous medium to time itself. See also the remarks Kant makes on number as an actual multiplicity in his inaugural dissertation of 1770, Kant 1992: 400.

11 This point is astutely brought out in Lindsay, 1911: 131ff., and upon whose account I shall draw.

12 On this confusion see also Plotinus, *The Enneads*, book III, 7: 'First there is space; the movement is commensurate with the area it passes through, and this area is its extent. But this gives us, still, space only, not Time' (Penguin edition 1991: 223).

13 Ayer holds that a simple appeal to mathematics is insufficient: 'The crucial point . . . is that the stages of a continuous series cannot be reached successively' (Ayer 1973: 20).

14 Bergson's thinking on this issue finds support in some fairly recent treatments of set theory and the infinite. See especially the excellent studies by Tiles 1989: 10–22 and Moore 1990: 103–4, 158.

15 As Čapek points out, within only a few years of writing his critique of Bergson in 1912 Russell publishes in 1915 an essay on time in *The Monist* in which his position is strikingly Bergsonian in recognizing an immanence of the past within the present: *'The present has no sharp boundaries . . .'*, Russell 1915: 223 (and cited in Čapek: 341–2). In this essay Russell draws a distinction between two time-relations, that obtaining between subject and object (relations of past, present, and future), and that obtaining between object and object (earlier, later, in short, succession). He presents this distinction as one between mental time and physical time. And he argues that, 'In a world where there was no experience there would be no past, present, or future, but there might be earlier and later' (1915: 212).

16 It is a similar conception of continuity that leads Richard Sorabji to the view that we can put to rest a bogey that has troubled commentators more than any other concerning Aristotle's definition of time as number in the *Physics*. This relates to the criticism made by Plotinus: how can the continuous nature of time be generated from number which is discrete? In other words, how can time, qua continuity, be number? Sorabji argues that while the stages which we choose to count are discrete this does not make time something discontinuous: 'On the contrary, it is infinitely divisible, in the sense that we can divide it at stages as close together as we please, and its infinite divisibility is precisely a mark of its continuity' (Sorabji 1983: 89). But this laying to rest of a bogey is only possible by construing time solely and simply in terms of an actual or discrete multiplicity. No other conception of multiplicity is allowed for. For Plotinus see *The Enneads* book III, 7, and the excellent treatment in Gerson 1994: 115–24, especially 120–1.

17 It is with this doctrine of relations that as early as 1953 Deleuze will champion empiricism, which for him is not about asserting the primacy of the sensible over the intelligible. Deleuze locates this empiricism of external relations not only in Hume but also in William James and in what he calls the realism of Russell (Deleuze 1991 [1953]: 99). See also the remarks on empiricism in *Dialogues*, Deleuze 1987: 54–9. I have questioned and challenged Russell's empiricism or realism in this essay in a way that was not entertained by Deleuze. The complex character of Bergson's own empiricism will be encountered in various essays of the volume. It is important to appreciate that Bergsonism, with its commitment to virtual multiplicities, has to think the nature of relations in a way quite different from Russell's logicism. For some insight into Bergson on relations see Karin Stephen, 1922: 62–5 and 70–4. Badiou completely ignores Deleuze's empiricism and construes the commitment to 'Relation' as confirmation of his reading of Deleuze as a closet Platonist (Badiou 2000a: 63). For Russell on relations see the important statements he makes in 1985: 68–70 and 170–4. For James see 'The Thing and Its Relations' in James 1912 (1996): 92–123, especially 110–16. For Hume on 'Relation' see *A Treatise of Human Nature*, book 1, part 1, section V. For the counter-view to this empiricism see Hegel 1812 (1999): 711ff.

18 Compare the 'image' Kant offers in his inaugural dissertation: '. . . space is also applied as an image to the concept of *time* itself, representing it by a *line* and its limits (moments) by points', (Kant 1992: 399).

19 The issue remains alive and well to this day. See, for example, the study by Guyer, 1987. For some highly original insights into the role of time in Kant's first Critique see Heidegger (see both 1997a and 1997b).

20 See Kant's letter to J. J. Lambert of September 2, 1770 in Kant 1967: 59. In his 'Kant' book of 1963 Deleuze holds that the 'phenomenon' in Kant should not, in fact, be taken to denote 'appearance' but rather 'appearing'. If the phenomenon appears in space and time then space and time are best conceived as *a priori presentations*: 'What presents itself is thus not only empirical phenomenal diversity in space and time, but the pure *a priori* diversity of space and time themselves' (Deleuze 1984: 8). This reading of Kant is taken up again in Deleuze's lectures on Kant of 1978. Here Deleuze argues that Kant has given a new sense to the transcendental and introduced something new into philosophy in his distinction between presentation and representation. Kant can be regarded as the founder of phenomenology since there is phenomenology 'from the moment that the phenomenon is no longer defined as *apparence* but as *apparition*'. The significance of the distinction is this: whereas appearance implies an essence lying behind it, 'apparition' implies no such essence but refers to 'what appears in so far as it appears'. On this model the transcendental subject is constitutive not of the apparition but of the conditions under what appears to it does, in fact, appear to it (see lecture dated 14 March 1978). For insight into Deleuze on Kant and the transcendental form of time see essay seven.

21 Heidegger's reading is also very helpful on this point (1997a: 100–11, especially pp. 101–2).

22 As we shall see in essay five Bergson does admit finality into our conception of evolution but only in a 'special sense'.

23 The work of Bergson's that presents special difficulties is *Duration and Simultaneity*, which will be treated in the next essay. Here Bergson wavers between a restriction of duration to a certain psychological consciousness and implicating the *durée* of this consciousness in the 'impersonal' time of a 'single duration' in which the human consciousness that initially laid out the field of duration is 'eliminated' (Bergson 1999: 32). Bergson goes on to add a qualifying remark: 'Impersonal and universal time, if it exists, is in vain endlessly prolonged from past to future; it is all of a piece; the parts we single out in it are merely those of a space that delineates its track and becomes its equivalent in our eyes; we are dividing the unfolded, not the unfolding.'

24 A reading of Bergson on the laws of thermodynamics can be found in chapter 1 of my *Germinal Life*, 1999: 60ff.

25 In this respect it complicates the manner in which William James attempted to define the 'most pregnant difference' between empiricism and rationalism, with empiricism being the habit of explaining wholes by parts, and thus having an inclination towards pluralism, and rationalism that of explaining parts by wholes and having an inclination towards monism. See James 1909: 7–8 and 1911 (1996): 35–7.

26 See Deleuze 2000: 131: '. . . there is no Logos that gathers up all the pieces, hence no law attaches them to a whole to be regained or even formed'. And: 'Time is precisely the transversal of all possible spaces, including the space of time' (130).

27 It should be noted that when Deleuze thinks nature under the aegis of Lucretian empiricism the task is defined as one of thinking 'the diverse as diverse' and he rules out all talk of a whole or a One that would assemble the diversity: 'Nature is not collective but distributive ... not attributive, but rather conjunctive: it expresses itself through "and", and not through "is"', 'Lucretius and the Simulacrum', Appendix 1 to Deleuze 1990: 266–7. If pressed, I would maintain that a Bergsonian thinking of the whole (even a Bergsonism of the One) is not incompatible with this empiricism and does not serve to reintroduce the (negative) theological form of a false philosophy. As will be argued in essay four, the Bergsonian open whole does not assemble what is given to it – in terms of a limited force – by the simple virtual.

28 Examples of external relations are provided by Russell in 1985: 171–2, and Deleuze 1986: 10–11 and 1997: 55. Russell insists that relation is not a 'third term' that is simply hooked on to the two terms that are implicated in a relation ('Giles is smaller than Bertie', or 'the wine is on the table'). If this was the case then it would no longer be concrete but abstract. See also James contra F. H. Bradley in James 1912 (1996): 107ff.

29 William James defined 'pluralistic empiricism' as the insight that 'everything is an environment' (James 1909: 90), and he provides the following insight into the significance of thinking in terms of the 'And': 'Pragmatically interpreted, pluralism ... means only that the sundry parts of reality *may be externally related.* Everything you can think of, however vast or inclusive, has on the pluralistic view a genuinely "external" environment of some sort or amount. Things are "with" one another in many ways, but nothing includes everything, or dominates over everything. The word "and" trails along after every sentence. Something always escapes' (ibid.: 321).

30 For the translation of this letter, as well as the translations of the letters from Bergson to Höffding and Delattre I utilize in essay five, I am deeply grateful to Melissa McMahon, who generously provided me with advance copies of the translations of Bergson's letters she has done for the forthcoming edition of *Bergson: Key Selected Writings*, ed. K. Ansell Pearson and J. Mullarkey (London, Continuum).

31 Kant, we may note, preferred to approach the scope of human reason in terms of the image of a *sphere* as opposed to a 'plane', simply because he held the horizon of knowledge to be limited to an equally narrow field of experience. On Kant's rejection of the plane see *Critique of Pure Reason*: A 762/B 790.

2 'A LIFE OF THE REAL' AND A SINGLE TIME: RELATIVITY AND VIRTUAL MULTIPLICITY

1 In his book *About Time* Paul Davies asks whether, in his adherence to determinism and denial that time flows, Einstein was really any different from Newton and Laplace (1995: 283). However, in my view he presents the problem inadequately when he suggests that the 'greatest outstanding riddle concerns the glaring mismatch between physical and subjective or psychological time'. But this is to suppose that we readily know what subjective or psychological time amounts

to, how it becomes constituted, and that all that can be said of the so-called 'phenomenological' experience of time is that it 'flows'.

2 Deleuze's conception of the 'pure empty form of time' (Aion), in which the privilege of the absolute present is radically displaced, has taken cognizance of the revolution of Relativity. See Deleuze 1990, especially the Twenty-Third series: 162ff.

3 Deleuze never ceased to maintain that science and philosophy are both separated and linked by their commitment to the two different kinds of multiplicity: 'Although scientific types of multiplicity are themselves extremely diverse, they do not include the properly philosophical multiplicities for which Bergson claimed a particular status defined by duration, "multiplicity of fusion", which expressed the inseparability of variations, in contrast to multiplicities of space, number, and time, which ordered mixtures and referred to the variable or to independent variables. It is true that this very opposition, between scientific and philosophical, discursive and intuitive, and extensional and intensive multiplicities, is also appropriate for judging the correspondence between science and philosophy, and their possible collaboration, and the inspiration of one by the other' (Deleuze and Guattari 1994: 127).

4 The poem is discussed in Plato's *Parmenides*.

5 See, for example, Morris 1997.

6 In addition to Bergson Popper might also be referring to the ideas of Samuel Alexander, which took the idea of emergent evolution from the 'emergent principle' of Lloyd Morgan. Alexander gave the Gifford lectures between 1916–18 which were published in 1920 as *Space, Time, and Deity*. An entertaining account of Alexander, Bergson, Einstein, Whitehead, *et. al.* can be found in Wyndham Lewis's *Time and Western Man*. The notion of emergent/creative evolution also figures in Popper and Eccles 1990: 15–16.

7 Deleuze produces a very different reading of Boltzmann in his *Logic of Sense*, where he reads him not as an apologist of a Parmenidean rationalism but rather as a physicist who opens up the time of Aion over Chronos. Aion cuts across the arrow of time that moves inexorably from past to future. Chronos is the time of the present which makes of past and future two oriented dimensions, in which the direction of movement is from one dimension to the other in terms of a series of presents that follow one another inside partial worlds and partial systems. But from the perspective of the 'whole' (the universe as the system of all systems) no such present can ever be fixed (Deleuze 1990 p. 77; see also Deleuze and Guattari 1988: 263ff.). Compare Deleuze on Boltzmann in 1994: 225–6.

8 As to whether this means that we have had 'cinema' all along, as the projection of a constant, universal illusion, see Deleuze 1986: 2.

9 See Plato, *Timaeus* (1971), section 7: 51–2. Plato notes that this moving image 'remains for ever at one' and that time was made 'as like as possible to eternity', which was its model. Thus, the relation between the 'eternal Living Being' (the model) and the actual universe (the copy) is one of *resemblance*. On the resemblance of the copy to the model see also 69–70.

10 It should be noted that Bergson was a close and gifted reader of Aristotle, writing his Latin dissertation on the concept of place in Aristotle (*Physics* IV) between the years 1883–8. At the same time as working on this piece of work

Bergson was working on his doctoral dissertation, *Les Données immédiates de la conscience* (*Time and Free Will*). In the former he is concerned to show the validity of a *mathematical* conception of empty and boundless space; the concern of the latter is with homogeneity of space in contrast to the heterogeneity of time. Kant's presentation of space in the *Critique of Pure Reason* mediates the approach Bergson adopts in both pieces of writing.

11 By describing the law of entropy as 'metaphysical' Bergson intends a positive meaning: the second law posits the general direction of the universe without an over-reliance on symbolic representation. For further insight into Bergson and the second law see my *Germinal Life* 1999: 60ff.

12 This criticism supposes that Bergson is not aware of the actual status of 'clocks' in the theory, which is clearly not the case: '"Clocks" and "observers" need not be anything physical; by "clock" we simply mean here an ideal recording of time according to definite laws or rules, and by "observer", an ideal reader of this ideally recorded time. It is nonetheless true that we are now picturing the possibility of physical clocks and living observers at every point in the system' (Bergson 1999: 28).

13 Support for my reading of Bergson can be found in Gunter 1971: 533ff.

14 Durie, Introduction to Bergson 1999: xxiii note 12.

15 For a critique of Bergson that takes up this point see Deleuze and Guattari 1994: 132: 'It is not enough to assimilate the scientific observer (for example, the cannonball traveller of relativity) to a simple *symbol* that would mark states of variables, as Bergson does, while the philosophical persona would have the privilege of the *lived* (a being that endures) because he will undergo the variations themselves. The philosophical persona is no more lived experience than the scientific observer is symbolic.'

16 Here there is a concordance between Bergsonism and current thinking in the 'philosophy of mind'. See especially the arguments put forward by Daniel Dennett in his essay 'Instead of Qualia' in Dennett 1998: 142–52. When in this essay Dennett responds to the claim that colour is not in the world but only exists in the eye and the brain of the beholder by pointing out that the eye and the brain are 'as much parts of the physical world as the objects seen by the observer' (142), he is close to the approach Bergson pursues in *MM*.

17 On this see my essay on Nietzsche and Boscovich, 2000d.

3 DURATION AND EVOLUTION:
THE TIME OF LIFE

1 The same explanation of novelty can be found in the writings of Peirce and his combined doctrines of 'tychism' and 'synechism', according to James. Indeed, he argues that Peirce's teaching 'means exactly the same thing as Bergson's 'évolution créatrice'. See W. James, 'On the Notion of Reality as Changing', 1909: 395–400, 399.

2 See my *Germinal Life* (1999) for insight into the changing configurations of 'evolution' in Deleuze's texts.

3 The issue remains alive in contemporary debates. See, for example, the study by Jablonka and Lamb, 1995.

4 On the role of contingency within Bergson's account of creative evolution see 1983: 255ff.: 'The part played by contingency in evolution is therefore great. Contingent are the forms adopted, or rather invented. Contingent, relative to the obstacles encountered in a given place and at a given moment, is the dissociation of the primordial tendency into such and such complementary tendencies which create divergent lines of evolution. Contingent the arrests and set-backs; contingent, in large measure, the adaptations.'

5 This is a view developed in almost identical terms in Heidegger's appraisal of the question of the organism: 'An eye taken independently is not an eye at all. This implies that it is never first an instrument which subsequently also gets incorporated into something else. Rather, the eye belongs to the organism and emerges from the organism, which of course is not the same as saying that the organism makes ready or produces organs' (Heidegger 1995: 221). Heidegger's reliance on 'potentialities' to explain a creative evolution has important affinities with Bergson's stress on tendencies.

6 In a consideration of novelty in the context of a treatment of causation James distinguishes three causes, the formal, the eminent and the virtual, and notes that unlike the formal cause a virtual cause does not resemble its effect and unlike an eminent cause it is not superior to its effect in perfection. See James 1911 (1996): 191–2. See Merleau-Ponty 1994: 92–3 for a discussion of Bergson and eminent causality. See also Kant's characterisation of a cause of the world that exists outside of the world as having a 'virtual', as opposed to a 'local', presence (Kant 1992: 403).

7 On the eye see Rose 1997: chapter 7, especially 193–4; and for a morphogenetic approach see Goodwin 1995: 147–54, and the classic study on 'growth and form' by D'Arcy Thompson first published in 1917 (1992).

8 How many times has the charge of 'subjective idealism' been cavalierly directed at strands of twentieth-century continental philosophy! (Husserl's phenomenology, for example, which is clearly not idealist in this sense, see Husserl 1931: 168–71).

9 Monod is a classic source for the more recent dismissal of Bergson and is the authority, for example, Sokal and Bricmont appeal to in order to discredit Bergson (1997, chapter 11: 165–85, 166).

10 In Deleuze it would seem that there does take place in his texts a shift away from the idea of a simple virtual (an original identity and simple totality) to the idea of a virtual whole that is constantly changing and that we might characterize as involving a move away from the virtual of the *élan vital* to the virtual of a 'plane of immanence' (the Open whole that is constantly changing but not changing in relation to an initial vital impulse). Some of the shifts away from Bergson are signalled as early as *Difference and Repetition* of 1968. The concern with distinguishing the virtual and the possible persists but now the virtual is conceived in terms of 'structure' and actualization concerns not tendencies of evolution but pre-individual singularities of various systems. For insight into this shift in Deleuze's work see my *Germinal Life*. Deleuze does not simply abandon the *élan vital* in his later work but appeals to it as a force of 'potent, pre-organic germinality' that is beyond the opposition of mechanism and organicism (Deleuze 1986: 51). In *DR* the virtual appears to have been supplanted by the eternal return – the doctrine of difference and repetition – as that which gives us internal difference, acts as the differentiator of difference (makes the difference)

in which difference in itself becomes difference for itself. It is perhaps not without significance, then, that Deleuze should return to Bergson and the virtual in the 1980s with the books on cinema and in *What is Philosophy?* In *DR* perhaps the most fundamental departure from Bergson that is signalled concerns the treatment of intensity, so that the most important field of differences for Deleuze now concerns the differences of intensity. Deleuze poses the question: is the difference between differences of degree and differences in kind itself one of degree or of kind? His answer is to say neither and to argue that between the two orders of differences, the lowest degree and the highest form, there is to be found all the degrees *of* difference and the 'entire nature of difference', namely, the intensive. See Deleuze 1994, 239–40 and my *Germinal Life* for further insight, especially 74–6.

11 In note 2 of chapter 5 of *Bergsonism*, the chapter that deals with *CE*, Deleuze explains his choice of preference for the term 'planes' over the term 'plans'. The difference is between ordinary conceptions of finalism and Bergson's special and complex conception in which the stress is on a virtual finality. 'Planes' refer to the degrees of levels of contraction that coexist in duration, and while there is directionality in life this is not the direction of a 'plan' or programme.

12 Bergson's critical perspective on the idea of an infinite universe might be relevant to the claim being made here: 'to speak of an infinite universe is to admit a perfect coincidence of matter with abstract space, and consequently an absolute externality of all the parts of matter in relation to one another' (1983: 244).

4 THE SIMPLE VIRTUAL: A RENEWED THINKING OF THE ONE

1 As Bussanich deftly draws out, this means that the negative way to the One ultimately contains a superior affirmation. For insight into the difficulties within Platonism of defining the One see Plato, *Parmenides*, Deductions one and two. The issues centre, among other things, on whether the One can have parts, can change, can admit of otherness and difference, and can be number. On the relation between neoPlatonism and the *Parmenides* see Dodds 1928. See also the genealogy of the transcendent One which Deleuze provides in his short piece 'Les plages d'immanence', 1985: 79–81.

2 May (1970: 631) has suggested that conceived as a 'one-many' the *élan vital* can be compared to the third hypostasis or World Soul of Plotinus. See Plotinus, *Enneads*, IV, 1. Bergson comments on the three hypostases in the third of his Gifford lectures (M: 1056–60), and a careful reading of what he has to say therein would show, I believe, that the comparison of the '*élan*' with the third hypostasis would have to be complicated. This is because in Bergson's metaphysics unity is a virtual multiplicity that can only proceed in terms of dissemination and dispersion, there can be no return to unity which is 'unity only'. This is why Deleuze always insists that the 'Whole' is never given and that we should be *glad* of this fact. Below I argue that there are, in fact, two different figurations of the whole in Bergson and Deleuze, and I insist that while the '*élan*' is given as a simple totality, the (virtual) whole of evolution as a creative process can never be given. Clearly it is imperative to think and take the two wholes together on the

level of ontology. Deleuze's 'gladness' is over the second whole. For a detailed study of the Bergson-Plotinus relation see Mosse-Bastide 1959. And see also Foubert 1973: 7–73.

3 Bergson mentions one of the courses of lectures he gave on Plotinus given at the Collège de France in 1897–8 in *CE* 353, where he says he tried to demonstrate the resemblances between Leibniz's monads and Plotinus' Intelligibles. Deleuze also makes a link between Plotinus and Leibniz in his *The Fold* (24).

4 On this see Henry 1991: lii: 'Plotinus identifies as a matter of course the Good of the *Republic* and the absolute One of the first hypothesis of the *Parmenides*. This identification which, in the words of Plato, situates the Good "beyond being" and which denies to the One all multiplicity – be it only virtual and logical, a multiplicity of names, attributes, forms, or aspects – constitutes the basis of the "negative theology" which, in Plotinus and in his disciples, plays so great a part in the doctrine of God and of the mystical experience.'

5 *TFW* unfolds a distinction between a 'true self' and a 'superficial self' that may initially strike one as either Plotinian or Kantian; but it is important to grasp that for Bergson the 'true self' does not reside outside time but can only become what it is in duration. On Bergson on links between Plotinus and modern metaphysics see also the essay 'The Perception of Change', in *The Creative Mind*, 1965: 139–42.

6 Bergson often 'distorts' (*détourné*), as he puts it, the terms of Spinoza's famous distinction. See for example *TSMR*: 58. It is interesting to note that although Bergson regularly gave lectures on the history of philosophy he accorded special treatment to Spinoza by always devoting a separate lecture course to him. For insight into the critical character of his rapport with Spinoza see *CE*: 347–54. Both Leibniz and Spinoza are said to present a 'systematization of the new physics, constructed on the model of the ancient metaphysics'; and in both, but especially in Spinoza, there are 'flashes of intuition' that break through the system. For further insight into Bergson on Spinoza see Zac 1968, who stresses the ambivalent character of Bergson's attitude towards Spinoza, and also the opening remarks in chapter 1 of Jankélévitch 1959: 5ff.

7 As Karl Jaspers notes, the Plotinian One cannot, strictly speaking, be thought and is not the 'subject' of thinking. It is what 'gives' thinking without giving anything of itself. This One is neither the number one nor the one contrasted with the other, 'for any attempt to think the One produces duality and multiplicity' (Jaspers 1966: 34).

8 Recent scholarship no longer favours using the term 'emanation' to describe Plotinus' doctrine on account of its Stoic connotations; rather, the creative process is now seen in terms of 'illumination' or 'irradiation'. See Dillon 1991: xci.

9 For a more recent upholding of this reading of Plotinus see Bussanich 1996: 60, where he makes it clear that while there is nothing discrete about the character of the One in Plotinus the move to univocity is not made: 'the One's properties are [not] univocally predictable of its products: the One's life is not life in the same sense or the same degree as Intellect's.' But he also notes that the One's products cannot then simply be said to be equivocal either. As ever, Plotinus presents his readers with an real interpretive dilemma.

10 The citation Badiou makes runs as follows: 'if the whole is not giveable, it is because it is the Open, and because its nature is to change constantly, or to give rise

to something new, in short, to endure' (Badiou 2000a: 49, quoting from Deleuze, *Cinema 1*, 1986: 9). Clearly, this whole that is subject to, and the subject of, constant change, can never be given; but this is a different virtual whole from the whole of the simple virtual. The two conceptions of the whole are both articulated by Bergson and both are at work in Bergson's *Creative Evolution* (see 1983: 53–5, 87 and 257 for a presentation of the first whole, and 10–11 for a presentation of the second whole; the two meet in the discussion that takes place on 86–7).

11 This is perhaps the principal theme of Deleuze's difference from Hegel – the difference that is at stake in *DR* – and it is expressed not only in the 1956 essay on Bergson but also in the 1954 review of Jean Hyppolite's *Logic and Existence*: 'can we not construct an ontology of difference which would not have to go up to contradiction, because contradiction would be less than difference and not more? Is not contradiction itself only the phenomenal and anthropological aspect of difference?' (Deleuze's review now appears as the appendix to the English translation of Hyppolite's text, Hyppolite 1997: 191–5).

12 See Bergson, 1983: 106: 'There is no manifestation of life which does not contain, in a rudimentary state – either latent or potential – the essential characters of most other manifestations.'

13 Like Badiou we waver between the two, Being and Life, in describing Deleuze's thinking. See the striking essay by Badiou called 'Of Life as a Name of Being, or, Deleuze's Vitalist Ontology', translated by Alberto Toscano in *Pli*, vol. 10, 2000b.

14 These difficulties are an essential part of any attempt to think with Bergson. See, for example, the admirable intellectual effort found in May (1970, especially 631–5), as when he writes: '. . . the original impetus or *élan*, remains transcendent to the movements or realities it engenders yet is at the same time immanent to them' (633); and, 'the *élan* precontains both consciousness and matter as interpenetrating virtualities, and it gives rise to both in the course of its actualization, in the course of giving rise to what is *other* than itself' (634).

5 THE *ÉLAN VITAL* AS AN IMAGE OF THOUGHT: BERGSON AND KANT ON FINALITY

1 Bergson lectured on all three of Kant's Critiques. His lessons on the *Critique of Pure Reason* provide a straightforward explication and can be found in *Bergson Cours III*, 1995: 131–201. For further insight see de Gruson 1959: 171–90, and Barthelmy-Madaule's study of 1966.

2 Russell endeavoured to explain away the antinomies by going beyond what he calls the 'inveterate subjectivism' of Kant's 'mental habits' (1914 [1922]: 161). In his lecture on the problem of infinity he locates this subjectivism in the way Kant sets up the problem of the antithesis of the first antinomy: the world can have no beginning in time since up to every instant an eternity has elapsed and this means that the world has passed by in terms of an infinite series of successive states; however, the problem with this, Kant argues, is that the infinity of a series can never be completed by a successive synthesis, and so a beginning of the world has to be assumed (Kant *CPR*: A 426/B 454). After remarking that the notion of infinity is a property of classes and only of series derivatively, Russell accuses Kant of confusing a mental series (which has no end) with a physical one (which

has an end but no beginning). It is the word 'synthesis' which gives Kant's game away for Russell, showing that what is being depicted is a mind trying to grasp a successive series of events in the reverse order to that in which they have, in fact, occurred. Russell then points out: '*This* series is obviously one which has no end. But the series of events up to the present has an end, since it ends with the present.' Now Russell's critique of Kant, which focuses on the need to go beyond our subjectivist mental habits, may strike us as having an affinity with Bergson's thinking. But a crucial difference remains, namely, that for all his talk of thinking beyond subjectivism Russell remains wedded to the idea of time as a discrete multiplicity, which is evident in the way he holds that the series comes to an end at the point of the present (1914 [1922]: 159–88: 184). For Bergson's teaching on the antinomies see Bergson 1995: 179–91.

3 This citation is from an essay of 1901 entitled 'Le parallélisme psycho-physique et la métaphysique positive', and can be found in Bergson, *Mélanges*, 1972: 463–502.

4 Bergson accounts for the vital basis of our forms of knowledge as follows: 'Before we speculate we must live, and life demands that we make use of matter, either with our organs, which are natural tools, or with tools, properly so-called, which are artificial organs . . . Science has pushed this labour of the intelligence much further, but it has not changed its direction. It aims above all at making us masters of matter' (1965: 38).

5 It is at this point in the text that Kant makes a distinction between the noumenon, things in themselves and the transcendental object. The transcendental object – the object which is posited by the understanding to denote the cause/ground of appearance – can be named the noumenon in the sense that its representation is not a sensible one. It remains, however, an empty representation and its only service is 'to mark the limits of our sensible knowledge and to leave open a space which we can fill neither through possible experience nor through pure understanding' (A 289/B 345; on the transcendental object see also A 190–1/B 235–6, A 109, A 250–3). On the need not to confuse the transcendental object with the thing in itself see Deleuze, lesson three, 28 March 1978 (1998b). See also Deleuze 1990: 97.

6 In *CE* intuition is, indeed, conceived in terms of instinct but one that has become disinterested and self-conscious, 'capable of reflecting upon its object and of enlarging it indefinitely' (1983: 176).

7 This has, in fact, been a feature of various histrionic readings of Bergson (ism) over the course of the past one hundred years from Wyndham Lewis to Alain Badiou. For Badiou's histrionic reaction to Bergsonism see Badiou 2000a: 99.

8 Compare Bergson *MM*, 1991: 185: 'the task of the philosopher . . . closely resembles that of the mathematician who determines a function by starting from the differential. The final effort of philosophical research is a true work of integration.'

9 Bergson's contention is that Kant's first Critique continues the old dream of approaching the real in terms of a universal mathematics: 'In short, the whole critique of pure reason leads to establishing the fact that Platonism, illegitimate if Ideas are things, becomes legitimate if ideas are relations, and that the ready-made idea, once brought down from heaven to earth, is indeed as Plato wished,

the common basis of thought and nature. The whole critique of pure reason rests upon the postulate that our thought is incapable of anything but Platonizing, that is, of pouring the whole of possible experience into pre-existing molds' (1965: 197).

10 Kant, of course, sought to show in precise terms that his project amounted to an *epigenesis* of pure reason and *not* 'a kind of *preformation-system* of pure reason' (*CPR*: B 167). The problem being confronted in the Critique is that of how to account for a *necessary* agreement of experience with the concepts of the objects of experience, and Kant's solution is to favour the system which will demonstrate that it is the categories of the understanding which make experience possible. This system of epigenesis is quite different from a preformation one in which the agreement between experience and concepts would be explained in terms of a subjective disposition implanted in us by a Creator. A preformation-system would have the effect of making the necessary agreement an arbitrarily subjective one: we are so constituted that we cannot think our representations in any other way than how we actually do. Kant has no desire to satisfy the skeptic on this issue and insists that the objective validity of our judgements does not rest on an illusion. It might prove productive to examine the critique of teleological judgement in relation to this problematic. See especially the movements at play in Kant's thinking in *CTJ*: sections 81 and 82.

11 See also the treatment of intellectual intuition in Bergson 1995: 172–4.

12 It would be an interesting exercise to compare this with Kant's critical reception of Spinozism in *CTJ*, not so much the remarks on hylozoism but those concerning the 'ontological reality', as Kant calls it, of the 'single, simple substance'. See Kant 1952: section 80: 81–2.

13 Although Kant acknowledges that the idea (or perhaps intuition) of a whole that contains 'the source of the possibility of the nexus of the parts' is a contradictory one for our discursive understanding, it can admit of a special 'representation' (1952: section 77: 64).

14 That Kant might be Bergson's predecessor on this and other issues at the heart of *CE* was noted by Höffding in his lectures on Bergson (see Höffding 1915: 274–5).

15 In a letter to Höffding of March 1915 Bergson distances himself from hylozoism. Its error, he says, is to confuse matter and life: the 'representation of matter' it gives uses 'images drawn from the world of life', *Mélanges*, 1972: 1148.

16 Bergson speaks of life as an intention in both *CE* (1983: 177) and *TSMR* (1977: 116). See also the discussion of chance in *CE*: 233ff.

17 I have put the claims of autopoiesis to critical test in a number of places. See, for example, Ansell Pearson 1997: 140–4, and 1999: 168–70.

18 In an article on Bergson's vitalism Maria and Alexander Wolsky show how the *élan vital* differs from the vitalism of Hans Driesch that postulates a vital force or entelechy *within* the organism. For Bergson, by contrast, the vital impetus is 'outside and above the organic world' (Wolsky and Wolsky 1992: 157). In his characterization of life in terms of a continuity of genetic energy that cuts across individuals, and his insistence that no mysterious vital principle can be appealed to, Bergson is, in fact, closer to Darwinism than conventional vitalism. For the original source of entelechy see Aristotle's *De Anima* II, 2: 'it is the nature of the entelechy of each thing to be in what is potentially it and in its own matter' (1986: 161). And on final causes in nature see Aristotle, *Physics* II. 8 (1996: 50–3).

19 For a contemporary up-take of Bergson's problematic see Grassé 1977.

20 That it might was first suggested by Höffding (1915: 277–8). Bergson responded to some of the issues Höffding raised in his lectures of 1913 in the letter to him dated 15 March 1915 that I discuss.

21 Santayana casually treats the *élan* on a level with Schopenhauer's Will in 1940: 70. Schopenhauer's defence of Kant on teleology can be found in section XXVI of the second volume of his *The World as Will and Representation*. Some excellent insights into the relation between the Will of Schopenhauer and the *élan vital* of Bergson can be found in Jankélévitch 1959: 135–44.

6 VIRTUAL IMAGE: BERGSON ON MATTER AND PERCEPTION

1 It is interesting to note that for Russell the notion of a pure perception implied a kind of ultra-realism on Bergson's part. See Russell 1914: 321–7, 329. More recently Bergson's position has been described as 'strongly realist' (as opposed to naively realist) and in the terms of the recent idiom of 'ultra-externalism': 'a perception just is those (*wholly external*) properties of an object which are selected by a body for a possible response' (Moore 1996: 32). See also the discussion in Lacey 1989: 89ff.

2 A recent study on 'mental Darwinism' provides valuable insight into the relation between Bergson's notion of selection and the Darwinian one, duly noting the similarities and the crucial differences. See McNamara 1999: 37–43.

3 Bergson comments on Book IV of *De Rerum Natura* and notes the way in which it seeks to show that objects cannot be thought independently of the *images* they send out in the universe: 'These particles are extremely minute; they come from everywhere and move with inconceivable speed' (Bergson 1884 [1959]: 20). In his treatment of the 'movement-image' in *Cinema 1* it is clear from the way that Deleuze stresses the identity of movement and image that he is returning to a Lucretian source. The following passage from Deleuze's short piece on 'The Actual and the Virtual' strongly supports this view: 'There is no object that is purely actual. All actuals are surrounded by a fog of virtual images. The particles are called virtual insofar as their emissions and absorptions, their creation and destruction, take place, in a time smaller than the minimum of thinkable continuous time [this is how Deleuze construes the time of aion in *The Logic of Sense*], and insofar as this brevity maintains them under a principle of uncertainty or indetermination', Deleuze 1996.

4 Bergson recognizes that transcendental idealism does not amount to transcendental illusionism. On Kant as a realist see also C. S. Peirce 1992: 90–1. For a clear account of Kant's commitment to transcendental idealism and empirical realism (unlike Berkeley Kant is not an empirical idealist) see the helpful discussion in Gardner 1999: 88–101. See also Guyer 1987: 20–5, 323–33, 413–17.

5 Dorothea Olkowski identifies the work of Antonio Damasio as falling into the internalist trap Bergson identitfied. See Olkowski 1999: note 28: 257–8; and see Damasio 1994 and especially the treatment of images in his recent study *The Feeling of What Happens* 1999, including the appendix: 317ff. The work of

Daniel C. Dennett is well known for its critique of Cartesian materialism, the view arrived at in the philosophy of mind when Descartes's mind–body dualism is discarded but the image of a central (and material) 'theatre' representing the locus of consciousness is retained (see Dennett 1991: 107). Dennett wishes to replace this idea of a Cartesian theatre with what he calls a 'Multiple Drafts' model (chapter 5, and p. 321). His position is materialist in that it adheres to the view that 'the mind is the brain' (33). In spite of the innovation it endeavours to make, however, it is not clear, for the Bergsonian at least, that this position completely escapes the predicaments of the Cartesian materialist. See also the remarks made in Dennett 1996: 72–3, 155–6.

6   See the helpful discussion in Moore 1996: 30–1.

7   For a wide-ranging treatment of these patterns see Mitchell 1984. Bergson's non-dependency on a subject–object duality is evidence of his idealism for Russell (1914: 345) and of his materialism for Deleuze.

8   As Moore notes, representation 'is a bad picture of perception' because a living body does not make a picture of an object but rather selects some of its properties in accordance with its needs and projects (its virtual actions) (Moore 1996: 27). If we suppose that it is necessary to ask after the conditions of image-perception (of picturability and perceptibility), we should not simply equate Bergson's position with either that of Kant or Wittgenstein, Moore argues. This is because on Bergson's model the conditions are 'shallower', arising not from either logical requirements of sense or meaning, or from *a priori* ones for the existence of a perceptible world, but rather 'from the (realised) possibility that the world contains objects which are capable of action like our own bodies' (26).

9   See Schopenhauer 1992: 81 and Nietzsche 1968: sections 567 and 636. For further insight into Nietzsche see my essay in *Nietzsche-Studien* 2000e, especially 159–60 and 165–70. Dennett is one current figure who espouses a subtractive theory of perception. See his contribution to Block 1981: 54–5. He has, however, been criticized for adhering to a spurious distinction between mental images and real images. See Mitchell 1984: 535.

10 The philosophical insight that 'all consciousness is something' informs Deleuze's reading of Michel Tournier's novel *Friday*, which reworks the Robinson Crusoe story: 'Consciousness ceases to be a light cast upon objects in order to become a pure phosphorescence of things in themselves. Robinson is but the consciousness of the island, but the consciousness of the island is the consciousness the island has of itself – it is the island in itself' (Deleuze 1990: 311).

11 Deleuze provides an account of the emergence of perception within matter – conceived as a difference in degree – in terms of a cooling-down of the plane of immanence: 'Even at the level of the most elementary living beings one would have to imagine micro-intervals. Smaller and smaller intervals between more and more rapid movements ... biologists speak of "primeval soup", which made living beings possible ... It is here that outlines of axes appear in an acentred universe, a left and a right, a high and a low. One should therefore conceive of micro-intervals even in the primeval soup. Biologists say that these phenomena could not be produced when the earth was very hot. Therefore one should conceive of a cooling down of the plane of immanence, correlative to the first opacities, to the first screen obstructing the diffusion of light. It is here that the first outlines of solids or rigid and geometric bodies would be formed' (Deleuze

1986: 63). On the significance of the interval in Bergson see Olkowski 2000. The specific contribution Olkowski makes, and it is a remarkably innovative one, is to construe the interval in terms of a sensory-motor occurrence positioned at the intersection of matter and memory, in which 'Its flow of affective sensations constitutes an ontological memory, a world memory in which nothing is originally separated from anything else, and the inside and outside are derivative conceptually as well as experientially' (82–3). It is with this construal of the 'interval' in terms of ontological memory that she seeks to re-think and to map anew sexual difference.

12 'cf. Bergson saying: we have already given ourselves the consciousness by positing the "images", and therefore we do not have to deduce it at the level of the "conscious" living being, which is *less* and not more than the universe of images, which is one concentration or abstraction of them — — It was meaningless to thus realize the consciousness before the consciousness. And this is why we say, for our part, that what is primary is not the diffuse "consciousness" of the "images" . . . it is Being' (Merleau-Ponty 1973: 251).

13 In a footnote to the text Deleuze qualifies his appreciation of Sartre's essay as follows: 'The idea of an "impersonal or pre-personal" transcendental field, producing the I and the Ego, is of great importance. What hinders this thesis from developing all its consequences in Sartre's work is that the impersonal transcendental field is still determined as the field of a consciousness, and as such must then be unified by itself through a play of intentionalities or pure retentions' (1990: 343–4, note 5).

14 See Paul Churchland's helpful discussion of identity theory in Churchland 1988: 26–36. His own eliminative materialism is often construed as a descendant of identity theory. However, it is clear that his materialism does not aim to come up with a set of complete one-to-one match-ups between the intuitions of folk psychology and the concepts of theoretical neuroscience; the aim is rather to 'eliminate' this psychology. The 'brain' of eliminative materialism would become truly interesting if the discussion moved out of the ineffable realm of qualia, which gets treated through a notion of representation in terms of vector coding and which has the effect of reducing perception to an interior vision, and its insights were linked up with the self-surveying brain (the brain as a rhizome and the brain as event) which Deleuze and Guattari focus on in the denouement to *What is Philosophy?* drawing on the work of Raymond Ruyer.

15 See Moore 1996: 52.

7 THE BEING OF MEMORY AND THE TIME OF THE SELF: FROM PSYCHOLOGY TO AN ONTOLOGY OF THE VIRTUAL

1 Merleau-Ponty does acknowledge the existence of a past that has never been present (1989: 242). He articulates the time of subjectivity as a dialectic: 'The duality of *naturata* and *naturans* is therefore converted into a dialectic of consti-tuted and constituting time' (240). While time 'exists only for a subjectivity' it is possible to say that 'this subject is time itself' (241). And note this remark: 'We are not in some incomprehensible way an activity joined to a passivity, an automatism

surmounted by a will, a perception surmounted by a judgement, but wholly active and wholly passive, because we are the *upsurge* of time' (428, my emphasis).

2 Deleuze's problem with phenomenology remains virtually the same from *Difference and Repetition* and *Logic of Sense* to *What is Philosophy?* Within the phenomenological project there takes place a limitation of the transcendental field to the requirements of common sense, with the result that it is not able to escape the domain of *doxa* but becomes a prisoner of *Ur-doxa* (Deleuze 1994: 137 and Deleuze and Guattari 1994: 142; see also Deleuze 1990, fourteenth series; see also Husserl 1970b: 155–6; 1973: 53ff., 387ff.). As a result philosophy becomes powerless to break with the form of common sense or to escape the tyranny of psychological and phenomenological clichés.

3 For insight into the differences between Deleuze's reconfiguration of the transcendental and Husserl's conception see the helpful chapter on Deleuze in Turetzky 1998, especially pp. 212ff.

4 For example, *Proust and* Signs (1964), Bergsonism (1966), *Cinema 2* (1985), *Foucault* (1986), and *What is Philosophy?* (1991).

5 See Bergson 1991: 168: 'There is not, in man at least, a purely sensori-motor state, any more than there is in him an imaginative life without some slight activity beneath it. Our psychical life . . . oscillates normally between these two extremes.'

6 It should be noted, however, that Russell had great problems trying to make sense of the notion of a pure past. His difficulties with the idea stem, I believe, from his failure to grasp the notion of the virtual at work in Bergson's thinking on memory. He mistakenly insists that whenever Bergson speaks of the past he can only mean a *present memory* of the past. See the discussion in Russell 1914: 341ff. In his major study on time Whitrow repeats Russell's myopic reading of Bergson on this issue: the difference is not between past and present but between perception and recollection both conceived as *present facts* (1980: 80–1). In his 1915 treatment of time, however, Russell seems positively open to the conjecture that the past is not simply dead and buried and that it is not only the present which has being: '. . . it is obvious that "past" expresses a relation to "present", i.e., a thing is "past" when it has a certain relation to the present, or to a constituent of the present. At first sight, we should naturally say that what is past cannot also be present; but this would be to assume that no particular can exist at two different times, or endure throughout a finite period of time. It would be a mistake to make such as assumption, and therefore we shall not say that what is past cannot also be present' (1915: 222–3). Deleuze's reading of the pure past, however, is clearly making a much stronger claim than this: the past exists on its own plane and not only in relation to a present (hence the need for a distinction between ontological memory and the psychological present). Mullarkey is one recent commentator who wishes to demote the role played by memory in Bergson's thinking on time, and his argument will be discussed in a later section of the essay.

7 Contemporary approaches in neuroscience work with the idea of there being multiple systems of memory with different brain organizations and that depend on different brain systems. For further insight see Squire 1998: 53–72. See also the study by Schacter 1996: 169ff.

8 See Bergson 1991: 168–9: 'memory, laden with the whole of the past, responds to the appeal of the present state by two simultaneous movements, one of

translation, by which it moves in its entirety to meet experience, contracting more
or less, though without dividing, with a view to action; and the other of rotation
upon itself, by which it turns toward the situation of the moment, presenting to it
that side of itself which may prove to be the most useful. To these varying
degrees of contraction correspond the various forms of association by similarity.'

9 Compare Husserl 1964: 77: '. . . the whole is reproduced, not only the then
present of consciousness with its flux but "implicitly" the whole stream of consciousness up to the living present. This means that as an essential *a priori*
phenomenological formation memory is in a continuous flux because conscious
life is in constant flux and is not merely fitted member by member into the
chain'.

10 We can make a contrast with Spinoza here: 'The human body can undergo many
changes, and nevertheless retain impressions, *or* traces, of the objects . . . and
consequently, the same images of things', *Ethics*, Book III, postulate 2.

11 For a similar critique of associationism see Husserl 1964: 78. In criticizing the
idea that we perceive and remember in terms of a 'mere chain of "associated"
intentions, one after the other', Husserl does not appeal to 'planes' but rather to
an intention within the context of a 'series of possible fulfillments'. One might
say that it is memory which gives time to perception.

12 Again, compare Husserl 1964: 53: 'The intuition of the past itself cannot be a
symbolization (*Verbildlichung*); it is an originary consciousness.'

13 Bergson's passage is misleading if it led us to suppose that perception is solely
actual while only memory has a virtual existence. As we saw in the previous essay
perception has to be credited with its own conditions of virtuality (perception
is bound up with virtual action, for example). Bergson extends the compass
of virtual perception in a novel way in a letter to G. Lechalas dated end of 1897:
'. . . in the case of memory I have positive reasons for affirming that recalled
memories are chosen from the totality of past states, which are conserved in an
unconscious form. By contrast, in the case of perception, I can see and I try to
show how the perceived image is taken from a wider field than that of actual
perception, but I have no means of determining how far this virtual perception
extends . . . we perceive virtually many more things than we perceive materially
and actually' (1972: 412).

14 It is on this point that Deleuze, in his 1956 essay on Bergson and difference,
draws a comparison between Bergson and Freud: 'In a different way from Freud,
but just as profoundly, Bergson saw that memory was a function of the future,
that memory and will were but one and the same function, that only a being
capable of memory could turn away from its past, detach itself, not repeat it, do
something new. In this way the word "difference" designates both *the particular
that is* and *the new which is made*' (1999: 56).

15 Sartre on temporality provides us with an example of a mode of thinking which
refuses to accept the difference between past and present could be anything other
than a difference of degree (Sartre 1989: 110). The later Merleau-Ponty, by
contrast, insists upon the need to mark their difference as one of nature (1973:
194).

16 Compare Husserl 1973: section 37: 'The unity of memory and its separation from
perception': 159–62. See also Husserl 1964: 84–5 on 'Memory of the Present',
1970: 19ff.; and James 1952: 411 and 425–7. In his treatment of temporality in

Being and Nothingness Sartre identifies Bergson and Husserl as the two thinkers who posit a being of the past. While recognizing the passivity of memory, the being of the past for Sartre can only be a 'not-being' for us: the past can only ever *be*, therefore, in terms of a past of some present and the project of the For-Itself (Sartre 1989: 109–10). On the immemorial past and its significance see Levinas: 'Does thought have meaning only through consciousness of the world? Or is not the potential surplus of the world itself, over and beyond all *presence*, to be sought in an immemorial past – that is, irreducible to a bygone present – in the trace left by this past which, perhaps, marks it out as a part of creation, a mark we should not be too quick to reduce to the condition of a causal effect and which, in any case, presupposes an otherness representable neither in terms of the correlations of knowledge nor in terms of the synchrony of re-presentation' (Levinas 1983: 106–7).

17 In a letter to James dated 15 February 1905 Bergson makes it clear that the existence of a reality 'outside of all actual consciousness' does not refer, in the manner of the old substantialism, to an *underlying* reality but rather to a reality which is intimately mingled with conscious life and '*interwoven with it*' (1972: 652).

18 Some helpful and astute insights into the relation between Bergson and Freud can be found in Game 1991: 103–9. In *DR* Deleuze makes a crucial observation with respect to repetition in Freud: 'Freud noted from the beginning that in order to stop repeating it was not enough to remember in the abstract (without affect), nor to form a concept in general, nor even to represent the repressed event in all its particularity: it was necessary to seek out the memory where it was, to install oneself directly in the past in order to accomplish a living connection between the knowledge and the resistance, the representation and the blockage. We are not, therefore, healed by simple anamnesis, any more than we are made ill by amnesia' (Deleuze 1994: 18–19).

19 For an instructive account of the history of associationism and a treatment of its contemporary manifestations see Sutton 1998. See also the history of psychology provided by Reed 1997. Neither texts mention or refer to Bergson. For a short and incisive account of Bergson's critique of associationist psychology see McNamara 1999: 42–4. See also Deleuze's discussion of the formal importance of an associationist psychology in Proust, Deleuze 2000: 55ff., and the discussion of Bergson and Hume in Deleuze 1994: 71 ff. See also the chapter on memory in James 1952: 421–52.

20 McNamara contends that Bergson's demand for a theory of the mechanism of association has largely been met within modern cognitive neuroscience: 'For modern theorists of the dynamics of associative networks, selection is largely accomplished via variations on the mechanisms of (1) lateral inhibition and (2) the search process . . . Bergson, I believe, would find such explanations congenial and impressive.'

21 For example, if I utter to myself a word from a foreign language this might make me think of this language in general or of a particular voice that I once heard pronounce it in a certain way. Such associations by similarity are not simply due to some accidental arrival of two different representations and in terms of some law of mechanical attraction applied to discrete recollections; rather, they are the result of two distinct degrees of tension within memory and 'answer to two

different mental *dispositions* . . .', in the one case nearer to the pure image, in the other more disposed to an immediate response and to action (Bergson 1991: 169).

22 See also Deleuze, 1986: 76–7: 'What can be more subjective than a delirium, a dream, a hallucination? But what can be closer to materiality made up of luminous wave and molecular interaction?'

23 See Crary 1999: 324; see also Deleuze 1986: 71–7. Where Crary sees Bergson as relying on a notion of a unified ego and a consciousness grounded in praxis (326), Game astutely shows that for Bergson 'there is no unitary, singular self' (1991: 102).

24 In *Cinema 2* Deleuze will speak of an absolute outside and inside confronting one another, and he argues that it is time-memory that makes relative insides and outsides communicate like interiors and exteriors (1989: 207). In his book on Foucault Deleuze insists that when time 'becomes a subject' it is always an 'outside' that is being folded, an outside of forces: disturbances, perturbations, shocks, etc. It is not as if the outside constitutes some ultimate spatiality deeper than time, but rather that time itself can be placed on the outside (time as other) and 'conditioned by the fold' (1988: 108; see also 118–19). The space of time is never that of a trip down memory lane. It is not simply a recollected past we return to, rather the past returns to us in a way we have never lived it: not a remembrance of things past but the search for lost time. This is truly uncanny and beyond a return of the repressed: as Deleuze says, the only crime is time itself. Badiou correctly notes of Deleuze's thinking of time: 'Were the past only an aftermath of the present, it would not be creation or power, but irremediable absence; it would be the production of the nothingness of the present-that-passes. Being would then have to be said, at the same point, in two different senses: according to its mobile-being and according to its absence. There would then be a *nostalgic* division of Being. Nothing is more foreign to Deleuze (or to Bergson) than this nostalgia. The past is the positive production of time' (Badiou 2000a: 61). Deleuze's deployment of Bergson's pure past is, however, even more radical than Badiou appreciates in this insight.

25 For those readers who are puzzled by my introduction of Heidegger into the reading of Deleuze at this juncture I refer them to note 33: 148 of the English translation of Deleuze's book on Foucault (Deleuze 1988), where it is clear that Deleuze has engaged with Heidegger's 1929 Kant book and that it is from this reading that he has derived the notion of time as 'auto-affection'.

26 In Sartre's *Transcendence of the Ego* Sartre speaks of the 'ego' in terms of a *virtual* locus of unity and of the human being as a sorcerer for itself. We are 'surrounded by magical objects' which conceal the spontaneity of consciousness and which also provide the ego with a passivity by which it is capable of being affected. See Sartre (1957): 81–2. Sartre is fully cognizant of the fact that he has made a phenomenological departure from Bergson and accuses Bergson of confusing freedom with 'object' rather than 'consciousness' (80). Deleuze will always go with Bergson over Sartre. On the significance of *Transcendence of the Ego* for Deleuze see Deleuze 1990, Fourteenth series: 98–9, where Deleuze describes it as 'decisive' and Deleuze and Guattari 1994: 47–8. On the transcendental field without a transcendental ego see also Sartre 1989: 235.

27 The notion of passive synthesis came to play an important role in Husserl's phenomenology. In developing his conception of it Deleuze draws primarily on

Hume and in relation to Bergson (the stress is on the syntheses afforded by contemplation and contraction). Deleuze does, however, refer to Husserl on retention in chapter 2 of *DR*. It should not be overlooked that Husserl's utilization of passive synthesis is also derived, in part, from a reading of Hume. In essence, Husserl transforms à principle of association from being a psychological and naturalistic one to being a transcendental-phenomenological one (an *Ur-konstitution*). For Husserl on passive synthesis see especially 1966: 51–8: 117ff.; see also Husserl 1973: 53ff., 156–7. On Hume see the crucial remarks in Husserl 1969: 256–60 and 1967: section 39. For Deleuze's early views on synthesis and relations see his first published book, on Hume, empiricism, and subjectivity, [1953] 1991: 100–1. See also Sartre on Husserl and passive synthesis in 1989: xxv. For insight into the difference between Deleuze and Husserl on passive syntheses see Turetzky 1998: 212.

28 See also Deleuze 1994: 75: 'Organisms awake to the sublime words of the third *Ennead*: all is contemplation!' See the *Enneads*, III, 8.

29 In *DR* Deleuze may be reworking of Bergson's distinction in *TFW* between the two selves, the self of duration and the self of public, clock time, now reconfigured as the self of virtual time and the self of sensori-motor habits. For Kant's presentation of the self or subject as appearance and 'not as it in itself' see *CPR*: B 156 and B 158–9.

30 Although saving the past in itself requires the being of involuntary memory Deleuze insists that art 'in its essence', art that is 'superior to life', is not simply based on this memory (neither is it based on the imagination). Signs of life and signs of art are to be distinguished in that the latter can only be explained in terms of 'pure thought as a faculty of essences' (Deleuze 2000: 55). Proust's search, therefore, is not simply an effort of recall or an exploration of memory: 'The Search for lost time is in fact a search for truth. If called a search for lost time, it is only to the degree that truth has an essential relation to time' (15).

31 On the fugitive character of recollections, and on their becoming materialized by chance and accidental determinations, see Bergson 1991: 106; for further artistic insight into pure memory see Bataille 1988: 141–3.

32 In his excellent book *Proustian Space* (1963, translated 1977), Georges Poulet seeks to show that not only is the hero of Proust's novel lost in time, he is also lost in space, not knowing who or where he is. As well as dealing with the complication of time, then, Proust's novel addresses itself to dislocations of space. Poulet reads the novel as challenging Bergson's theses on time and space, in particular the claim that we are always projecting time into space whenever we juxtapose our psychic states. But Poulet's thinking moves too quickly in seeking to establish this point. The following remark from Deleuze should always be borne in mind when encountering Bergson on time and space: '. . . the question of space will need to be reassessed on new foundations. For space will no longer simply be a form of exteriority, a sort of screen that denatures duration . . . Space itself will need to be based in things, in relations between things and between durations . . . This was to be the double progression of the Bergsonian philosophy' (Deleuze 1991: 49). Significant in regard to this whole issue are the movements of thought being made by Heidegger in his later text, *Time and Being*. These are movements which radically complicate the idea of there being some 'actual' space or place of time. These movements of thought would benefit from an encounter with Bergsonism.

33 Film explores the expressionism of the crystal in which the movement of expression is from the mirror to the seed. If *Citizen Kane* can be credited with being the first great film of a cinema of time it is because in it time is not subordinated to movement but rather movement to time: 'The hero acts, walks, and moves; but it is the past that he plunges himself into and moves in . . .' (Deleuze 1989: 106). In Welles's film 'depth of field' effects a deformation of both space and time, involving dilations and contractions and exploring virtual zones of the past. The 'depth' is not a mere technique, but serves as a figure of temporalization that gives rise to the adventures of memory – adventures, Deleuze insists, that are not so much psychological accidents but more like 'misadventures in time, disturbances of its constitution' (110). Through the use of montage Welles does not give us an indirect image of time on the basis of movement, but rather its direct image that organizes an order of non-chronological coexistences and relations. The pure recollection, 'Rosebud', serves not to identify the true or authentic past, but to 'cast suspicion on all the sheets of the past which have been evoked by various characters . . .' 'Rosebud' is without meaning, and even when our focus is on the shattering of the glass ball that leaves the hand of the dying Kane, we do not glimpse the future but only a non-germinal life. What the film explores is not the triumph of a life, but its failure: Kane dies alone, 'recognizing the emptiness of his whole life, the sterility of all his sheets' (112) When we reach the sheets of the past we find ourselves carried away 'by the undulations of a great wave' for here 'time gets out of joint, and we enter into temporality as a state of *permanent crisis*' (ibid.). But if there is a dimension of time missing from this classic of modern cinema, it is that of the future.

34 David Rodowick makes an astute point about the use of flashback that is worth noting: 'Flashbacks present an interesting test case. As a recollection-image, the flashback detours time the better to restore a linear causality. One plunges from the end to the beginning to restore understanding of the sequence of events through which destiny brought us to this point . . . The recollection-image . . . "actualizes virtuality" by plumbing strata of pure memory, seeking out an image from the past through which to represent itself' (1997: 91). We should also pay heed to these remarks of Welles: '. . . a flashback implies a sustained narrative and the effect of a continuity within its own framework which I think should be carefully avoided . . . Memories are like the uncut rushes of a movie. They make their own patterns, unlike the patterns of drama. The emphasis is never the emphasis of a script writer – so that a loaf of bread, or a cup of cocoa – a lithograph on a wall – a shrine – any inconsequential blade of grass may find itself a star performer in one's memories of thing's past. The unities find no special observances in Memory' (Welles cited in Callow 1996: 528).

35 Conceived as a labyrinthine line of time Aion offers another way of showing the dislocations of time and the pathological character of a lived duration: today there is only the day before and the day after; something has just happened and something is about to happen, but it is not happening now. In *Logic of Sense* Deleuze describes the time of Aion as 'independent of all matter' (it is an empty form) and 'incorporeal', it is even an 'instant', one without thickness and extension which 'subdivides each present into past and future, rather than vast and thick presents which comprehend both future and past in relation to one another' (1990: 62, 164–5). It is in the terms of this strange time that Deleuze approaches

the time of the event, which he conceives, paradoxical as it may sound, as a *dead time*, a time of the meanwhile (*entre-temps*) which insists when nothing seems to be happening, an infinite awaiting in reserve. Although nothing happens in the event it is the immensity of its reserve (a pure virtual) that makes it possible for things to become and change. Deleuze defines the event as 'immaterial, incorporeal, unlivable, pure reserve' (Deleuze and Guattari 1994: 156). It can be comprehended only in terms of the 'strange indifference of an intellectual intuition' (ibid.). For further insight into this time of the event see Ansell Pearson 2000c: 141–56.

36 On the three metamorphoses see the opening discourse of part one of Nietzsche's *Thus Spoke Zarathustra*, 1969: 54–6.

37 For some important remarks on the relation of the other (time) to Eros and power see Levinas 1987: 90.

38 The relation between the line and the circle as Deleuze depicts it is a little more complicated than I am indicating here; see Deleuze 1994: 91, 115ff and 298ff. Nevertheless, in *DR* Deleuze's commitment is to the line and not to the circle of time or life, and he argues that the circular reading of eternal return belongs to the spirit of gravity, not to Zarathustra, However, in *Ecce Homo* Nietzsche does refer to himself as the 'advocate of the circle'.

39 See Heidegger, 'Who is Nietzsche's Zarathustra?': 'What is left for us to say, if not this: Zarathustra's doctrine does not bring redemption from revenge. We do say it. Yet we say it by no means as a misconceived refutation of Nietzsche's philosophy. We do not even utter it as an objection against Nietzsche's thinking. But we say it in order to turn our attention to the fact – and the extent to which – Nietzsche's thought too is animated by the spirit of prior reflection' (Heidegger 1984: 229).

40 This empty time refers to the form of time (including its formlessness) and not to the time that is void of change and of events and to which Kant denies any reality (A 192/B 237).

41 Deleuze had already complicated the straight line of time in these terms in *The Logic of Sense*. See Deleuze 1990, tenth series, especially 62. On the labyrinth see also Deleuze 1983: 188: '. . . the labyrinth is becoming, the affirmation of becoming.'

BIBLIOGRAPHY

Where two dates are given the one given in square brackets refers to the original date of publication.

The references in the text to 'Bergson 1920' and 'Bergson 1965' refer to two volumes of his essays without specifying the dates of the individual essays within them and which are given below.

Adamson, G. Dale (1999), 'Henri Bergson: Time, Evolution, and Philosophy', *World Futures* (54:1), 135–62.

—— (2000), 'Science and Philosophy: Two Sides of the Absolute', *Pli: The Warwick Journal of Philosophy* (9), 53–86.

Adolphe, L. (1952), 'Bergson et l'Élan Vital', *Les Études Bergsoniennes*, vol. 3: 81–138.

Adorno, T. W. (1966), *Negative Dialektik*, Frankfurt am Main, Suhrkamp.

—— (1991), *Notes to Literature (Volume One)*, trans. S. W. Nicholsen, New York, Columbia University Press.

Agamben, G. (1999), *Potentialities. Collected Essays in Philosophy*, Stanford, Stanford University Press.

Alliez, E. (1998), 'On Deleuze's Bergsonism', *Discourse* (20:3), 226–47.

Ansell Pearson, K. (1997a), *Viroid Life: Perspectives on Nietzsche and the Transhuman Condition*, London, Routledge.

—— (1997b), 'Living the Eternal Return as the Event', *Journal of Nietzsche Studies* (14), 64–98.

—— (1998), 'Nietzsche contra Darwin', in D. W. Conway (ed.), *Nietzsche: Critical Assessments*, London, Routledge, vol. 3: 7–32.

—— (1999), *Germinal Life: The Difference and Repetition of Deleuze*, London, Routledge.

—— (2000a), 'Spectropoieis and Rhizomatics: Learning to Live with Death and Demons', in G. Banham and C. Blake (eds), *Evil Spirits: Nihilism and the Fate of Modernity*, Manchester, Manchester University Press: 124–46.

—— (2000b), 'Thinking Immanence: On the Event of Deleuze's Bergsonism', in G. Genosko (ed.), *Deleuze and Guattari: Critical Assessments*, London, Routledge, vol. 2: 1343–73.

—— (2000c), 'Pure Reserve: Deleuze, Philosophy, and Immanence', in M. Bryden (ed.), *Deleuze and Religion*, London, Routledge: 141–56.

—— (2000d), 'Nietzsche's Brave New World of Force: Thoughts On the Time Atom Theory Fragment and Boscovich's Influence on Nietzsche', *Journal of Nietzsche Studies* (20), 5–33.

—— (2000e), 'The Miscarriage of Life and the Future of the Human: Thinking Beyond the Human Condition with Nietzsche', *Nietzsche-Studien* (19), 153–77.

—— (2001), (co-ed. with J. Mullarkey), *Bergson: Key Selected Writings*, London, Continuum.

Aristotle, *De Anima (On the Soul)* (1986), trans. H. Lawson-Tancred, Harmondsworth, Middlesex, Penguin.

—— *Physics* (1996), trans. R. Waterfield, Oxford, Oxford University Press.

—— *Metaphysics* (1998), trans. H. Lawson-Tancred, Harmondsworth, Middlesex, Penguin.

Ayer, A. J. (1973), *The Central Questions of Philosophy*, Harmondsworth, Middlesex, Penguin.

Bachelard, G. (1999) [1950], *The Dialectic of Duration*, trans. M. MacAllister Jones, Manchester, Clinamen Press.

—— (2000), 'The Instant', in R. Durie (ed.), *Time and the Instant*, Manchester, Clinamen Press: 64–96.

Badiou, A. (1988), *L'être et l'événement*, Paris, Éditions du Seuil.

—— (1994), 'Gilles Deleuze, *The Fold: Leibniz and the Baroque*', in C. V. Boundas and D. Olkowski (eds), *Gilles Deleuze and the Theater of Philosophy*, London, Routledge: 51–73.

—— (1999), *Manifesto for Philosophy*, trans. N. Madarasz, New York, SUNY Press.

—— (2000a), *Deleuze. The Clamour of Being*, trans. L. Burchill, Minneapolis, University of Minnesota Press.

—— (2000b), 'Of Life as a Name of Being, or Deleuze's Vitalist Ontology', trans. A. Toscano, *Pli: The Warwick Journal of Philosophy* (10), 174–91.

Barbour, J. (1999), *The End of Time*, London, Weidenfeld & Nicolson.

—— (2000), 'Time, Instants, Duration and Philosophy', in R. Durie (ed.), *Time and the Instant*, Manchester, Clinamen Press: 96–112.

Barthelmy-Madaule, M. (1966), *Bergson, adversaire de Kant: Étude Critique de la Conception Bergsonniene du Kantisme*, Paris, PUF.

Bataille, G. (1988) [1954], 'Digression on Poetry and Marcel Proust', *Inner Experience*, trans. L. A. Boldt, New York, State University of New York Press: 135–52.

Baugh, B. (1993), 'Deleuze and Empiricism', *Journal of the British Society for Phenomenology* (24:1), 15–31.

Benda, J. (1954), *Sur le succès du Bergsonisme*, Paris, Mercvre de France.

Benjamin, W. (1973), 'The Image of Proust', *Illuminations*, trans. H. Zohn, London, Collins: 203–19.

Bergson, H. (1920), *Mind-Energy*, trans. H. Wildon Carr, New York, Henry Holt.

—— (1920) [1901], 'Dreams', in *Mind-Energy*: 104–34.

—— (1920) [1904], 'Brain and Thought: A Philosophical Illusion', in *Mind-Energy*: 231–57.

—— (1920) [1908], 'Memory of the Present and False Recognition', in *Mind-Energy*: 134–86.

—— (1920) [1911], 'Life and Consciousness', in *Mind-Energy*: 3–37.

—— (1959) [1884], *The Philosophy of Poetry: The Genius of Lucretius*, trans. W. Baskin, New York, Philosophical Library.

—— (1959), *Oeuvres*, Paris, Presses Universitaires de France.

—— (1960) [1889], *Time and Free Will*, trans. F. L. Pogson, New York, Harper & Row.

—— (1965), *The Creative Mind*, trans. M. L. Andison, Totowa, Littlefield, Adams, & Co.

—— (1965) [1903], 'Introduction to Metaphysics', in *The Creative Mind*: 159–201.

—— (1965) [1904], 'The Life and Work of Ravaisson', in *The Creative Mind*: 220–52.

—— (1965) [1911], 'Philosophical Intuition', in *The Creative Mind*: 107–30.

—— (1965) [1911], 'The Perception of Change', in *The Creative Mind*: 130–59.

—— (1965) [1913], 'The Philosophy of Claude Bernard', in *The Creative Mind*: 201–9.

—— (1965) [1922], 'Introduction I and II', in *The Creative Mind*: 11–30, 30–91.

—— (1965) [1930], 'The Possible and the Real', in *The Creative Mind*: 91–107.

—— (1970) [1889], *Aristotle's Concept of Place*, trans. J. K. Ryan in *Studies in Philosophy and the History of Philosophy*, vol. 5: 13–72.

—— (1972), *Mélanges*, Paris, PUF.

—— (1977) [1932], *The Two Sources of Morality and Religion*, trans. R. Ashley Audra and C. Brereton, University of Notre Dame Press.

—— (1983) [1907], *Creative Evolution*, trans. A. Mitchell, Lanham MD, University Press of America.

—— (1990), *Cours I: Leçons de Psychologie et de Métaphysique (Clermont-Ferrand 1887–8)*, Paris, PUF.

—— (1991) [1896], *Matter and Memory*, trans. N. M. Paul and W. S. Palmer, New York, Zone Books.

—— (1995), *Cours III: Leçons d'histoire de la philosophie moderne et Theories de l'âme*, Paris, PUF.

—— (1999) [1922], *Duration and Simultaneity*, trans. L. Jacobson and M. Lewis, with an introduction by R. Durie, Manchester, Clinamen Press.

Berkeley, G. (1962) [1710], *The Principles of Human Knowledge*, ed. G. J. Warnock, London, Fontana.

Block, N. (ed.) (1981), *Imagery*, Cambridge, Mass., MIT Press.

Boundas, C. V. (1996), 'Deleuze-Bergson: an Ontology of the Virtual', in P. Patton (ed.), *Deleuze: A Critical Reader*, Oxford, Basil Blackwell: 81–107.

Burwick, F. and Douglass, P. (eds) (1992), *The Crisis in Modernism: Bergsonism and the Vitalist Controversy*, Cambridge, Cambridge University Press.

Bussanich, J. (1996), 'Plotinus's Metaphysics of the One', in L. P. Gerson, *The Cambridge Companion to Plotinus*, Cambridge, Cambridge University Press: 38–66.

Butler, S. (1981) [1910], *Life and Habit*, London, Wildwood House.

Cache, B. (1995), *Earth Moves*, trans. A. Boyman and M. Speaks, Cambridge, Mass., MIT Press.

Cairns-Smith, A. G. (1985), *Seven Clues to the Origin of Life*, Cambridge, Cambridge University Press.

Callow, S. (1996), *Orson Welles: The Road to Xanadu*, London, Vintage.

Calvin, W. H. (1997), *How Brains Think*, London, Weidenfeld & Nicolson.

Canguilhem, G. (1943), 'Commentaire au troisième chapitre de *L'Évolution Créatrice*', *Bulletin de la Faculté Lettres de Strasbourg* (21), 126–43.

Čapek, M. (1970), *Bergson and Modern Physics*, Dordrecht, Nijhoff.

Caygill, H. (1995), *A Kant Dictionary*, Oxford, Basil Blackwell.

Chevalier, J. (1928), *Henri Bergson*, trans. L. A. Clare, London, Rider & Co.

Churchland, P (1988), *Matter and Consciousness* (revised edition), Cambridge, Mass., MIT Press.

Clark, A. (1997), *Being There: Putting Brain, Body and World Together Again*, Cambridge, Mass., MIT Press.

Cobb, Jr., J. B. and Griffin, D. R. (1978), *Mind in Nature: Essays on the Interface of Science and Philosophy*, Washington DC, University Press of America.

Collingwood, R. G. (1945), *The Idea of Nature*, Oxford, Clarendon Press.

Coveney, P. and Highfield, R. (1995), *Frontiers of Complexity*, London, Faber & Faber.

Crary, J. (1999), *Suspensions of Perception. Attention, Spectacle, and Modern Culture*, Cambridge, Mass., MIT Press.

Damasio, A. (1994), *Descartes's Error*, London, Macmillan Papermac.

—— (1999), *The Feeling of What Happens*, London, Heinemann.

Davies, P. (1995), *About Time: Einstein's Unfinished Revolution*, Harmondsworth, Middlesex, Penguin.

Deck, J. N. (1967), *Nature, Contemplation, and the One: A Study in the Philosophy of Plotinus*, Toronto, University of Toronto Press.

de Gruson, François Fabre Luce (1959), 'Bergson, Lecteur de Kant', *Les Études Bergsoniennes*, vol. 5: 171–90.

de Landa, M. (2001 forthcoming), *Intensive Science and Virtual Philosophy*, London, Continuum.

Delattre, F. (1948), 'Bergson et Proust: Accords et Dissonances', *Les Études Bergsoniennes*, vol. 1: 13–127.

Deleuze, G. (1981), *Francis Bacon: Logique de la Sensation*, Paris, Éditions de la Différence.

—— (1984) [1963], *Kant's Critical Philosophy: The Doctrine of the Faculties*, trans. H. Tomlinson and B. Habberjam, London, Athlone Press.

—— (1985), 'Les plages d'immanence', in A. Cuzenave and J. F. Lyotard, *L'Ort des confins*, Paris, PUF: 79–81.

—— (1986) [1983], *Cinema 1: The Movement-Image*, trans. H. Tomlinson and B. Habberjam, London, Athlone Press.

—— (1987) [1977], *Dialogues*, trans. H. Tomlinson and B. Habberjam, London, Athlone Press.

—— (1988) [1986], *Foucault*, trans. S. Hand, London, Athlone Press.

—— (1989) [1985], *Cinema 2: The Time-Image*, trans. H. Tomlinson and R. Galeta, London, Athlone Press.

—— (1990) [1969], *Logic of Sense*, trans., M. Lester with C. Stivale, London, Athlone Press.

—— (1991) [1953], *Empiricism and Subjectivity: An Essay on Hume's Theory of Nature*, trans. C. V. Boundas, New York, Columbia University Press.

—— (1991) [1966], *Bergsonism*, trans. H. Tomlinson and B. Habberjam, New York, Zone Books.

—— (1992) [1968], *Expressionism in Philosophy: Spinoza*, trans. M. Joughin, New York, Zone Books.

—— (1993) [1988], *The Fold: Leibniz and the Baroque*, trans. T. Conley, London, Athlone Press.

—— (1994) [1968], *Difference and Repetition*, trans. P. Patton, London, Athlone Press.

—— (1995) [1990], *Negotiations*, trans. M. Joughin, New York, Columbia University Press.

—— (1996), 'L'actuel et le virtuel', in *Dialogues*, second edition, Paris, Flammarion: 179–85.

—— (1997) [1995], 'Immanence . . . A Life', trans. N. Millett, *Theory, Culture, and Society* (14:2), 3–7.

—— (1998a) [1986], 'On Four Poetic Formulas that Might Summarize the Kantian Philosophy', in Deleuze, *Essays Critical and Clinical*, trans. D. W. Smith and M. A. Greco, London, Verso: 27–36.

—— (1998b), *Lessons on Kant*, March 14, March 21, March 28, April 4, trans. M. McMahon (imaginet.fr/deleuze).

—— (1998c), 'The Brain is the Screen: Interview with Gilles Deleuze', *Discourse* (20:3), 47–56.

—— (1998d), 'Boulez, Proust and Time: "Occupying without Counting"', trans. T. S. Murphy, *Angelaki* (3:2), 69–74.

—— (1999) [1956], 'Bergson's Conception of Difference', trans. M. McMahon, in J. Mullarkey (ed.), *The New Bergson*, Manchester, Manchester University Press: 42–66.

—— (2000) [1972], *Proust and Signs* (the complete text), trans. R. Howard, London, Athlone Press.

Deleuze, G. and Guattari, F. (1988) [1980], *A Thousand Plateaus*, London, Athlone Press.

—— (1994) [1991], *What is Philosophy?*, trans. H. Tomlinson, London, Verso.

Dennett, D. C. (1991), *Consciousness Explained*, London, Allen Lane.

—— (1993) [1969], *Content and Consciousness*, London, Routledge.

—— (1995), *Darwin's Dangerous Idea: Evolution and the Meanings of Life*, London, Allen Lane.

—— (1996), *Kinds of Minds*, London, Weidenfeld & Nicolson.

—— (1997), *Brainstorms: Philosophical Essays on Mind and Psychology*, Harmondsworth, Middlesex, Penguin.

—— (1998), *Brainchildren: Essays on Designing Minds*, Middlesex, Penguin.

Descartes, R. (1996) [1641], *Meditations on First Philosophy*, Cambridge, Cambridge University Press.

Dewey, J. (1912), 'Perception and Organic Action', *The Journal of Philosophy, Psychology, and Scientific Methods* (IX:24), 645–68.

Dillon, J. (1991), 'Plotinus: An Introduction', *Plotinus: The Enneads*, Harmondsworth, Middlesex, Penguin: lxxxiv-cii.

Dodds, E. R. (1928), 'The *Parmenides* of Plato and the Origin of the Neoplatonic One', *Classical Quarterly* (22), 129–43.

Durie, R. (2000), 'Splitting Time: Bergson's Philosophical Legacy', *Philosophy Today* (44), 152–68.

—— (2000a) (ed.), *Time and the Instant*, Manchester, Clinamen Press.

Eigen, M. (1992), *Steps Towards Life: A Perspective on Evolution*, Oxford, Oxford University Press.

Einstein, A. (1999) [1920], *Relativity: The Special and the General Theory*, London, Routledge.

—— (1998), *Einstein's Miraculous Year: Five Papers that changed the face of Physics*, ed. J. Stachel, Princeton, Princeton University Press.

Elsasser, W. (1953), 'A Reformulation of Bergson's Theory of Memory', *Philosophy of Science* (20), 7–21.

Fawcett, E. D. (1912), 'Matter and Memory', *Mind* (21), 201–32.

Foubert, J. (1973), 'Mystique plotinienne. Mystique bergsonniene', *Les Études Bergsoniennes*, vol.10: 7–73.

Frege, G. (1997), *The Frege Reader*, ed. M. Beaney, Oxford, Basil Blackwell.

Freud, S. (1991), *One Metapsychology*, Harmondsworth, Middlesex, Penguin.

Gallois, P. and Forzy, G. (1997), *Bergson et les Neurosciences*, Le Plessis Robinson, Institut Synthelabo.

Game, A. (1991), *Undoing the Social: Towards a Deconstructive Sociology*, Milton Keynes, Open University Press.

Gardner, S. (1999), *Kant and the 'Critique of Pure Reason'*, London, Routledge.

Gazzaniga, M. S. (1998), *The Mind's Past*, Berkeley, University of California Press.

Gerson, L. P. (1994), *Plotinus*, London, Routledge.

—— (1996), *The Cambridge Companion to Plotinus*, Cambridge, Cambridge University Press.

Gleick, J. (1987), *Chaos: Making a New Science*, London, Abacus.

Goethe, J. W. von (1988), *Scientific Studies* (vol. 12 of *The Collected Works*), ed. and trans. D. Miller, Princeton, Princeton University Press.

Gombrich, E. H. (1982), *The Image and the Eye*, Oxford, Phaidon Press.

Goodwin, B. C. (1995), *How the Leopard Changed Its Spots*, London, Phoenix.

Grassé, P. (1977), *Evolution of Living Organisms: Evidence for a New Theory of Transformation*, New York, Academic Press.

Gross, D. (1985), 'Bergson, Proust, and the Revaluation of Memory', *International Philosophical Quarterly* (25:4), 369–80.

Gunn, A. (1920), *Bergson and His Philosophy*, London, Methuen & Co.

Gunter, P. A. Y. (ed.) (1969), *Bergson and the Evolution of Physics*, Knoxville, University of Tennessee Press.

—— (1971), 'Bergson's Theory of Matter and Modern Cosmology', *Journal of the History of Ideas*, (XXXII:4), 525–43.

—— (1991), 'Bergson and Non-linear Non-equilibrium Thermodynamics: An Application of Method', *Revue Internationale de Philosophie* (45:2), 108–22.

Guyer, P. (1987), *Kant and the Claims of Knowledge*, Cambridge, Cambridge University Press.

Haas, A. (2000), *Hegel and the Problem of Multiplicity*, Evanston, Northwestern University Press.

Hadot, P. (1993), *Plotinus or The Simplicity of Vision*, trans. M. Chase, Chicago, University of Chicago Press.

Hardt, M. (1993), *Gilles Deleuze: An Apprenticeship in Philosophy*, London, UCL Press.

Harward, J. (1918/1919), 'What does Bergson Mean by Pure Perception?', *Mind* (27), 203–7 and (28), 463–70.

Hayden, P. (1995), 'From Relation to Practice in the Empiricism in Gilles Deleuze', *Man and World* (28:3), 281–302.

Hayles, N. K. (1999), *How We Became Posthuman: Virtual Bodies in Cybernetics, Literature, Informatics,* Chicago, University of Chicago Press.

Hegel, G. W. F. (1995) [1840], *Plato and the Platonists: Lectures on the History of Philosophy Volume 2*, trans. E. S. Haldane and F. H. Simson, Lincoln, University of Nebraska Press.

—— (1999) [1812], *Science of Logic*, trans. A. V. Miller, New York, Humanities Books.

Heidegger, M. (1972), *On Time and Being*, trans. J. Stambaugh, New York, Harper Torchbooks.

—— (1978) [1916], 'The Concept of Time in the Science of History', trans. H. S. Taylor and H. W. Uffelmann, *Journal of the British Society for Phenomenology* (9:1), 3–10.

—— (1984), *Nietzsche Volume Two: The Eternal Recurrence of the Same*, trans. D. F. Krell, New York, Harper & Row.

—— (1992) [1924], *The Concept of Time*, trans. W. McNeill, Oxford, Basil Blackwell.

—— (1995), *The Fundamental Concepts of Metaphysics* (1929–30 lecture course), trans. W. McNeill and N. Walker, Bloomington, Indiana University Press.

—— (1997a), *Phenomenological Interpretation of Kant's 'Critique of Pure Reason'* (1927–8 lecture course), trans. P. Emad and K. Maly, Bloomington, Indiana University Press.

—— (1997b) [1929], *Kant and the Problem of Metaphysics* (enlarged fifth edition), trans. R. Taft, Bloomington, Indiana University Press.

Heim, M. (1993), *The Metaphysics of Virtual Reality*, Oxford, Oxford University Press.

Henry, P. (1991), 'The Place of Plotinus in the History of Thought', *Plotinus: The Enneads*, Harmondsworth, Middlesex, Penguin: xlii–lxxxiv.

Höffding, H, (1915), *Modern Philosophers and Lectures on Bergson*, trans. A. C. Mason, London, Macmillan.

Horkheimer, M. (1934), 'Zur Bergsons Metaphysik der Zeit', *Zeitschrift für Sozialforschung* (3:3), 321–43.

Hulme, T. E. (1949), *Speculations: Essays on Humanism and the Philosophy of Art*, London, Routledge & Kegan Paul.

Hume, D. (1985) [1739–40], *A Treatise of Human Nature*, Harmondsworth, Middlesex, Penguin.

Husserl, E. (1931) [1913], *Ideas: General Introduction to Pure Phenomenology*, trans. W. R. Boyce Gibson, London, Allen & Unwin.

—— (1964) [1928], *The Phenomenology of Internal Time-Consciousness*, ed. M. Heidegger, trans. J. S. Churchill, The Hague, Martinus Nijhoff (based on lecture courses 1893–1917).

—— (1966), *Analysen zur Passiven Synthesis*, The Hague, Martinus Nijhoff (lecture courses 1918–26).

—— (1969) [1929], *Formal and Transcendental Logic*, trans. D. Cairns, The Hague, Martinus Nijhoff.

—— (1970a) [1929/33], *Cartesian Meditations*, trans. D. Cairns, The Hague, Martinus Nijhoff.

—— (1970b) [1954], *The Crisis of the European Sciences and Transcendental Phenomenology*, trans. D. Carr, Evanston, Northwestern University Press.

—— (1970c) [1900/1913/1921], *Logical Investigations I and II*, trans. J. N. Findlay, London, Routledge & Kegan Paul.

—— (1973) [1938], *Experience and Judgement: Investigations in a Genealogy of Logic*, trans. J. S. Churchill & K. Ameriks, London, Routledge & Kegan Paul.

Hyppolite, J. (1997) [1952], *Logic and Existence*, trans. L. Lawlor & A. Sen, New York, SUNY Press.

Jablonka E. and Lamb, M. J. (1995), *Epigenetic Inheritance and Evolution: The Lamarckian Dimension*, Oxford, Oxford University Press.

James, W. (1909), *A Pluralistic Universe*, London, Longmans, Green, & Co.
—— (1952) [1890], *The Principles of Psychology*, Chicago, William Benton
—— (1996) [1911], *Some Problems of Philosophy*, Lincoln, University of Nebraska Press.
—— (1996) [1912], *Essays in Radical Empiricism*, Lincoln, University of Nebraska Press.
—— (1988), *Manuscript Essays and Notes*, Cambridge, Mass., Harvard University Press.
Jankélévitch, V. (1959), *Henri Bergson*, Paris, PUF.
Jaspers, K. (1966), *Anaximander, Heraclitus, Parmenides, Plotinus, Lao-Tzu, Nagarjuna*, ed. H. Arendt, trans. R. Mannheim, New York, Harcourt Brace Jovanovich.
Jay, M. (1993), *Downcast Eyes. The Denigration of Vision in Twentieth-Century French Thought*, Berkeley, University of California Press.
Jubak, J. (1992), *In the Image of the Brain*, Boston, Little Brown & Co.
Kampis, G. (1993), 'Creative Evolution', *World Futures* (38), 131–7.
Kant, I. (1950) [1781/1787], *Critique of Pure Reason*, trans. N. Kemp Smith, London, Macmillan.
—— (1952) [1790], *Critique of Judgement*, trans J. C. Meredith, Oxford, Oxford University Press.
—— (1967), *Kant: Philosophical Correspondence 1759–99*, ed. A. Zweig, Chicago, University of Chicago Press.
—— (1992), *Kant: Theoretical Philosophy 1755–70*, trans. D. Walford, Cambridge, Cambridge University Press.
Lacey, A. R. (1989), *Bergson*, London, Routledge.
Leibniz, G. W. (1973) [1715–16], 'Correspondence with Clarke', *Leibniz: Philosophical Writings*, trans. M. Morris and G. H. R. Parkinson, London, Everyman: 205–39.
Le Roy, E. (1913), *A New Philosophy: Henri Bergson*, London, Williams & Norgate; New York, Henry Holt.
Levinas, E. (1983), 'Beyond Intentionality', in A. Montefiore (ed.), *Philosophy in France Today*, Cambridge, Cambridge University Press.
—— (1987), *Time and the Other*, trans. R. A. Cohen, Pittsburgh, Duquesne University Press.
—— (1998), *Entre Nous*, trans. M. B. Smith and B. Harshav, London, Athlone Press.
—— (1999), *Alterity and Transcendence*, trans. M. B. Smith, London, Athlone Press.
Levy, P. (1998), *Becoming Virtual: Reality in the Digital Age*, trans. R. Bononno, London, Plenum.
Lewis, W. (1927), *Time and Western Man*, London, Chatto & Windus.
Lindsay, A. D. (1911), *The Philosophy of Bergsonism*, London, J. M. Dent & Sons Ltd.
Lucretius (1994), *On the Nature of the Universe*, trans. R. E. Latham, Harmondsworth, Middlesex, Penguin.
Lyotard, J. F. (1991) [1954], *Phenomenology*, trans. B. Beakley, New York, SUNY Press.
McNamara, P. (1999), *Mind and Variability. Mental Darwinism, Memory, and Self*, London, Praeger.
Maritain, J. (1943), *Redeeming the Time*, London, The Centenary Press.
—— (1955), *Bergsonian Philosophy and Thomism*, trans. M. L. Andison, New York, Philosophical Library.
May, William E. (1970, 'The Reality of Matter in the Metaphysics of Bergson', *International Philosophical Quarterly* (10:4), 611–42.

Meissner, W. W. (1967), 'The Problem of Psychophysics in Bergson's Critique', *Journal of General Psychology* (66), 301–9.

Merleau-Ponty, M. (1964), *The Primacy of Perception*, trans. J. M. Edie, Evanston, Northwestern University Press.

—— (1973) [1959–60], *The Visible and the Invisible*, trans. A. Lingis, Evanston, Northwestern University Press.

—— (1988) [1953], *In Praise of Philosophy and Other Essays*, trans. J. Wild and J. Edie, Evanston, Northwestern University Press.

—— (1989) [1945], *Phenomenology of Perception*, trans. C. Smith, London, Routledge.

—— (1994), *La Nature: Notes Cours du Collège de France*, Paris, Éditions de Seuil.

Mitchell, W. J. (1984), 'What is an Image?', *New Literary History* (XV:3), 503–37.

Monod, J. (1971), *Chance and Necessity*, trans. A. Wainhouse, New York, A. A. Knopf.

Moore, A. W. (1990), *The Infinite*, London, Routledge.

Moore, F. C. T. (1996), *Bergson. Thinking Backwards*, Cambridge, Cambridge University Press.

Moran, D (2000), *Introduction to Phenomenology*, London, Routledge.

Morris, P. and Gruneberg, M. (eds) (1994), *Theoretical Aspects of Memory* (second edition), London, Routledge.

Morris, R. (1997), *Achilles in the Quantum Universe: The Definitive History of Infinity*, London, Souvenir Press.

Mullarkey, J. (1995), 'Bergson's Method of Multiplicity', *Metaphilosophy* (26:3), 230–59.

—— (1999), *Bergson and Philosophy*, Edinburgh, Edinburgh University Press.

Murphy, T. S. (1999), 'Beneath Relativity: Bergson and Bohm on Absolute Time', in J. Mullarkey (ed.), *The New Bergson*, Manchester, Manchester University Press: 66–84.

Niess, R. J. (1956), *Julien Benda*, Ann Arbor, University of Michigan Press.

Nietzsche, F. (1968), *The Will to Power*, trans. W. Kaufmann and R. J. Hollingdale, New York, Random House.

—— (1969), *Thus Spoke Zarathustra*, trans. R. J. Hollingdale, Harmondsworth, Middlesex, Penguin.

—— (1974), *The Gay Science*, trans. W. Kaufmann, New York, Random House.

—— (1979), *Ecce Homo*, trans. R. J. Hollingdale, Harmondsworth, Middlesex, Penguin.

Olkowski, D. (1999), *Gilles Deleuze and the Ruin of Representation*, Berkeley, University of California Press.

—— (2000), 'The End of Phenomenology: Bergson's Interval in Irigaray', *Hypatia*, (15:3), 73–91.

Papa-Grimaldi, A. (1998), *Time and Reality*, Aldershot, Ashgate.

Papanicolaou, A. C. and Gunter, P. A. Y. (eds), *Bergson and Modern Thought*, London, Harwood.

Peirce, C. S. (1992), *The Essential Peirce: Selected Philosophical Writings. Volume 1 (1867–1893)*, ed. N. Houser and C. Kloesel, Bloomington, Indiana University Press.

—— (1998), *The Essential Peirce: Selected Philosophical Writings: Volume 2 (1893–1913)*, ed. The Peirce Edition Project, Bloomington, Indiana University Press.

Plato (1977), *Timaeus*, trans. D. Lee, Harmondsworth, Middlesex, Penguin.

—— (1987), *Theaetetus*, trans. R. A. H. Waterfield, Harmondsworth, Middlesex, Penguin.

—— (1996), *Parmenides*, trans. M. L. Gill and P. Ryan, Indianapolis, Hackett.

Plotinus (1966–1988), *The Enneads* (seven volumes), trans. A. H. Armstrong, Cambridge, Mass., Harvard University Press (Loeb Classical Library).

—— (1991), *The Enneads*, Harmondsworth, Middlesex, Penguin.

Popper, K. R. (1992), *The Logic of Scientific Discovery*, London, Routledge.

—— (1998), *The World of Parmenides*, ed. A. F. Petersen and J. Mejer, London, Routledge.

Popper, K. R. and Eccles J. C. (1990), *The Self and Its Brain: An Argument for Interactionism*, London, Routledge.

Poulet, G. (1977), *Proustian Space*, trans. E. Coleman, Baltimore, Johns Hopkins University Press.

Prigogine, I. and Stengers, I. (1985), *Order out of Chaos*, London, Flamingo.

Proust, M. (1983), *Remembrance of Things Past* (*In Search of Lost Time*) (3 volumes), trans. C. K. Scott Moncrieff, T. Kilmartin and A. Mayor, Harmondsworth, Middlesex, Penguin.

Rajchman, J. (1998), *Constructions*, Cambridge, Mass., MIT Press.

—— (2000), *The Deleuze-Connections*, Cambridge, Mass., MIT Press.

Reed, E. S. (1997), *From Soul to Mind: The Emergence of Psychology from Erasmus Darwin to William James*, New Haven, Yale University Press.

Riemann, G B (1873), 'On the Hypotheses which Provide the Grounds for Geometry', trans. W. K. Clifford, *Nature* (8), 14ff.

Rodowick, D. N. (1997), *Gille Deleuze's Time Machine*, Durham, Duke University Press.

Rodriguez-Consuegra, F. A. (1996), 'Russell's Perilous Journey from Atomism to Holism 1919–1951', in R. Monk and A. Palmer, *Bertrand Russell and the Origins of Analytical Philosophy*, Bristol, Thoemmes Press, 217–45.

Rose, S. (1992), *The Making of Memory: From Molecules to Mind*, London, Bantam Press.

—— (1997), *Lifelines: Biology, Freedom, and Determinism*, London, Allen Lane.

—— (1998) (ed.), *From Brains to Consciousness? Essays on the New Sciences of the Mind*, London, Allen Lane.

Ruiz, M. (1997), 'Psychophysical Parallelism in the Philosophy of G. Deleuze', PhD thesis, University of Warwick.

Russell, B. (1912), 'The Philosophy of Bergson', *The Monist* (22:3), 321–47 (reprinted in *The Collected Papers of Bertrand Russell*, vol. 6, London, Routledge, 1992: 313–38).

—— [1912] (1992), 'On Matter', in *Collected Papers of Bertrand Russell*, vol. 6, ed. J. G. Slater, London Routledge: 80–95.

—— [1913a] (1992), 'Metaphysics and Intuition', in *The Collected Papers of Bertrand Russell*, vol. 6, ed. J. G. Slater, London, Routledge: 338–42.

—— [1913b], 'Mr Wildon Carr's Defence of Bergson', ibid.: 342–9.

—— [1914] (1922), *Our Knowledge of the External World*, London, Allen & Unwin.

—— [1914] (1986), 'Mysticism and Logic', in *Collected Papers of Bertrand Russell*, ed. J. G. Slater, London, Allen & Unwin, vol. 8: 30–49.

—— (1915), 'On the Experience of Time', *The Monist* (25), 212–33.

—— (1985) [1918/1924], *The Philosophy of Logical Atomism*, ed. with an Introduction by D. Pears, Chicago, Open Court.

—— (1992) [1903, 1937], *The Principles of Mathematics*, London, Routledge.
—— (1992) [1927], *The Analysis of Matter*, London, Routledge.
—— (1993) [1925], *ABC of Relativity*, London, Routledge.
—— (1995) [1919], *Introduction to Mathematical Philosophy*, London, Routledge.
Ruyer, R. (1952), *Neo-finalisme*, Paris, PUF.
Safranski, R. (1991), *Schopenhauer and the Wild Years of Philosophy*, trans. E. Osers, Cambridge, Mass., Harvard University Press.
Santayana, G. (1940), *Winds of Doctrine: Studies in Contemporary Opinion*, London, Dent (first published 1913, new edition 1940).
Sartre, J. P. (1957) [1936–7], *The Transcendence of the Ego*, trans. F. Williams and R. Kirkpatrick, New York, Farrar, Straus, and Giroux.
—— (1962) [1936] *Imagination*, Ann Arbor, University of Michigan Press.
—— (1989) [1943], *Being and Nothingness: An Essay on Phenomenological Ontology*, trans. H. E. Barnes, London, Routledge.
—— (1995) [1940], *The Psychology of the Imagination*, London, Routledge.
Schacter, D. L. (1996), *Searching for Memory: The Brain, the Mind, and the Past*, New York, Basic Books.
Scheler, M. (1973), *Selected Philosophical Essays*, trans. D. R. Lachterman, Evanston, Northwestern University Press.
Schelling, F. W. J. (1988) [1797/1803], *Ideas for a Philosophy of Nature*, trans. E. E. Harris and P. Heath, Cambridge, Cambridge University Press.
—— (1997) [1813], *Ages of the World*, trans. J. Norman, Ann Arbor, University of Michigan Press.
Schlick, M. (1968), *Philosophy of Nature*, trans. A. von Zeppelin, New York, Greenwood Press.
Schopenhauer, A. (1969) [1819/1844], *The World as Will and Representation* (two volumes), trans. E. F. J. Payne, New York, Dover.
—— (1992) [1836], *On the Will in Nature*, trans. E. F. J. Payne, New York, Berg.
Schrödinger, E. (1992) [1944], *What is Life?*, Cambridge, Cambridge University Press.
Scott, J. W. (1917), 'Bergsonism in England', *The Monist* (27:2), 179–204.
Seager, W. (1999), *Theories of Consciousness*, London, Routledge.
Sheldrake, R. (1981), *A New Science of Life: The Hypothesis of Formative Causation*, London, Granada, 1983.
Sokal, A. and Bricmont, J. (1997), *Impostures Intellectuelles*, Paris, Éditions Odile Jacob.
Sorabji, R. (1983), *Time, Creation and the Continuum*, London, Duckworth.
—— (1988), *Matter, Space, and Motion*, London, Duckworth.
Squire, L. R. (1998), 'Memory and Brain Systems', in S. Rose (ed.), *From Brains to Consciousness?*, London, Allen Lane: 53–72.
Stephen, K. (1922), *The Misuse of Mind: A Study of Bergson's Attack on Intellectualism*, London, Kegan Paul, Trench, Trubner & Co.
Sutton, J. P. (1998), *Philosophy and Memory Traces*, Cambridge, Cambridge University Press.
Thompson, D'Arcy (1992) [1917], *On Growth and Form*, Cambridge, Cambridge University Press.
Tiles, M. (1989), *The Philosophy of Set Theory: An Historical Introduction to Cantor's Paradise*, Oxford, Basil Blackwell.

Trusted, J. (1999), *The Mystery of Matter*, London, Macmillan.

Turetzky, P. (1998), *Time*, London, Routledge.

Wesson, R. (1991), *Beyond Natural Selection*, Cambridge, Mass., MIT Press.

Weyl, H. (1987) [1918], *The Continuum: A Critical Examination of the Foundation of Analysis*, trans. S, Pollard and T Bole, New York, Dover.

Whitrow, G. J. (1980), *The Natural Philosophy of Time*, Oxford, Clarendon Press.

Wickham, H. (1933), *The Unrealists*, London, Sheed & Ward.

Wiener, N. (1961) [1948], 'Newtonian and Bergsonian Time', *Cybernetics, or Control and Communication in the Animal and the Machine*, Cambridge, Mass., MIT Press: 30–44.

Wildon Carr, H. (1992), 'On Mr Russell's Reasons for supposing that Bergson's Philosophy is not True', in *The Collected Papers of Bertrand Russell*, ed. J. G. Slater, London, Routledge, 1992: 456–60 (originally published in *The Cambridge Magazine* (2), 1913).

Wolsky, M. and Wolsky, A. (1992), 'Bergson's Vitalism in the Light of Modern Biology', in F. Burwick and P. Douglass, *Bergson and the Vitalist Controversy*. Cambridge, Cambridge University Press: 153–70.

Worms, F. (1997), *Introduction à 'Matière et mémoire' de Bergson*, Paris, PUF.

Wright, S. (1964), 'Biology and the Philosophy of Science', *The Monist* (48): 265–90.

Zac, S. (1968), 'Les thèmes Spinozistes dans la philosophie de Bergson', *Les Études Bergsoniennes*, vol. 8: 123–58.

INDEX